WAR, VIOLENCE, AND POPULATION

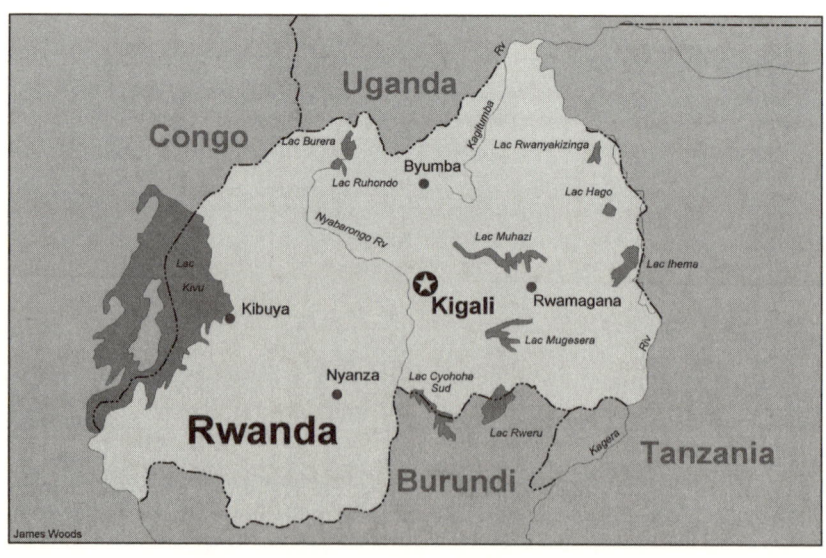

War, Violence, and Population
Making the Body Count

JAMES A. TYNER

Foreword by CHRIS PHILO

THE GUILFORD PRESS
New York   London

© 2009 The Guilford Press
A Division of Guilford Publications, Inc.
72 Spring Street, New York, NY 10012
www.guilford.com

All rights reserved

No part of this book may be reproduced, translated, stored in
a retrieval system, or transmitted, in any form or by any means,
electronic, mechanical, photocopying, microfilming, recording,
or otherwise, without written permission from the Publisher.

Printed in the United States of America

This book is printed on acid-free paper.

Last digit is print number: 9 8 7 6 5 4 3 2 1

Library of Congress Cataloging-in-Publication Data

Tyner, James A., 1966–
  War, violence, and population : making the body count / by James A Tyner.
    p. cm.
  Includes bibliographical references and index.
  ISBN 978-1-60623-037-4 (pbk.) — ISBN 978-1-60623-038-1 (hardcover)
  1. Genocide. 2. Political atrocities. 3. War crimes. 4. Crimes against humanity. 5. Violence. I. Title.
  HV6322.7.T95 2009
  364.15′1—dc22

2008034366

FOREWORD

I am delighted to provide a foreword to this important new work by James A. Tyner, not least because I believe that *War, Violence, and Population: Making the Body Count* is that rare beast—a book that can genuinely double both as a lively and accessible student textbook and as a major contribution to the research literature of population geography (and, more broadly, of all social sciences concerned with population issues). And more than both of these two angles, perhaps, the book is a sustained, intelligent, challenging, and, in places, moving critical introduction to events and processes absolutely central to the making, for good and (all too often) ill, of our contemporary world.

To my mind, this book tackles head-on issues that have been skirted around in the subdiscipline of population geography over recent years, arguing in twin intellectual and ethicopolitical registers that all scholars interested in the geographies of human population *must* take far more seriously than hitherto the often violent, terrifying, and sometimes gut-wrenching dimensions to how whole populations—defined in various ways, perhaps delimited as aliens or "others," whether by their own supposed country-kin or by foreign powers—become disciplined and regulated at the "point" of a gun (or knife, club, fist, bomb). The book hence comprehensively displaces a safe, comfortable, uncontroversial version of population geography, one couched in the somewhat arid terms of fertility, morbidity, and mortality, captured in statistical representations and paraded in simple diagrams and models (the age pyramids and transition models of countless classroom exercises). It demands instead a more edgy version of population geography, one that will and should deeply trouble its readers and practitioners, asking critical questions (possibly as an explicit "education for peace") and putting flesh, blood, and bones on the skeletal figures, graphs, and maps of population dynamics and distribution, even as it is then shown how human bodies are sometimes stripped of their flesh, drained of their blood, and their bones crushed by *actual* practices of population "management" on the ground.

Without making the book conceptually overburdened, Tyner offers an expressed turn to social theory in reformulating population geography, and more particularly he proposes a loosely Foucauldian approach—after the French intellectual Michel Foucault (1926–1984)—concerned with how bodies are disciplined and populations regulated at the heart of an ever-contested *biopolitics* of life and death, notably, at the hands of emergent nation-states or other collectivities claiming control over or aiming to "influence" territories and their occupant populations. Through a critical review of population geography as conducted to date, querying both its content and its conceptual resources, Tyner sets up his alternative vision: a defiant attunement to new "objects" of study, specifically, how populations are indeed "managed" more or less directly in many world situations through the violence of armed struggle, clandestine operations, and routine brutalities. Such a vision demands an engagement with diverse social theories, Foucauldian ones to be sure, and what can also be found here, clearly doing "work" in the text, are a range of postcolonial, feminist, and political–economic varieties of social critique.

This book, if I can put it like this, "kicks you in the guts," since it immediately brings readers into contact with the most appalling of human actions, the junctures between "enacted violence"—the atrocities of the "killing fields" performed immediately on helpless bodies (most horrifyingly perhaps, children)—and "structural violence"—the more mundane and unalleviated structural inequities underlying the grinding poverty, hunger, and ill health faced by certain populations. Tyner constantly moves attention from bodies to populations and back again, so that at one moment he might describe the terrible embodied experiences of individuals housed in detention camps or "strategic hamlets," whereas at the next moment he might analyze forced migrations from urban areas, the carpet-bombing of whole regions, or plans to remove all designated "enemies" from every inch of a national soil. This scale-jumping is also in part designed to trace out the complex relations involved, leading to the dawning realization of how much "we"—or at least the apparently respectable, educated equivalents of "us" in other times and place—can become deeply enmeshed in all manner of abuses, often because we more or less consciously subscribe to an imagined geography of "us" and "them" which sanctions such abuses, ultimately perhaps the deaths, of others not like "us" (whether far away or next door).

The heart of the book is three substantive chapters that might be conceived of as case studies, but whose cumulative effects arguably do something more than what such a labeling (as case studies) might imply. Tyner examines in turn the excesses of applied "biopolitical" population geography: in Vietnam (chiefly how the United States sought continually to up the "body count" in its futile bloody campaign to bludgeon North Vietnam into accepting the legitimacy of its U.S.-sponsored southern neighbor); in Cambodia (how the Khmer Rouge sought to eradicate all "enemies," including countless supposed potential enemies to be found in various ethnic, class, occupational, generational, etc., peoples and alliances); and in Rwanda (how the Hutu nationalists sought to construct Tutsis as fundamental "blockages" to the proper flows of the Rwandan "body politic," thus necessitating the most savage of "unblocking" practices). At every turn, the author's loosely Foucauldian framework serves to illuminate and to provoke, allowing the empirical materials their full meaning and horror, but always insisting that the reader is engaged, responding, thinking, and feeling. This is not easy reading but it is compelling: I doubt whether any other work of population geography would have me leafing through the pages so fast. It is, to adopt the same metaphor again, a series of blows to the guts, deeply troubling and upsetting, with contents that will haunt the reader for some time to come. I should maybe add, though, that Tyner handles this difficult material in as sensitive, nonsensationalist a fashion as possible.

It is maybe too much hyperbole on my part, but population geography—in fact, more widely, all geographical and social studies of population—can never be the same again. Indeed, put down all other books and papers about population geography, and read this one first! Through paying sustained attention to the biopolitical manipulations of morbidity, mortality, migration, marriage, and much else besides, and with reference to the tragedies of mass violence and genocide in Vietnam, Cambodia, and Rwanda, Tyner renders the spatial study of human population a fundamental matter of life and death. His book demands to be read.

CHRIS PHILO
Professor of Geography
University of Glasgow

Acknowledgments

In my office I have a small but growing collection of peace buttons, many of which include catchy slogans. One, for example, encourages us to "Prepare for peace, not for war." Another asks us to "Give our children a world without war." My favorite, however, is a small green and yellow button that simply states: "Will work for world peace." As a professor, this button resonates with me because it acknowledges that peace is something that we must work toward achieving. Peace is not easy to attain. Indeed, one quickly finds that peace activists are often represented as starry-eyed dreamers, idealists, utopians, cowards, or wimps, and are portrayed as stupid, ignorant, misinformed, and/or dangerous.

When Kristal Hawkins first approached me to write a book on population geography, she asked me what works were called for in the field. A *critical* population geography, I responded. Within population geography, as the writings of Adrian Bailey, Elspeth Graham, and Paul Boyle (among others) indicate, there had been a long-standing engagement with social theory, and yet the majority of population geography texts and monographs were largely silent on these developments. My first prospectus, therefore, reflected a synthesis of "traditional" population concepts with more recent, critical approaches and applications. One anonymous reviewer, however, encouraged me to go further. My initial reaction to this comment—and her or his recommendation to substantially revise my prospectus—is not printable. However, on later reflection, I began to see what the reviewer was looking for—but did not find—in my initial proposal. For a population text, or any manuscript, to be truly critical, it must promote change. It must be provocative and stimulating; it must question. My initial proposal, whereupon I set out to *respond* to previous approaches, was simply not critical.

So how was I to proceed? One avenue seemed obvious enough: Population geography is about people. But what happens to these people? As I contemplated this question, every day brought new accounts of people dying, people being killed, people killing other people. I had just completed one book on the business of war and America's occupation in Iraq and was working on another book examining the Cambodian genocide. Where, I wondered, were these stories in our population geographies? Sure, we population geographers talk about mortality (usually in the abstract); we mention (often in passing) events such as war and genocide. But we rarely talk about rape. War rape? Forget it. On such topics we are mostly silent. And so *War, Violence, and Population: Making the Body Count* is not the book that I initially proposed, but it is the book that I was most compelled to write. Consequently, my first thanks must go to both Kristal—for her continued support of this project—and to that anonymous reviewer who initially read my proposal. Thank you both for giving me the opportunity to speak my mind and to facilitate my work toward achieving peace.

As always, many heartfelt thanks go to the many graduate students whom I have been fortunate to work with over the years. It is a cliché to write that I've learned more from my students than they have from me. And it is a cliché to write that it's still true, despite being a cliché. So be it. Therefore, let me thank Olaf Kuhlke, Donna Houston, Josh Inwood, Rob Kruse, Gabe Popescue, Sutapa Chaddopaya, Steve Butcher, Steve Oluic, Rob Schwartz, Stacey Wicker, and Andrew Shears. Thanks also to Jim Woods for the preparation of the maps that appear at the beginning of this book.

Thanks also to the many geographers who have influenced my thinking about war, genocide, and violence over the years. Were it not for the efforts of individuals such as, but not limited to, Gerard Toal, Carl Dahlman, Shannon O'Lear, Colin Flint, Derek Gregory, William Wood, Don Mitchell, and Amy Ross, this book would never have materialized. There *is* a strong geographical tradition in the study of violence, a tradition that is unfortunately sometimes overlooked. I am humbled to contribute in some small way to this tradition.

Closer to home I thank Bond (my now 6-year-old puppy) and Jamaica (my cat) for their unspoken encouragement and support—or were they asking for food? I thank also my parents, Dr. Gerald Tyner and Dr. Judith Tyner. Even after all these years, they continue to provide invaluable support and encouragement. Thanks also to my brother, David, and my aunt, Karen. Still closer to home, I thank my wife, Belinda, for her support and inspiration. Given my double faults of procrastination and absent-mindedness, I would not be able to function without Belinda. Special thanks are extended to our daughters, Jessica and Anica Lyn. They are still very young—just 6 and 7 years old, respectively. Now, their problems center on broken toys, or of trying to stay up past bedtime. In time, however, they will learn about the violence that is part of many people's everyday realities. I hope, in some way, that this book will help them understand their ever-expanding world, and that this book will contribute to the ongoing discussions and initiatives to bring about a more peaceful world, not only for my children, but for all children. And it is because of this hope that I dedicate this book to Jessie and Anica.

Contents

1 Journeys from the Killing Fields   1
    A Retheorized Population Geography   7
    Toward a Philosophical Reorientation   15
    An Embodiment of Population Geography   17
    Violence and Spaces of Moral Exclusion   33
    Why I Write   42

2 Biopower in Vietnam   46
    The Context of the Vietnam War   51
    The Demographics of State Building   54
    Population and the Rostow Doctrine of War   58
    Rostow's Air Campaign of Terror   66
    (De)Population Forecasting   74
    Population and (the Destruction of) the Environment (Part I)   81
    Population and (the Destruction of) the Environment (Part II)   92
    The Control of Populations   97
    Embodied Instruments of Warfare   104
    Conclusions   107

3 Death and the Erasure of Space   109
    Sowing the Killing Fields   111
    The Other Killing Fields   120
    The Birth of Democratic Kampuchea   127
    The Place-Death of Cambodian Cities   129
    We Are Family, You Are Not   133
    Subjugating the Political Body   142
    Conclusions   149

4 Spaces of Planned Violence   151
Colonial Constructions   153
Independence   158
Preparations for a Genocide   164
Genocide Unleashed   170
The Embodiment of Rwanda's Genocide   172
The Biopolitics of Genocidal Rape   179
Conclusions   184

5 Population and Peace Education   186
Educating for Peace   194
Concluding Thoughts   199

Notes   201

References   205

Author Index   220

Subject Index   223

About the Author   226

1
JOURNEYS FROM THE KILLING FIELDS

It was impossible to walk without stepping on shards of bone and broken teeth. It was mid-April in 2001 and I was at Choeung Ek, 15 kilometers southwest of Cambodia's capital of Phnom Penh. Choeung Ek is perhaps the most infamous of Cambodia's killing fields, although by no means the only site. The Cambodian Genocide Program, based at Yale University, maintains a database of 158 prisons, 309 mass-grave sites—including approximately 19,000 grave pits—and 76 sites of post-1979 memorials to the victims of the genocide

During the years of the Khmer Rouge (1975–1979), Democratic Kampuchea—as Cambodia was then called—witnessed a genocide of remarkable proportions (see Chandler, 1999; Kiernan, 1996). An estimated one to three million people, out of a base population of perhaps eight million, died from starvation, disease, and execution.

The peacefulness and solitude of Choeung Ek today belie its horrific past, a history that nonetheless may be tangibly grasped upon closer inspection. The landscape at Choeung Ek is a rolling field of grass-covered mass graves—86 in all. A marker at Grave No. 7 explains that 166 victims were found buried without heads. Their crime? Traitors to the party. Nearby, at Grave No. 5, the bodies of more than 100 women and children were exhumed. On the edge of a slight depression I knelt down. Embedded in the dry, dusty earth was a piece of faded cloth: the remnants of a shirt or perhaps a pair of pants. I looked closer at the ground and saw more pieces of cloth. And bones. Splinters mostly. Pieces of bone fragments bleached by the sun, vivid reminders of the horrors that occurred here. Some of the pits—such as Graves Nos. 5 and 7—have been excavated; many more have not. The mounds and depressions remain as earthen memorials to the dehumanizing practices of the Khmer Rouge.

Nearby is a gnarled chankiri tree. Surrounding the trunk are small, white kernels: teeth. Hundreds of baby teeth glittering in the sunlight. During the genocide, the Khmer Rouge simply smashed infants and small children against trees—a technique cheaper than using bullets. And for what reason? The infants and children were murdered because their parents were accused of "crimes" against the Khmer Rouge. It was death by association.

Visually, Choeung Ek is dominated by a tall, glass-faced, *stupa*-shaped mausoleum that has been erected to commemorate those who died. Approximately 9,000 skulls and other human remains are arranged, tier upon tier, organized by age and sex. Most of the skulls reveal visible fractures, cuts, or bullet holes. The display is a grim visualization of the demographics of death.

While the Khmer Rouge were in power, prisoners from Tuol Sleng—a former school converted into a secret interrogation and torture facility—were trucked to a Chinese graveyard: Choeung Ek. According to David Chandler (1999: 139 passim), the site was equipped with electric power to illuminate the executions and to allow the guards from the prison to read and sign the rosters that accompanied prisoners to the site. The number of people executed at Choeung Ek on a daily basis varied from a few dozen to over 300. Trucks would arrive, often at night, carrying three or four guards and perhaps 20 to 30 prisoners. Those condemned would assemble in a small building where their names were verified against an execution list. Prisoners were then led in small groups to ditches and pits that had been dug earlier by workers stationed at Choeung Ek. Him Huy, a former Khmer Rouge guard, describes the scene: "They were ordered to kneel down at the edge of the hole. Their hands were tied behind them. They were beaten on the neck with an iron ox-cart axle, sometimes with one blow, sometimes with two..." (quoted in Chandler, 1999: 140).

One of the most chilling aspects of the Cambodian genocide, and similar to the Holocaust, was the systematic management of torture and executions. The prison at Tuol Sleng, for example, contained three main units: interrogation, documentation, and defense. Chandler (1999: 27) explains that the documentation unit, which included a photography subunit, was responsible for "transcribing tape-recorded confessions, typing handwritten notes, preparing summaries of confessions, and maintaining the prison's voluminous files." The photography subunit "took mug shots of prisoners when they arrived, pictures of prisoners who died in captivity, and pictures of important prisoners after they were killed." Over 6,000 photographs and 4,000 "confessions" have survived. Between April 1975 and January 1979 at least 14,000 men, women, and children were held at Tuol Sleng; only seven are known to have survived.

On leaving Choeung Ek I was surrounded by a half dozen Cambodian children. Their faces were dirty, their clothes tattered. With hands outstretched, they asked for dollars. These children embody the past, present, and future of Cambodia—as well as dozens of other war-ravaged countries. As Cambodia begins the 21st century, its population continues to struggle with its past. Cambodia ranks among the world's worst countries in terms of infant and maternal mortality. Today, approximately 97 per 1,000 infants in Cambodia will die before their first birthday. The under-5 mortality rate is estimated to be as high as 135 per 1,000 live births and the maternal mortality ratio is 437 per 100,000 live births; some hospitals report rates in excess of 785. The lifetime risk for Cambodian women of dying from maternal causes is 1 in 50 (Yanagisawa, 2004: 113). Most women and children die from preventable diseases, compounded by an ill-equipped medical system. Many more people are grievously injured or killed as a result of land mines or unexploded ordinance.

During the reign of the Khmer Rouge there was a saying: "If you live there is no gain. If you die there is no loss." This phrase encapsulates many of the personal motives that underlie both my teaching and my research, and the writing of this book in particular. The phrase speaks to the wanton disregard for human life, the indiscriminate killing of human beings, the discipline of individual bodies, and the regulation of populations. Personal testimonies, such as Haing Ngor's disturbing and haunting autobiography, *Survival in the Killing Fields* (2003), and the collections contained in Dith Pran's *Children of Cambodia's Killing Fields* (1997), give voice to a massive and tragic experiment of population control and social engineering.

The deaths associated with the Khmer Rouge occupy but one place within an increasingly violent world. In 2001 three researchers associated with the Centers for Disease Control and the World Health Organization published a paper entitled "Epidemiology of Violent Deaths in the World." Noting that the extent of global violence had never been described, Avid Reza, James Mercy, and Etienne Krug set out to describe the patterns of violence-related mortality (including suicide, homicide, and war) for the world and its major regions. Restricting their study to just one year (1990), they found an estimated 1.8 million violence-related deaths worldwide (35.3 per 100,000). Overall, their findings reveal that violence-related deaths were highest in sub-Saharan Africa and lowest in the established market economies. Indeed, violence accounted for a greater proportion of total deaths in sub-Saharan African than in any other region of the world (Reza et al., 2001: 105). Among their various other findings, Reza and colleagues (2001: 107) found that there were an estimated 211,000 and 291,000 war-related deaths among females and males, respectively, and that the war-related death rate for females in the world was highest for 0–4 year olds.

The Reza and colleagues study is important for two main reasons. First, it strikes at the heart of my concerns, namely, the geography of population. Second, it highlights one particular form of oppression that is often overlooked by theorists of social justice: violence. Iris Young (1990: 61) points out that many groups suffer the oppression of systematic violence. Members of some groups, often times marginalized, such as gays and lesbians, are subject to harassment, intimidation, physical and verbal abuse, and murder. And geographers have made substantial contributions to this area of study (Koskela and Pain, 2000; Pain, 1997; Valentine, 1989). However, despite the scale and scope of violent acts, Young (p. 61) wonders rhetorically why discussions on various theories of justice are usually silent about violence. She suggests that violence and harassment are usually viewed at the level of the individual, as singular acts perpetrated by people; violence typically is not viewed as involving institutions as found in the exploitation of groups (structural inequalities in the capitalist division of labor) or marginalization (resultant from systemic racial prejudices or patriarchy). And yet, for Young (p. 61; emphasis added), "What makes violence a face of oppression is less the particular acts themselves ... than the social context surrounding them, which makes them possible and even acceptable. *What makes violence a phenomena of social injustice, and not merely an individual moral wrong, is its systematic character, its existence as a social system."*

My goal in writing *War, Violence, and Population: Making the Body Count* is both narrow and broad. First, and more narrowly, I propose a particular agenda for population studies—and especially those that fall under the domain of "population geography." This is not, therefore, a population geography text (although I do envision this as a critical supplement to existing texts). Nor is this a "history" of population studies or population geography—although mention is made throughout the course of this book. Numerous review articles and books exist on this subject and I believe that the field is well plowed (see, for example, Bailey, 2005; Gober and Tyner, 2004; White et al., 1989).

More broadly, this book is an attempt to promote solidarity between those scholars (geographers and nongeographers) who are fundamentally concerned with questions of social justice and those who are interested in the discipline of populations. Considerable work within academia, both inside and outside of geography, is being conducted on population-related issues. Many practitioners, however, do not consider themselves "population geographers," nor is their work considered in reviews of population geography.

Why is this salient? I believe there are two reasons. First, I agree that academic labels are not terribly relevant—unless one is speaking to a university administrator. Throughout my academic career, for example, I have been labeled (both by myself and by others) as a population geographer, a political geographer, a social geographer, a gender geographer, and an Asian geographer. Certainly the bulk of my work, both research and teaching, falls under these categories, but I would be hard-pressed to separate any particular article or book into just one domain. My writings on the politics of gendered Philippine labor migration, for example, overlap easily in all of the aforementioned subdisciplines of geography. Nevertheless, labels also indicate the existence of "communities" of scholars; these communities, moreover, do have histories and geographies. Knowledge is produced (not discovered) within these communities and it is necessary to understand the construction of these knowledges. In other words, communities of scholars contribute to discursive formations, and it is through an understanding of these formations that we may better understand *why* some questions are asked as opposed to others.

Second, it is important to consider the labeling or "marking" of population geographers because it indicates how ideas or approaches may be marginalized. As I demonstrate throughout this book, many areas of study—such as sexuality—have been excluded from population geography (or geography more generally) because they are not considered part of the field. And yet, outside of the circumscribed field of population geography, we find many scholars forwarding important contributions to the study of population-related issues, many of which do in fact fall within the traditional domain of population geography. These include war-related deaths and rapes, aerial bombing campaigns, or state-sanctioned terrorism. My questions thus echo those working in feminist and queer studies, those who study critical race theory and Marxism, and those informed by poststructuralism and postcolonialism. Consequently, *War, Violence, and Population: Making the Body Count* speaks to *one* audience; this audience is not composed of population geographers or nonpopulation geographers. It is composed of those who want to intervene in the struggle against societal injustices and specifically violence.

My hope is to maintain a balance between being critical and being complimentary. On the one hand, I want to acknowledge the significant contributions of earlier work. Research does not proceed in a vacuum. Indeed, I could not conduct my own work were it not for the earlier foundation laid, for example, by Wilbur Zelinsky, Elspeth Graham, Allan Findlay, Paul Boyle, Victoria Lawson, Rachel Silvey, Emily Skop, and Adrian Bailey. On the other hand, there is space to expand, clarify, or even to forsake certain ideas, attitudes, or avenues of research. I agree, in part, with Don Mitchell (2000: xv) that "learning, like political change, proceeds through struggle" and that "only by engaging with ideas, debates, and intellectual and political positions, does knowledge advance." Consequently, I draw on a range of ideas developed by scholars who may not consider themselves to be population geographers, such as Geraldine Pratt, Kim England, and Robyn Longhurst.

Wilbur Zelinsky, in 1966, asked: "Where do people live, and why do they live there? How many and what sorts of people inhabit different parts of the world? What meanings lie behind these areal patterns?" (p. 1). These questions dominated conventional population geography for the better part of four decades. It is time, however, to concentrate on other questions, questions that grapple with the killing fields of Cambodia and the rape of Tutsi women. How, for example, is space manipulated to facilitate the disciplining of people? For what purposes are populations constructed and subsequently regulated by institutions? How are the so-called demographic events of fertility, mortality, and migration modified for political and economic purposes? Or, to paraphrase Zelinsky, "Where do people die, and why are they killed there?" These questions encompass my call for a retheorized population geography and provide the terrain over which I travel.

Before setting off, however, a roadmap is in order. The remainder of this chapter is a lengthy and rather winding path that will visit the various themes and concepts that guide subsequent chapters. First, I revisit the calls of Paul White, Peter Jackson, Elspeth Graham, and Paul Boyle, among others, for a retheorized population geography. Next I provide the basis for a philosophical reorientation, one that is buttressed by insights provided by poststructuralism and postcolonialism. I argue that population geography must place the body at the center of its concerns. Consequently, the third section details the parameters of an "embodied" population geography. Fourth, and consistent with my concern with violence, war, and genocide, I provide an overview of violence and the spaces of moral exclusion. Lastly, I return to where I began, the killing fields of Cambodia, and reaffirm why I write and why I argue that a retheorized population geography is required.

A RETHEORIZED POPULATION GEOGRAPHY

In 1995 Paul White and Peter Jackson issued a wake-up call for population geographers. They argued that "population geography would profit greatly from a recognition of developments in and beyond the wider discipline" (p. 111). Specifically, it was their contention that population geography had remained steadfastly isolated from current theoretical debates in human geography and that any serious engagement with feminism, structuration theory, postmodernism, or postcolonial studies was all but absent.

Population geographers, White and Jackson (1995: 111) lamented, had "paid insufficient attention to recent philosophical and methodological discussions that make their mark elsewhere in human geography, and in the rest of the social sciences." Consequently, population geography as a subfield had ignored to its own detriment many of the key debates that were invigorating other parts of the discipline.

What precipitated this "crisis of relevancy" that seemed to plague some population geographers through the 1990s and into the 21st century? The answer, of course, is complex and multifaceted. A good starting point, however, is Cleveland, Ohio, with Glenn Trewartha's 1953 presidential address delivered before the Association of American Geographers (AAG). Trewartha (p. 71) began with a simple statement: "The geography of population has been, and continues to be neglected, to the injury of geography in general." Consequently, he called for "a serious and sustained effort [to] be made to develop a working concept of population geography which may be applied broadly in teaching and research." Trewartha urgently observed that there was a "paucity of professed specialists in population geography who might bring to the discussion a superior wisdom derived from experience." He believed that "the neglect of population geography constitutes a fundamental weakness in the general approach to modern geography."

In his address Trewartha (1953: 83) argued that "population is the point of reference from which all the other elements are observed and from which they all, singly and collectively, derive significance and meaning. It is population which furnishes the focus." Looking back on Trewartha's address, Graham (2004: 290) observes two salient points. First, she is struck by Trewartha's conviction that geography is a unitary science. This is not surprising, given Trewartha's background as a climatologist. Second, Graham highlights the situatedness of Trewartha's plea within a North American—and specifically United States—context. As such, the influence of Richard Hartshorne's notion of geography figures prominently in Trewartha's case for population geography. Geography was the study of areal differentiation and the focus was largely anthropocentric. Population, with a focus on resources, would provide the link between physical and cultural geography.

"Geography is a unitary science," argued Trewartha (1953: 79). "Its single focus is its concern with the areas which comprise the earth's surface and no convenient organizational subdivision should be permitted to destroy this basic unity." However, Trewartha did not slavishly follow the Harthshornian tradition. Instead, as Bailey (2005: 64) writes, Trewartha (among others) was well aware of the growing prominence of, and respect for, the field of demography. Given the importance of earlier demographic work being conducted by the United Nations' precursor, the League of Nations, Trewartha saw an important opportunity for geographers to contribute to and benefit from developments in demography (p. 65).

Trewartha proposed a tripartite conceptualization of geography, with population bridging the "cultural earth" and the "physical earth." The epistemology of population geography, Trewartha suggested, would be both topical and regional. He (p. 87) explained that "just as areal differentiation is the theme of geography in general, so it is of population geography in particular." However, he emphasized that the concept of differentiation applied to a wider range of population attributes than most geographers usually included. Distribution patterns and arithmetic densities alone were insufficient; instead, he suggested that population geographers study a gamut of characteristics, including areal natality and mortality patterns and differentials; areal change and variability of population; age pyramids as indicators of future growth; areal patterns involving crude rates of natural increase and net reproduction rates; population distribution by settlement types; patterns of migration; and qualities of population (for example, body size, form, color, sex balance, health and disease, marital status, customs, and so forth) and their regional patterns of distribution (pp. 88–89).

And geographers heeded Trewartha's call. Population geographic research from the 1950s onward was dominated by a descriptive and inferential approach; studies considered "measures of and depictions of population concentration and dispersion; the relative size and proximity of urban areas within a population; density and overpopulation; [and] the decomposition of population characteristics, including flows of population" (Bailey, 2005: 73; see other reviews in James, 1954; Jones, 1990; White et al., 1989). By the 1960s several population geography texts had appeared and the number of population-related papers at the annual meetings of the AAG steadily increased (Jones, 1990: 2).

In 1966 Wilbur Zelinsky published a slim volume entitled *A Prologue to Population Geography*. Bailey (2005: 69–71) suggests that Zelinsky's contribution, often widely overlooked as a think-piece on the nature of population geography, is influential in at least four main ways. First, Zelinsky linked population geography to broader social agendas. In his conclusion, for example, Zelinsky (p. 129) wrote that "perhaps [the] most important item on the agenda of the population geographer ... is the study of the effects of population phenomena, and particularly change, upon the nondemographic phases of geography." Zelinsky (p. 129) explained:

> Little as yet has been done in this direction, but it is safe to predict that geographers will soon become immersed in such problems as how population structures and dynamics act differently in different places to affect habitat and resources; how the population factor reacts upon the economic behavior of a community and, particularly, the type and direction of its current economic development; its impact upon the political and other aspects of social geography; and the effects of changing population characteristics upon the basic structure of the total culture.

Second, Bailey finds in Zelinsky's work a recognition that if population geography were to be useful, it would have to be effective—foreshadowing the relevancy crisis. Third, Zelinsky believed that culture was the key element in an account of population geography. Fourth, he stressed the development of appropriate methodologies. These were largely positivist, with the mapping of population attributes assuming a key role. Zelinsky (p. 3) explained that "the demographer is ... concerned with the intrinsic nature, the universal attributes, of populations, with the systematic principles governing their composition, socioeconomic correlates, behavior, and changes; the spatial dimension is incidental to this central purpose." Population geography, conversely, was defined by Zelinsky (p. 5) as "the science that deals with the ways in which the geographic character of places is formed by, and in turn reacts upon, a set of population phenomena that vary within it through both space and time as they follow their own behavioral laws, interacting one with another and with numerous non-demographic phenomena." Methodologically, his approach was largely conservative, with research driven by readily available statistics. He explained (p. 7):

> For practical purposes, we may equate the resulting list of human characteristics [to be studied] with those appearing in the census enumeration schedules and vital registration systems.... These are such facts as can be quickly and reliably collected from individual respondents by enumerators or registrars with only a moderate amount of training.

Zelinsky (p. 7) continued that

> for the most part, then, the demographic characteristics are those readily perceptible in individuals or families, while other equally important characteristics, detectable only by skillful or protracted observation of the larger group or by intensive study of individuals, lie beyond the limits of population geography and are largely the cultural geographer's responsibility.

During the 1970s Zelinsky's conception of population geography was steadily refined. In keeping with broader intellectual trends in social science and human geography, George Demko and his coauthors clarified Zelinsky's view to focus on spatial analysis, logical positivism, and quantitative methods (Gober and Tyner, 2004: 186). Such an emphasis was strengthened by population geography's continuing ties with demography. By the early 1980s, Bailey (2005: 103) contends, population geography had come of age. He writes:

> The field was moving from inductive to deductive ways of contributing positivist knowledge and had made some brief forays into feminist and political economic literatures. It had contributed both macro-level and, increasingly, micro-level analyses of population behaviors, notably migration. Its most distinctive achievement, however, was convergence around a single vision—Zelinsky's vision.

In 1989 Stephen White, along with several luminaries of population geography, provided an overview of "1980s" population geography for Gary Gaile and Cort Willmott's (1989) ambitious and monumental *Geography in America*. In a survey of 769 articles that appeared in the *Annals of the Association of American Geographers*, the *Geographical Review*, and the *Professional Geographer*, White and his coauthors noted that 77 (10 percent) focused on population-related topics. Of these, 53.3 percent emphasized migration; 30.6 percent examined changing patterns of population distribution, density, or urban growth; and 14.7 percent dealt with patterns of specific population characteristics (White et al., 1989: 259). Furthermore, they noted that there was an increased use of inferential statistics and quantitative methods, although more than half of the articles were essentially descriptive or review pieces. Six themes dominated population geography: residential mobility, urban housing, counterurbanization, internal migration, international migration, and the relationship between population change and economic development. In their conclusion, White and colleagues (p. 281) identified "the need to frame population-geography research in such a way as to increase its emphasis on social relevance." No specific mention is made of various social theories, although the final paragraph of their review is striking:

> Geographers might disagree about the most significant topics within population geography, the most appropriate research questions, and certainly the most appropriate research methodologies. However, it is clear that despite these honest differences, population-geography research has grown rapidly since 1953, and shows no signs of slowing. Undoubtedly, population geography is pivotal to an understanding of the cultural landscape. (p. 282)

I find three aspects of this statement of interest. First, there is no mention of philosophical sea changes within population geography, nor is there any sense that such a philosophical reorientation is necessary. Population geography, for over three decades, had been dominated by empiricist and positivist approaches. And while there was a call for greater social relevancy, there was no indication that this entailed either an epistemological or an ontological change. Second, the legacy of Zelinsky remained. Population geography had a mission to facilitate an understanding of the cultural landscape and the areal differentiation of demographic events. Third, and perhaps most salient, is the overall optimistic spirit of the review. If there were concerns over the current health and future prognosis for population geography, the symptoms were not identified. Admittedly, a review chapter appearing in *Geography in America* may not have been considered an appropriate place to air one's dirty laundry. Nonetheless, it is remarkable to juxtapose the White et al. piece with the later writings of Paul White, Peter Jackson, Allan Findlay, and Elspeth Graham. It is also extremely important to note that many of the challenges to population geography originated not in the United States, but in the United Kingdom, Canada, Australia, and New Zealand.

Population geography, by the late 1980s and early 1990s, had reached a crossroads (Bailey, 2005: 116). Bailey (p. 116), in fact, identifies three commonly expressed views about the field at the time. Some population geographers advocated a continuity in focus and approach; a second group of population geographers saw the field as supporting pluralistic approaches to familiar topics; and a third, more critical, group pressed for a radical shift in the field to include more explicitly recent developments in feminist and social theory. Unfortunately, as Bailey (p. 116) finds, "Discussions of boundaries between the field and medical geography, spatial ecology, demography and population studies appeared as border disputes rather than forward-looking attempts to develop theory."

Throughout the 1990s a handful of population geographers made repeated demands for a retheorization. A call went out for population geographers to engage in the broader debates that permeated other disciplines, namely, an incorporation with social theory. One early call was for a direct engagement with feminist thought. In 1993 Ruth Fincher addressed the importance of gender relations and the geography of migration. She had been asked, "What had geographers, long involved in analyses of migration processes internal and international, contributed to this issue?" When she turned to the Population Specialty Group (PSG of the AAG), she could find no mention of gender and migration. To be sure, population geographers had addressed "sex differentials" of migration patterns. But any direct and explicit engagement with *gender* was lacking. Fincher was forced to look elsewhere. She wrote: "Even if those geographers most directly concerned with migration issues through their study of population have to date been little concerned with matters of gender, there are signs that feminist geographers are appreciating the significant of migration for women, and indeed the significance of women in migration movements" (p. 1703). In conclusion, Fincher (pp. 1704–1705) declared: "Though the geographic literature of migration is certainly not replete with references to the gendered nature of migration processes, there are signs that feminist geography may be claiming migration as a significant new context for its work."

And Fincher's challenge to integrate gender and migration in 1993 was not new at the time. In their 1991 review of population geography (published in *Progress in Human Geography*), Allan Findlay and Elspeth

Graham questioned, "Where is the definitive population geography of women?" Although this did not (and, arguably, still has not) appeared, the next decade did witness a flourishing of work that incorporated feminist ideas into the subject of gendered migration. The work of the aforementioned geographers Rachel Silvey, Victoria Lawson, Geraldine Pratt, and Kim England stands out for its relevance.

Nearly a decade later Elspeth Graham and Paul Boyle (2001: 389), however, felt that the ongoing attempts had borne little fruit. They claimed that "the changing landscape of academic geography [had] increasingly marginalised the study of population to the extent that our particularly adjectival niche [had] been relegated, at best, to the second division." Allan Findlay (2003: 178) could say only that "some progress has been made in introducing social theory in population geography," but that "there has been strikingly little innovation by most researchers in their approach to population studies." Indeed, outside of migration studies, population geographers exhibited very little engagement with social theory.

Such a pessimistic overview may be overstated. There are, in fact, many young (particular female) scholars who have successfully escaped established norms and have moved beyond the traditional (and limited) confines of population geography. Rachel Silvey (2004), for example, finds that critical geography *has* assessed, among other topics, the interconnections of gender-differentiated migration processes (Tyner, 1994, 2004); the construction of citizenship and transnationalism (for example, Bailey et al., 2002; Kofman and England, 1997; Willis and Yeoh, 1999; Wright et al., 2000); the reification of sociospatial boundaries defining race and ethnicity (for example, Nagar, 1998; Nagel, 2001); the regulation and meanings of sexuality and sex work (e.g., Tyner, 2002a, 2002b; Tyner and Houston, 2000); and the production of belonging, exclusion, and identity (for example, Secor, 2002; Yeoh and Huang, 2000). Consequently, I find myself in agreement with Findlay's (2003) plea to move the debate in population geography forward from the now weary call to engage with social theory. For Findlay (p. 179), the "time has come for population geography to get over the neurosis it [has] developed in relation to its self-perceived marginality to social theory in geography and to engage in a self-confident and self-aware fashion." Such a move requires an engagement with the philosophical grounding of population geography (Graham, 1999; Underhill-Sem, 2001).

TOWARD A PHILOSOPHICAL REORIENTATION

I agree with Findlay's (2003: 182) contention that "population questions lie at the heart of many contemporary social theories." Indeed, Pat Gober and I argue that much population geography is actually being done by scholars who do not identify themselves as population geographers. For me, this raises two key issues. On the one hand, ongoing work is testimony to the salience of topics that broadly fall within the realm of population studies, including the trinity of fertility, mortality, and migration. On the other hand, the unwillingness to be identified as a population geographer suggests something of the use of labels and categories to define our work. As Bailey (2005: 165) argues, the division between contemporary scholars identifying with the term "population geographer" and those desisting often reflects ontological rather than ideological disagreements.

For a retheorized population geography, it is imperative to critically evaluate the philosophical underpinnings of our work. Why have certain questions been asked by demographers, population geographers, and other researchers concerned with population-related topics? Why are other questions and topics seemingly shunned? Often, the asking of these questions will reveal a particular understanding or belief about the way in which the world works, and the way in which future worlds should be.

Population geography and demography have almost always been empirical disciplines. Indeed, writing of demography specifically, Caldwell (2001) maintains that population studies are somewhat unique in their adherence to 19th-century positivist attitudes throughout the 20th century. He explains that most demographers have been "happy to carry out analyses within a minimalist theoretical framework and have been deeply suspicious of disciplines that built theoretical structures upon unproven, theoretical bases" (p. 21).

I propose a population geography situated within a context of poststructural and postcolonial ontology and epistemology. Poststructuralism, first, refers to a collection of theories based largely on the writings of Michel Foucault, Jacques Derrida, Roland Barthes, and Judith Butler, among others. Poststructuralists ask fundamental questions about language, meaning, and subjectivity; more specifically, they disrupt meanings, labels, and categories and challenge terms that are assumed to be natural and unchanging. Poststructuralism—and, relatedly, some feminist theory and queer theory—forwards the idea that all knowledges are partial and situated. All knowledge-claims, and hence all truth-claims, are contextual, contingent, and often contested. Poststructuralists thus are interested in how some knowledge-claims come to be seen as natural, normal, and truthful.

Postcolonialism, relatedly, provides a critique of knowledge. However, postcolonialism more specifically has been concerned with the elaboration of theoretical structures that contest the dominance of Western ways of approaching knowledge (Young, 2003: 4). Postcolonialists, according to Young (2003: 6), are concerned with "developing the driving ideas of a political practice morally committed to transforming the conditions of exploitation and poverty in which large sections of the world's population live out their daily lives." As such, postcolonialism comprises a set of related perspectives; it is not a coherently elaborated set of principles. Rather, postcolonialism seeks "to intervene, to force its alternative knowledges into the power structures of the west as well as the non-west. It seeks to change the way people think, the way they behave, to produce a more just and equitable relation between the different peoples of the world" (p. 7).

Within this sentiment, I suggest, lies another reason why population geographers (and other social "scientists") have failed to engage in social theories such as postcolonialism. Social theory is radical; it is revolutionary. Social theory seeks to disrupt meanings, to challenge authority, and to advocate change that are largely socialist in orientation. Postcolonial and poststructural perspectives critique the status quo, one that is still dominated largely by structures of patriarchy, white privilege, Eurocentrism, and heterosexual normativities. Academia in general and geography in particular—despite repeated claims by certain political administrations—are very conservative institutions. Change comes slowly, in part because those in the mainstream are not willing to relinquish their hegemonic positions. As Young (2003: 7) concludes, many people do not like postcolonialism because "it disturbs the order of the world. It threatens privilege and power. It refuses to acknowledge the superiority of western cultures. Its radical agenda is to demand equality and well-being for all human beings on this earth."

AN EMBODIMENT OF POPULATION GEOGRAPHY

What, exactly, is the subject matter of population geography? Why are some subjects addressed (for example, the geographic variation of fertility differentials) while others are not?

Established practices in academic disciplines, David Sibley (1995) writes, favor the cautious and the conservative. In other words, "knowledge which has gained legitimacy, which has become part of the currency of academic communities, has often maintained its status to the exclusion of conflicting ideas" (p. 115). The concerns of Sibley reverberate throughout discussions of academia and the conduct of research. Aside from questions of "appropriate" methodologies and "sources" of data, we are confronted more immediately with questions about questions. In other words, what research questions are considered appropriate for study? To what extent might we ask questions "outside the box"?

As Matt Bradshaw and Elaine Stratford (2005: 68) explain, "None of us ever formulates research questions or undertakes research in a vacuum. We are all members of interpretive communities that involve established disciplines with relatively defined and stable areas of interest, theory, and research methods and techniques." And as described earlier, the interpretive community of population geographers—from Trewartha and Zelinsky onward—has been fairly narrow in its conception of what constitutes its area of study. If one were to ask what is the subject matter of population geography, one would get a relatively straightforward answer. By convention, most population geographers study *population-related events*, namely, fertility, mortality, or migration.

It is ironic that population geographers rarely study *people*. Indeed, as John McKendrick (2001: 461) exclaims, "it is surprising to find so little reflection on the nature of populations" within population geography. McKendrick notes that practitioners generally are concerned with the standardized classifications that are routinely deployed. "The goal," he argues (p. 461), "is to justify the population classification, rather than to understand that population; the population group is a means to an end, as opposed to an end in itself."

Such a clear-cut distinction, of course, may be exaggerated. James Newman and Gordon Matzke (1984), for example, argue that there exists a divergence of opinion as to the broader field of population geography. They note (p. 5), for example, that "some population geographers would include a range of social and economic indicators," while others would "stress the importance of considering population in its broader human context—that is, of examining important issues like population and resources, population and environmental quality, population and politics, and population policy." Likewise, Gary Peters and Robert Larkin (1999: 1) concede that "it is not always easy to distinguish population geography from other disciplinary contributions." Nevertheless, both sets of authors gravitate to a position of population geography encompassing questions of how spatial variations in the distribution and composition of populations and related events are related to other spatial variations.

The more one deviates from an established position, the more one is likely to be marginalized from the interpretive community. Consequently, those scholars who work outside the accepted boundaries may be subjected to various forms of exclusion, harassment, or potentially even violence (Dear, 2001; Longhurst, 2001; Valentine, 1998). Consider, for example, the topic of sexuality. Given the traditional domains of population studies—most especially fertility and nuptuality—one would assume that population geographers would have much to say on the topic of sex and sexuality. And yet, as Chris Philo (2005: 327) writes, "The subdiscipline of population geography has always talked about phenomena that transparently relate to sex, circulating around the messy realities of sexual activity integral to fertility and overall population dynamics, but it might be claimed that sex itself has remained curiously absent." Indeed, practitioners within population geography are in step with the mainstream of geography and many of the social sciences in exhibiting a "suspicion of and squeamishness around sex and sexuality" (Binnie, 1997: 225).

In part, population geographers' minimal engagement with sexuality results from a methodological conservatism identified by Elspeth Graham and Paul Boyle (2001). The dominant interpretive community of population geographers has not, in general, deemed sexuality a fundamental area of enquiry. Philo (2005: 327) explains that "the quantitative and spatial-analytical tools used" and the "research questions being asked about demographic events" combine to leave the "situated content and understanding of the sexual relations themselves somewhat marginal." He continues:

> Sex acts, what sex itself entails in its many possible permutations, but also the specifics of how sex is translated into the discourses of medicine, health and public policy: all of these components of the box marked "sex," and many more ... remain very much on the sidelines of population geography in its present subdisciplinary guise, even when expressly concerned with fertility, birth control, sexual health and the like. (pp. 327–328)

However, the neglect is also related to a long-standing conservatism—at times bordering on the puritanical—within geography. Consider, for example, geography's engagement both with feminism and Marxism. Beginning in the late 1960s and continuing especially throughout the 1980s, a handful of remarkable individuals, including David Harvey, Gordon Clark, Michael Dear, Richard Peet, William Bunge, Ron Horvath, Wilber Zelinsky, Susan Hanson, and Janice Monk, among others, attempted to incorporate diverse perspectives into the field. In 1973 Wilbur Zelinsky brought attention to the existence of gender inequalities within geography. Still later, in 1982, Monk and Hanson attempted to "identify some sexist biases in geographic research and to consider the implications of these for the discipline as a whole." They were respectful of the discipline, pointing out that their intent was not to "accuse geographers of having been actively or even consciously sexist in the conduct of their research" or to "castigate certain researchers or their traditions." However, they did assert that "through omission of any consideration of women, most geographic research [had] in effect been passively, often inadvertently, sexist" (Monk and Hanson, 1982: 11).

These attempts to include "half of the human in human geography" were parallel with efforts to incorporate Marxist and other "radical" ideas into geography. The founding of *Antipode* at Clark University in 1969 and the publication of Harvey's (1973) *Social Justice and the City* were crucial milestones in the formation of critical perspectives that explicitly sought to challenge societal inequalities. Steen Folke (1972: 14) pointed out that a "new trend of critical reexamination has finally entered the field of human geography." Differences, to be sure, were found, even among the so-called radical geographers. In the late 1970s Richard Peet, Michael Dear, and Gordon Clark, in particular, waged a lengthy war of words regarding the future of radical geography (see Clark and Dear, 1978; Peet, 1977, 1978). Curiously, all three questioned why contemporary geography "ignored" the call of radical geographers—a situation not unlike the laments of contemporary population geographers.

The incorporation of feminist and Marxist thought, however, was not merely ignored; indeed, it was vehemently attacked. George Carter (1977), for example, wrote in the *Professional Geographer* that he was "dismayed" by the "appearance of tables representing various strange groups attending meetings of the Association of American Geographers." Specifically, he was referring to "Marxist Geographers and Gay Geographers." He asked, What next? "Are we going to have a table for Whores in Geography, and Russian Communist Geography? If we admit the first two, on what basis do we exclude the next?" For Carter, "Geography is and should be geography and as a profession we should not be in the business of Gay or un-Gay, or Marxist or non-Marxist." Clearly not one to foreshadow the salience of positionality or reflexivity, Carter elaborated on the existence of a "gay geography": "The Gay movement has to do with life style and morality. It has nothing to do with geography as such and should be excluded from our meetings as irrelevant to geography." With respect to Marxist geographers, Carter explained that while it is possible that theirs could be a "theoretical position," he believed otherwise: Marxist geography "is instead a politically oriented one and as such is disruptive to the Association of American Geographers." Carter saw no problem with exclusion. He explained that at professional meetings, "we should flatly refuse any such groups the right to such representations. When engaging in their gay behavior they are not acting as geographers. Our exclusion of such groups cannot be taken as a moralistic stand on the part of the Association, but simply as a professional one. It is not our business to support the Gay or the Street Walkers, or the Democrats or the Republicans" (Carter, 1977: 101–102; see the replies by Chappell, 1977; Harvey, 1977; and Rodrigue, 1977).

The comments of Carter were not isolated (see, for example, the commentary by Wolf Roder, 1977); nor are these attitudes absent from contemporary research. Michael Dear (2001) and Gill Valentine (1998) have each been harassed—both publicly and through other, more sinister means (for example, silent telephone calls, threatening voice mail messages)—for their attempts to bring "alternative" perspectives into the discipline. Given such a climate, is it any wonder that some academics may self-censor their research questions? The history of geography indeed reveals itself to be a contestation of inclusion or exclusion: What counts as legitimate scholarship? What topics are acceptable?

Both poststructuralism and postcolonialism are concerned with the construction of knowledge and the attendant truth-claims that are forwarded to justify certain actions (for example, colonial policies and practices). These claims may be those of American military strategists conducting war in Vietnam, or the Khmer Rouge and Hutu extremists justifying the slaughter of thousands upon thousands of men, women, and children. Likewise, these claims may be those of a few practitioners of geography in their attempt to establish normative standards for generations to come. Consequently, I find in both approaches (postcolonialism and poststructuralism) an opportunity to set a new agenda for population geography. Therefore, to rephrase my opening statement to this section, What is the subject matter of population geography to be? One such approach is a population geography that is sympathetic to the concerns of social justice, violence, and the building of peace. As such, it must by necessity begin with the body.

Population geography should focus, first and foremost, attention on the body. Such a repositioning would place the field in line with recent advances in social theory, and especially those informed by poststructuralism and postcolonialism. As Linda McDowell (1999: 36) argues, the body has become a major theoretical preoccupation across the social sciences, as well as an object for scrutiny and regulation by society as a whole (see also Longhurst, 2001). She explains (p. 34) that "while bodies are undoubtedly material, possessing a range of characteristics such as shape and size and so inevitably taking up space, the ways in which bodies are presented to and seen by others vary according to the spaces and place in which they find themselves." In other words, "the body is not simply the bearer of some pre-given cultural categories" (Nast and Pile, 1998: 3).

For most demographers and statisticians, however, the conception and explanation of "bodies" has been based on a scientific approach that posits physical, biological, and chemical features of the material body as the functional basis for human life (Kulke, 2004: 57). Too often population geographers continue to uncritically use and refine standard demographic analyses (Graham, 2000; Underhill-Sem, 2001). Such uncritical usage is found within the genealogy of population studies and an academic inertia that has stunted the asking of alternative questions.

Recently Chris Philo (2001, 2005) and Stephen Legg (2005) have argued for the importance of a Foucauldian engagement with population geography. Philo (2001: 486), for example, maintains that "in thinking about the interleaving of populations, bodies, institutions, and space," population geographers "might wish to take a more sustained look at ... Foucault." Legg (2005: 138) concurs, finding within the writings of Foucault "a distinctive and fascinating population geography ... which is detectable in his empirical studies, his methodological tactics, and his very epistemological questioning of the nature and genealogy of 'population.'"

For Foucault (1980: 98), the "individual is not to be conceived as a sort of elementary nucleus ... on which power comes to fasten or against which it happens to strike, and in so doing subdues or crushes individuals. In fact, it is already one of the prime effects of power that certain bodies, certain gestures, certain discourses, certain desires, come to be identified and constituted as individuals." Thus, rather than seeing individuals as stable entities—objects to be objectively measured, counted, and categorized—Foucault draws attention to the discursive processes through which bodies are constituted (Mills, 2003: 83).

Foucault's project was to create a history of the different modes by which human beings are made productive subjects. This is an ontological position that critiques biological essentialism and the belief in a transcendental subject. Significantly, Foucault (1980: 73) forwards the idea that "the individual is not a pre-given entity which is seized on by the exercise of power. The individual, with his [sic] identity and characteristics, is the product of a relation of power exercised over bodies, multiplicities, movements, desires, forces." The terms, or discourses, which are inscribed onto bodies are also fluid; meanings are contextual and contingent. To label a body as "male" or "female," for example, entails a host of assumptions and practices that relate to what being "male" and "female" means. In this way, men and women, to continue the example, literally embody norms of masculinity and femininity—or are assumed to embody or are expected to embody them (Domosh and Seager, 2001: 111).

Foucault therefore does not deny the materiality of the body, but neither does the body's materiality exist outside a disciplinary framework, in terms of both knowledge and practices. Victoria Pitts (2003: 29), herself influenced by the writings of Foucault, explains that many contemporary theorists "reject such notions as the body's universality, naturalness, and subordinate relationships to a rational actor as deeply logocentric." She continues (p. 28):

> Post-essentialist theories of the body, expressed in cultural studies, feminism, postmodernism, poststructuralism, and other areas of thought, reject the notion that there is an "essential," proper, ideal body. Instead, the body, along with social laws, nature, and the self, is seen as always open to history and culture, and always negotiable and changing. Instead of one truth of the body or of ontology, there are competing truths that are productions of time, space, geography, and culture.

That said, it is important to not lose sight of the materiality of the body. Glenda Laws (1997: 49), for example, writes that "geographers need to attend to both the conceptualization and material construction of bodies because *our bodies make a difference in our experience of places*: whether we are young or old, able-bodied or disabled, Black or White in appearance does, at least partly, determine collective responses to our bodies." Robyn Longhurst (2001: 223) elaborates that it is essential that geographers address more than simply the "body" as a stable, secure construct. This requires an engagement with the "messiness" of bodies. She writes: "Geographers seldom refer to the actual materiality and fluidity of the body itself.... [It] is still not acceptable for the flesh and boundaries of fluid, volatile, messy, leaky bodies to be included in geographical discourse." Indeed, she explains (p. 23) that "there is little in the discipline that attests to the runny, gaseous, flowing, watery nature of bodies. The messy surfaces/depths of bodies, their insecure boundaries, the fluids that seep and leak from them, that which they engulf, the insides and outsides that sometimes collapse into each other remain invisible in the geographical canon. When geographers speak of the body they still often fail to talk about a body that breaks its boundaries—urinates, bleeds, vomits, farts, engulfs tampons, objects of sexual desire, ejaculates and gives birth."

For feminist scholars, Foucault's notion of the material body as a surface for social inscription has been particularly productive (McDowell, 1999). Indeed, as McDowell (p. 51) highlights, feminists recognize that both women and men are subject to disciplinary power and regimes of corporeal production, albeit to different degrees and in different ways. The challenge, as Yvonne Underhill-Sem (2001: 453) correctly identifies, "has become to work with notions of embodiment that extend beyond any assumed naturalness of biological bodies." Drawing on the work of Michel Foucault, Donna Haraway, and Elizabeth Grosz, among others, Underhill-Sem (p. 454) reminds us that "it is not simply a matter of either a discursive or a material body, but that the material exists both through the way it is talked about and through the way it is not talked about." In short, population geographers need to work with bodies that are not just biological constants, but bodies as situated in historical processes within particular places (Underhill-Sem, 2001: 454).

Many of Foucault's early writings addressed the disciplinary techniques by which bodies were subjected and discursively made. The subjected body, according to Foucault (1979: 25) "is directly involved in a political field: power relations have an immediate hold upon it; they invest it, mark it, train it, torture it, force it to carry out tasks, to perform ceremonies, to emit signs." He continues (pp. 25–26):

> This political investment of the body is bound up in accordance with complex reciprocal relations, with its economic use: it is largely as a force of production that the body is invested with relations of power and domination; but, on the other hand, its constitution as labour power is possible only if it is caught up in a system of subjection (in which need is also a political instrument meticulously prepared, calculated and used); the body becomes a useful force only if it is both a productive body and a subjected body.

This is what Foucault terms an "anatomopolitics" of the human body.

Discipline, according to Foucault (1979: 215), is a type of power; it is a technique for its exercise, "comprising a whole set of instruments, techniques, procedures, and levels of applications." Consequently discipline may be appropriated by various institutions, such as prisons, schools, hospitals, the military, or even "migrant" institutions. The subjugation of bodies, however, is not necessarily repressive. Indeed, Foucault goes to great lengths to show that the exercise of power through discipline is often very productive. The question, of course, is: Who benefits from any particular exercise of power? A well-known example is the discipline meted out by parents to their children. Children must be taught to look before crossing a street, to not touch a hot stove, and so forth. Discipline, in this context, is restrictive, yes. The child is not *allowed* to cross the street "at will" or to touch the stove. But it is probably understood that this, in the long run, is a beneficial form of discipline for the child. The point, therefore, is to consider the context and the contingency of discipline.

Discipline, from a Foucauldian perspective, is not random. Instead, disciplinary techniques are used for specific purposes by specific individuals, groups, or institutions. Discipline, though, *is* directed at bodies. As explained by Foucault (1979: 25), "it is always the body that is at issue—the body and its forces, their utility and their docility, their distribution and their submission." For Mills (2003: 43), Foucault's work on "disciplined bodies" is of great interest "since rather than simply seeing regimes as being oppressive, he analyses the way that regimes exercise power within a society [on bodies] through the use of different institutions such as the hospital, the clinic, the prison and the university."

Having established bodies as subjects, it becomes possible to consider the construction of populations. This occurs, in general, through the classification of bodies into larger collectives, including both social groups and populations. Population as a term is thus dependent on the establishment of practical equivalences among subjects, objects, or events (Curtis, 2002: 508). It is concerned with aggregates and regularities. Bailey (2005: 118) concurs, noting that "essentialist approaches to populations as groups not only infer group meaning from component characteristics, but regard these components as fixed, naturalized and stable elements." Curtis (pp. 508–509) elaborates:

> As an object of knowledge, population is primarily a statistical artefact. The establishment of practical equivalences means that population is connected to the law of large numbers, which causes individual variation to disappear in favour of regularity.

> In its developed forms, population is bound up with the calculus of probabilities. Population makes it possible to identify regularities ... and such things may be both analytic tools and objects of intervention, such as birth, death, or marriage rates.

It was this political–statistical concept of population that preoccupied much of Foucault's writings, although, as Curtis (2002) and Mitchell Dean (1999) suggest, the French philosopher erred in some key elements.[1] Dean (p. 94), for example, explains that "for Foucault, population is a strongly marked term and it is here that we should be wary about following him." Notwithstanding the disparate uses of "population" by Foucault, what is most important for our present purpose is Curtis's discussion on the presence of "population" from the 18th century onward. Population, he (p. 529) argues, "depends upon the establishment of equivalences among the subjects within a particular territory"; political–scientific knowledge consequently "depends on the discipline of potential objects of knowledge. It is only on the grounds of constructed and enforced equivalences that one body comes to equal another, that each death, birth, marriage, divorce, and so on, comes to be the equivalent of any other." Curtis (p. 529) concludes that "it is only on the grounds of such constructed equivalences that it is possible for statistical objects to emerge in the form of regularities and to become the objects of political practice. Population is coincident with the effective capacity of sovereign authority to discipline social relations."

Between the 17th and 18th centuries, Foucault identified a shift in disciplinary focus. It was during this period, in particular, that the first steps were taken toward a "scientific" study of population (James and Martin, 1981: 102). Furthermore, the scientific study of population—as manifested in the writings of John Graunt, William Petty, William Farr, and Thomas Malthus—coincided with an ideological shift concerning the nature of governance. In particular, governments increasingly supplemented their concern with singular bodies with that of whole populations. As Stephen Legg (2005: 141) writes, "Here was a government that became obsessed with statistics concerning birth rates, morbidity and endemics, supplanting the earlier fear of epidemics." Now, a focus on the body revealed it as being imbued with the mechanics of life and serving as the basis of various biological processes: propagation, births and mortality, the level of health, life expectancy, and longevity (Foucault, 1990: 139).

There emerged the concept of a population, a large body of people constituting some kind of definable unit to which measurements pertain (Caldwell, 2001: 20). The German scholar Johann Peter Süssmilch (1707–1767), for example, first demonstrated the existence of certain statistical regularities in population data (James and Martin, 1981: 102). While searching for a divine order, or evidence of God's planning, Süssmilch—who was a clergyman and published a book titled *The Divine Ordinance Manifested in the Human Race through Birth, Death, and Propagation*—examined masses of demographic data. In his quest for regularities, Süssmilch discerned the balance of births and deaths and subsequently produced a life table that was used for actuarial purposes well into the 19th century (Caldwell, 2001: 22; James and Martin, 1981: 102).

Süssmilch of course was not the first individual to ponder the meanings and patterns of life and death. Population-related issues had long occupied human thought. From Plato to Confucius, from St. Augustine to St. Thomas Aquinas, philosophers and political theorists considered the implications of population growth and stability as matters of society and governance. However, it was only during the Renaissance that governments finally undertook the collection of population data, and that statistical studies based on these data were rapidly improved (James and Martin, 1981: 102–103). In so doing, the ontological belief in a discrete and essential "population" came into being.

The timing was not happenstance. The elaboration of a notion of the population was a gradual process that was both technical and theoretical, relying on the development of statistics and census taking, and the techniques of epidemiology, demography, and political philosophy (Dean, 1999: 108). The emergent field of demography blossomed during postfeudalistic Europe for several interrelated reasons. First, the economic changes that accompanied the period were vitally important to the development of population studies. In particular, disciplinary control and knowledge of bodies and populations were unquestionably connected to the rise of capitalism (Dreyfus and Rabinow, 1983: 135). Although subject to debate, there is general agreement that the transition from feudalism, through merchant capitalism, to capitalism in Europe was the result of "a phase of economic, demographic and political 'crisis' [that] brought about the combination of steady population growth, modest technological improvements and limited amounts of usable land" (Knox, Agnew, and McCarthy, 2003: 127; see also Legg, 2005).

The doctrine of mercantilism, or merchant capitalism, is premised on the idea that a nation's wealth is determined by the amount of precious metals (for example, gold and silver) it had in its possession. Colonialism was fundamental to mercantilism. Colonies provided instant wealth, access to resources, cheap labor in the form of indentured servitude and slavery, and ready-made markets (Weeks, 2005: 73). Indeed, it was this "economic 'logic' that justified not only overseas colonization but also the coercion of plantation labour and the prohibition of manufacturing in the colonies" (Knox et al., 2003: 132).

Merchant capitalism was a self-propelling growth system in which the continued expansion of trade was vital: without it neither merchants nor those dependent on their success—producers, consumers, financiers, and so on—could maintain their position, let alone advance it (Knox et al., 2003: 127). Consequently, mercantilist writers sought to encourage population growth by a number of means, including penalties for nonmarriage, encouragements to get married, lessening penalties for illegitimate births, limiting outmigration, and promoting inmigration of productive laborers (Weeks, 2005: 73). Hence, on sugar plantations and in silver mines, in textile factories and dockyards, it was the disciplining of populations that underlay the growth, spread, and (ultimately) triumph of capitalism as an economic venture. Without the insertion of disciplined, orderly individuals into the machinery of production, the new demands of capitalism would have been impossible without the fixation, control, and rational distributions of populations on a large scale (Dreyfus and Rabinow, 1983: 135).

Furthermore, the ascension of mercantilism and, later, capitalism in Western Europe led to the widespread practice of insurance and life annuities. As Paul Knox and his coauthors (2003: 130–131) explain, "in the fifteenth and sixteenth centuries, a series of innovations in business and technology contributed to the consolidation of merchant capitalism." These included, among others, banking, loan systems, credit transfers, shares in stock, speculation in commodity futures, and insurance. Many of these financial transactions were directly related to the "probability" of life and death. Consequently, as Bourdelais (2004: 100) explains, the "disappointments of some cities that had to modify the rate during the duration of local loans quickly revealed the advisability of having life tables based on actual observation of the life span of the population." As a result, the first life tables, covering each age, appeared in England and Holland at the end of the 17th and the beginning of the 18th centuries (Bourdelais, p. 101).

Dean (1999) explains that the construction of demography coincided with liberalism as a political economic philosophy. Governments were no longer primarily concerned with the proper distribution of things, by which Dean means an ordering and regulation of humans in their relations to various heterogeneous entities (for example, wealth, industry, land) and orderly settlement and movements between and within territories. Rather, "the point at which population ceases to be the sum of the inhabitants within a territory and becomes a reality *sui generis* with its own forces and tendencies is the point at which this dispositional government of the state begins to meet a government through social, economic, and biological processes" (pp. 95–96). In other words, *population* becomes its own entity. From this point forward, it becomes possible to speak of a state's "population," as if that population had a transcendental existence and experience above and beyond the government. Furthermore, it is here that we can locate the construction of populations into subgroups that contribute to or retard the general welfare and life of the population as a whole. For Dean (p. 100), it is this proclivity that led to the discovery among the population *writ large* of criminal classes, for example, or the feebleminded and the imbeciles, the inverts and the degenerates, the unemployable and the abnormal.

It is the notion of a "population," according to Dean (1999: 107) that makes possible the elaboration of distinctively liberal governmental techniques and rationalities. As Dreyfus and Rabinow (1983) explain, the history, geography, climate, and demography of a particular country became more than mere curiosities. These became

> crucial elements in a new complex of power and knowledge and, subsequently, the development of academic fields such as demography, sociology, and geography.[2] The government, particularly the administrative apparatus, needed knowledge that was concrete, specific, and measurable in order to operate effectively. This

enabled it to ascertain precisely the state of its forces, where they were weak and how they could be shored up. (p. 137)

Not surprisingly, certain data were jealously guarded by governments. Most secret was the size of the population. As Caldwell (2001: 19) writes, "State strength was dependent on population numbers, especially those males of military age." Consequently, many authorities responsible for the collection and dissemination of data, such as the Danish census takers, were under strict orders not to include members of the army in that the king did not want to disclose the army's strength (Johansen, 2004: 26).

The concept of population introduces several key elements that will have broad ramifications on the art of governance. First, the idea of population introduces a different conception of the governed. The members of a population are no longer subjects bound together in a territory who are obliged to submit to their sovereign. Instead, they are also conceived as living and working social beings, with their own customs, habits, and histories. Second, populations are defined in relation to matters of life and death, health and illness, propagation and longevity, all of which can be *known* by statistical, demographic, and epidemiological instruments (Dean, 1999: 107). Third, the concept of population imparts the idea of a collective entity, the knowledge of which is irreducible to the knowledge that any of its members may have of themselves. In other words, the "population is not just a collection of living, working and speaking subjects; it is also a particular objective reality of which one can have knowledge" (Dean, 1999: 107). This is a crucial ontological shift in the formation of population studies. As John Caldwell (2001) writes, those scholars who came to identify themselves as demographers were suspicious of the study of individuals and small groups; they believed that such bodies were significant only when it could be shown what fraction of a larger population they constitute. Demographers, consequently, would look for regularities in populations or subpopulations, as well as for contrasts between subpopulations (p. 21).

Given such an ontological position on population, Dean (1999: 107) explains that now one could ask

> about the historical development of certain aspects of the population; its marriage customs, the number of marriages that are usu-

ally conjoined, at what ages, how many children are produced by these marriages, the customs that take place within the family, the price of labour and its variation, and the happiness of the working population at a given time. In short, we can know a population, and its industry, customs and history, as a collective identity that is not constituted by political or governmental institutions or frameworks.

Supervision of these population processes was effected through a series of interventions Foucault terms "biopolitics." *Biopolitics* entails "a set of processes such as the ratio of births to deaths, the rate of reproduction, the fertility of a population, and so on. It is these processes—the birth rate, the mortality rate, longevity, and so on—together with a whole series of related economic and political problems ... [that] become biopolitics' first objects of knowledge and the targets it seeks to control" (Foucault, 2003: 243). Not surprisingly, it was at this point that demographers began to measure these population events in statistical terms. The individual, to the extent that bodies were considered, was "of interest exactly insofar as he [sic] could contribute to the strength of the state. The lives, deaths, activities, work, miseries, and joys of individuals were important to the extent that these everyday concerns became politically useful" (Dreyfus and Rabinow, 1983: 139).

Biopolitics emerged with the constitution of *the population* as a field of knowledge (as seen in political economy, statistics, and the like) and a domain of regulation and action in technologies of the management of its health, hygiene, and welfare (Dean, 1999: 94). This emergence was predicated on the institutionalization and standardization of censuses and population-related concepts. As Bruce Curtis (2002: 259) explains, "It is only on the grounds of constructed and enforced equivalences that one body comes to equal another, that each death, birth, marriage, divorce, and so on, comes to be the equivalent of any other. It is only on the grounds of such constructed equivalences that it is possible for statistical objects to emerge in the form of regularities and to become the objects of political practice."

Unlike the disciplining of bodies, biopolitics addresses the population, with population as a political–economic problem. New technologies of power—including population forecasts, statistical estimates, and various other demographic measures and concepts—were applied not to individual bodies, but to a "global mass," collectivities and aggregates, or, simply put, populations. And the purpose of these techniques, according to Foucault (2003: 246), was not to modify any given phenomenon as such, or to modify a given body insofar as he or she is an individual, but essentially to intervene at the level at which these general phenomena are determined. For example, the "mortality rate" or the "birthrate" were to be modified. This could be accomplished through various regulatory mechanisms that operate at a larger aggregate scale.

For population geographers, we now see that two technologies of power exist: one technique is disciplinary and centers on the body. This exercise of power produces individualizing effects and manipulates the body as a source of forces that have to be rendered both useful and docile. A second set brings together the mass effects characteristic of a population, and tries to control the series of random events that can occur in a living mass (for example, births, deaths, and illnesses) (Foucault, 2003: 249). Biopolitics therefore does not exclude considerations of the anatomopolitics of the human body. Rather, the two forms of power are seen as complimentary; they exist on different levels, one directed toward the body, the other toward the population. Indeed, the combination of the two contributes to a particular era of "biopower," marked by an explosion of numerous and diverse techniques for achieving the subjugation of bodies and the control of populations.

A retheorized population geography therefore has two overlapping concerns: the disciplining of bodies (that is, an anatomopolitics) and a regulation of populations (that is, biopolitics). Consequently, we see a combined "biopower" that "has taken control of both the body and life in general, with the body as one pole and the population as the other" (Foucault, 2003: 253). What, though, is the specific contribution that *population geographers* can make? My agenda, as indicated earlier, prefigures an intervention in the struggle against societal injustices and, specifically, violence. My intent is to highlight the underlying population geographies that are made in the discipline of bodies and the regulation of populations through the control of space. Concurrently, it will be possible to develop a theoretically informed population geography that may more fully engage in overturning structures of injustice and work toward the building of a more peaceful society.

VIOLENCE AND THE SPACES OF MORAL EXCLUSION

Foucault (1980: 77) concluded, at the end of an interview, that "geography must indeed necessarily lie at the heart of [his] concerns." By this he meant that the exercise of power (for example, the disciplining of people and the regulation of populations) was inherently spatial. Indeed, Elden (2001: 152) writes:

> In terms of Foucault's own work I have argued that Foucault's historical studies are spatial through and through, and that this is a fundamental legacy of his work to those interested in the question of space.... Understanding how space is fundamental to the use of power and to historical research into the exercise of power allows us to recast Foucault's work not just as a history of the present but as a mapping of the present.

Foucault's spaces, however, have not been the spaces of population geography. We need to establish, therefore, a respatialized population geography while we concurrently retheorize population geography. Such a repositioning, likewise, will entail an engagement with the body.

David Delaney (1998: 4) introduces a concept he terms *geographies of experience*. He writes:

> Our lives are, in a sense, made of time. But we are also physical, corporeal, mobile beings. We inhabit a material, spatial world. We move through it. We change it. It changes us. Each of us is weaving a singular path through the world. The paths that we make, the conditions under which we make them, and the experiences that those paths open up or close off are part of what makes us who we are.

Delaney prefigures a discussion of self and space and opens a window on the idea of embodied practice. Through our daily activities we encounter other peoples and other places; our thoughts and actions are influenced by these encounters. Concurrently, however, our presence, our interactions, likewise reflect back upon those spaces. Just as we are transformed through our daily activities, so too are the spaces that we inhabit transformed. In short, we produce and are produced by space just as we produce and are produced by discourse (Tyner, 2006b: 63).

The meanings and uses of space are never separate from the contestations over bodies and populations: Who, or which group, is granted or denied access to certain spaces? What activities are deemed acceptable or not? And who has the authority, the ability, to define such spaces? Philosopher Henri Lefebvre (1991) suggests that space may be viewed in two basic forms: *representations of space* and *representational spaces*. The former refers to conceptualized spaces, the spaces of scientists and planners. These constitute the "dominant" or authorized spaces and carry with them certain rules and regulations for use. In this light, space is purposefully representational of certain societal ideals, and therefore the holders of these ideals attempt to control its use (Lefebvre, 1991). The Khmer Rouge leadership, for example, developed particular ideals as to the spaces of Democratic Kampuchea: Cambodia was to be remade as a modern, socialist utopia (Tyner, 2008). Consequently, this entailed a massive project of social engineering. Likewise, the Hutu perpetrators of the Rwandan genocide worked with a particular representation of a post-Tutsi society.

Representations of space are not simply produced via the machinations of state institutions. Often we are socialized, or trained, into a recognition and understanding of these representations of space. The work of David Sibley, in particular, has explored these various *geographies of exclusion* whereby the presence of certain "groups" is deemed acceptable or not. Public parks, for example, are considered to be appropriate for children and families but generally inappropriate spaces for teenagers. These socially produced divisions of space—which may be physically demarcated through signs, gates, or other markers—become naturalized and normalized. This does not negate, however, the observation that these spaces remain highly regulated and contested spaces. Authorities often expend considerable investment in the policing of these spaces.

Despite the efforts of those in dominance, representations of space are far from complete. Attempts to normalize space are never complete; the hegemonic control of space is always open to exposure, confrontation, reversal, and refusal through counterhegemonic or disidentifying practices (Natter and Jones, 1997: 150). Consequently, representational spaces are "sites of resistance, and of counter-discourses which have not been grasped by apparatuses of power" (Stewart, 1995: 611). According to Lefebvre (1991: 41), representational spaces "need obey no rules of consistency or cohesiveness. Redolent with imaginary and symbolic elements, they have their source in history—in the history of a people as well as in the history of each individual belonging to that people."

Both representations of space and representational spaces are not mutually exclusive. Rather, the two spaces coexist—albeit tenuously and contested. Don Mitchell (1995: 115) writes that "public space often, though not always, originates as a representation of space" but "as people use these spaces, they also become representational spaces, appropriated in use." As Lefebvre (1991: 85) explains, "Space is never produced in the sense that a kilogram of sugar or a yard of cloth is produced." Instead, space is "the product of competing ideas (discourses) about what constitutes that space—order and control or free, and perhaps dangerous interaction" (Mitchell, 1995: 115).

The construction of community and the bounding of social groups are part of the same problem as the separation of self and other (Sibley, 1995: 45). As Young (1990) explains, the social ontology underlying many contemporary theories of justice is methodologically individualistic; it presumes that the individual—the self—exists ontologically prior to the social group. However, one of the main contributions of poststructural philosophy has been to challenge this ontological assumption, to "expose as illusory this metaphysics of a unified self-making subjectivity, which posits the subject as an autonomous origin or an underlying substance to which attributes of gender, nationality, family role, intellectual disposition, and so on might attach" (Young, 1990: 45).

Such a challenge is critical because, at the social level, as at the individual level, an awareness of group boundaries serves to marginalize and exclude other people (Sibley, 1995). According to Young (1990: 43), a social group (or population) is a collective of persons differentiated from at least one other group by cultural forms, practices, or way of life. More precisely, groups are expressions of social relations; groups exist only in relation to other groups. However, as Young (p. 53) elaborates, many groups find themselves marginalized. Indeed, a "whole category of people may be expelled from useful participation in social life and thus potentially subjected to severe material deprivation and even extermination."

Susan Opotow (2001) suggests that norms, moral rules, and concerns about rights and fairness govern our conduct toward other people. However, not every person or group is necessarily included within the scope of justice. Rather, she explains that "inclusion in the scope of justice means applying considerations of fairness, allocating resources, and making sacrifices to foster another's well-being." Conversely, moral exclusion "rationalizes and excuses harm inflicted on those outside the scope of justice. Excluding others from the scope of justice means viewing them as unworthy of fairness, resources, or sacrifice, and seeing them as expendable, undeserving, exploitable, or irrelevant" (p. 156).

Three dimensions of moral exclusion are particularly salient: extent, severity, and engagement. First, there is the *extent* of moral exclusion. This refers to the scope of collective inclusion or exclusion and is seen, for example, in sociospatial practices that marginalize both people and groups of people. It is especially prevalent in "us–them" thinking. According to social psychologists, the process of *us–them thinking* originates with social categorizations. These mental constructs (for example, man/woman, black/white, citizen/noncitizen) are cognitive tools that segment, classify, and order our social environment (Waller, 2002: 239). Waller (pp. 239–240) suggests that the use of social categorizations in assigning people to populations has four salient effects: assumed similarity, outgroup homogeneity, accentuation, and ingroup bias. First, people who identify themselves as part of an ingroup tend to perceive other ingroup members as more similar than outgroup members. Second, people likewise perceive members of outgroups as all alike; generalizations, moreover, are often based on one or two members. Third, perceived differences between ingroups and outgroups tend to be accentuated, or exaggerated. These differences, furthermore, may be augmented spatially. The imposition of black codes in the United States following Emancipation, and later, Jim Crow laws, were attempts to fix the meaning of space, reflecting a hegemonic cultural norm (that is, white supremacy). Spaces in this sense were color-coded and imbued with particular meanings. Fourth, the mere act of dividing bodies into groups (or populations) inevitably sets up a bias in group members in favor of the ingroup and against the outgroup (p. 240).

The process of social categorization does not proceed based on natural divisions of humanity. Rather than presuming that such categorizations (for example, racial and ethnic) are simply present, social categories do not simply *include* groups, but rather *produce* those groups. In other words, there are no ontological bases to social categories. There is, consequently, an immediate spatiality to the process of social categorization. As Waller (2002: 239) writes, "Not only do social categorizations systemize our social world; they also create and define our place in it." Social categorizations, in effect, *produce* population geographies.

To be sure, certain physical markers, presumed as natural, have been widely utilized (for example, skin color), but even here, people must be socialized into a belief that this is an appropriate marker of distinction. Rare is the child who "naturally" divides his or her classmates based on eye color. Subsequent examples will further clarify this point. During the months and years leading up to the Rwandan genocide, for example, differences between Tutsis and Hutus were routinely played up, with deadly consequences.

One extreme form of moral exclusion, also readily evident in the Rwandan genocide, is the outright denial of self as manifested in practices of dehumanization. This involves the categorizing of a group as inhuman either by using categories of subhuman creatures (for example, cockroaches) or by using categories of negatively evaluated nonhuman creatures (for example, demons and monsters). Moreover, this process of dehumanization is most likely to occur when target groups can be readily identified as a separate category of people (Waller, 2002: 245). The Chams, a minority people living in Cambodia, for example, were visually easy targets for Khmer Rouge violence. Likewise, the tendency of American soldiers in Vietnam to identify the enemy as "gooks" or "dinks" contributed to the violence that engulfed that country.

Through practices of dehumanization isolated groups are stigmatized as alien. Waller (2002: 245) elaborates that such dehumanization facilitates practices of exclusion, oppression, discrimination, and violence. Once dehumanized, one's body "possesses no meaning. It is a waste, and its removal is a matter of sanitation. There is no moral or emphatic context through which the perpetrator can relate to the victim." As such, a dehumanized body facilitates the process of moral exclusion. This is seen vividly in the historical stigmatization of Jewish victims prior to the Holocaust. Waller (p. 246) explains that

> in the Holocaust ... the Nazis redefined Jews as "bacilli," "parasites," "vermin," "demons," "syphilis," "cancer," "excrement,"

"filth," "tuberculosis," and "plague." In the camps, male inmates were never to be called "men" but *Haftlinge* (prisoners), and when they ate the verb used to describe it was *fressen*, the word for animals eating. Statisticians and public health authorities frequently would list corpses not as *corpses* but as *Figuren* (figures or pieces), mere things, or even rags. Similarly, in a memo of June 5, 1942, labeled "Secret Reich Business," victims in gas vans at Chelmno are variously refereed to as "the load," "number of pieces," and the "merchandise."

There is, likewise, a spatial counterpart to these dehumanization practices. For Waller (2002: 247), "linguistic dehumanization is complemented by physical machinations that make the victims seem less than human. These degrading, often ritualistic, processes remake the individual self in the institutional image of something less than a full person." Consider, for example, the strategic hamlets established during the Vietnam War, or the isolated work camps of the Khmer Rouge. Both served to physically and symbolically separate and dehumanize perceived outgroups. More concretely, the placement of bodies in cages or other torture facilities serves, symbolically, to further dehumanize people. In Cambodia, during the killing times, people were forced to live in work camps that worked to dehumanize people. Roeun Sam (1997: 78) describes her experiences:

> A doghouse was better than where we were staying. Bushes were our walls. We slept on rice hay. Thick bags made of hemp that held rice seed were our blankets. The bags smelled, and mine was completely stained and falling apart.... Every night I could hear the footsteps of Khmer Rouge soldiers walking around. They were laughing and drinking, and they enjoyed the killing.... One night ... I got into my bag.... A rat came in and ate my toenail. I slept so heavy I didn't even know.

Those prisoners confined to torture facilities fared worse (if such a statement can be made). Those interned at Tuol Sleng, or any of the other centers throughout the country, were kept chained to the floor, in make-shift cells. Both prior to and during their interrogations—and before their near inevitable executions—prisoners were made to lie in their own urine and feces. Such practices served to dehumanize the prisoners. As Waller (2002: 248) writes, such people "become emaciated figures of total misery, lice-infested, soiled, and wrapped in rags, furthering their dehumanization in the eyes of the perpetrators."

Apart from discussions of the extent of moral exclusion, it is possible to identify a second dimension, namely, the *severity* of moral exclusion. As explained by Opotow (2001: 158), these may range from rude, degrading behavior, to mild injury, to severe injury, to torture, to irreversible injuries, to mutilation, and to murder. Of particular importance is how violence is enacted toward morally excluded bodies and groups. An exercise of violence is totalizing. When violence is applied to a body, subjugation is complete. It removes the possibilities for active subjects to resist. To this end, Barker (1998: 38) explains that "violence involves a direct application of force upon the body of the other, reducing every possibility for independent action. Violence is applied directly to a body, but more than this it is applied to a body which is not recognized as being in a 'relationship' that would allow it to act autonomously."

It is possible, furthermore, to distinguish between "direct" and "structural" violence. Direct violence, in Opotow's (2001: 151) view, "is immediate, concrete, visible, and committed by and upon particular people" or bodies. This contrasts with structural violence, which "occurs as inequalities structured into a society so that some have access to social resources that foster individual and community well-being—high quality education and health care, social status, wealth, comfortable and adequate housing, and efficient civic services—while others do not." Consequently, "structural violence normalizes unequal access to political and economic resources" (p. 151) in favor of one group over another. Furthermore, structural violence does not necessarily maim or kill directly, but it has the potential to do so, and sets up divisions.

Practices of moral exclusion and political violence are legitimized and sustained through complex imaginative geographies (Graham, 2006; Gregory, 1994, 2004). Indeed, both direct violence (that is, those practices applied to bodies) and structural violence (that is, those practices applied to groups or populations) are justified and spatialized through the forwarding of particular representations of "difference" between *bodies in space*. As Derek Gregory (2004: 17) explains, imaginative geographies "are constructions that fold distance into difference through a series of spatializations. They work ... by multiplying partitions and enclosures that serve to demarcate 'the same' from 'the other.'" As a spatial practice of moral exclusion, imaginative geographies construct 'gaps' or 'differences' between social groups by designating certain spaces as 'ours' or 'theirs.' In Rwanda, for example, Hutu extremists categorized the Tutsi as "invaders" and "occupiers"; only the Hutu were considered the rightful inhabitants of the country.

Lastly, we may refer to one's *engagement* in moral exclusion, or, in other words, a person's responsibility for, and response to, exclusionary practices. Opotow (2001: 158) suggests that engagement may range from unawareness to ignoring, allowing, facilitating, executing, or devising moral exclusion. Consequently, questions of engagement relate directly to the idea of impunity. Strictly defined, impunity refers to the exemption from accountability, penalty, punishment, or legal sanctions for a crime. Such an understanding necessarily focuses attention on alleged perpetrators of violence (for example, Pol Pot in Cambodia). More broadly, though, we can speak of a "culture of impunity." This occurs when impunity is institutionalized and widespread, when torture, crimes against humanity, and mass murder are overtly or tacitly condoned and unpunished as result of amnesties, pardons, indifferences, or simply "looking the other way" (Opotow, 2001: 150). It is a "culture of impunity" that permits mass violence and genocide to continue unabated; it is a culture of impunity that allows other governments and global citizens to ignore—and, consequently, condone—the continuation of direct and structural violence in other places.

A culture of impunity is supported by imaginative geographies. As Joseph Nevins (2005: 11–13) explains, geographic proximity, power, and distance (both social and geographic) must be accounted for in discussions of political violence. He argues that social distance and geographic distance combine to make the plight of others more peripheral and, by extension, less relevant. The violence in Darfur, we say to ourselves, is unfortunate; but it is *their* problem, *not ours*. Likewise, the "indifference by the international community to earlier massacres of Tutsi by Hutu" in Rwanda offered "encouragement to the growing elites that the Hutu could commit genocide [in 1994] and get away with it" (Smith, 1999: 4). Through such reasoning, "people [and institutions] who have the intellectual, financial, or social resources to hinder harm-doing choose to remain aloof, disinterested, or uninformed" (Opotow, 2001: 158).

A lack of engagement operates within and simultaneously produces a culture of impunity. Once established, a culture of impunity serves to legitimate nonaction. Opotow (2001: 157) identifies a particular form of denial whereupon one attempts to exonerate oneself. This is evident in such examples as "deindividuation (believing one's contribution to harm doing is undetectable), displacing responsibility (identifying others, such as higher authorities, as legitimate decision-makers responsible for harms), and diffusing responsibility (denying personal responsibility for harm by seeing it as the result of collective rather than individual decisions and actions)."

A culture of impunity may also work to blame the victims of violence for their own plight. Various studies have documented the tendency of both participants and bystanders of mass violence to blame the victims (Waller, 2002). Similar findings have been forwarded by studies of rape, domestic abuse, homelessness, and HIV/AIDs. Accordingly, social psychologists, among others, have grappled with the observation that "victims" are often classified by participants and bystanders into two broad categories: those who deserve suffering and those who do not. To capture this concept, Melvin Lerner (1980) coined the term "just-world phenomenon" in reference to the practice of people believing that the world is just and that *other* people "get" what they deserve. In other words, the social categorization of bodies into populations, and the concomitant dehumanization of people, not only recategorizes bodies into subhuman groups, it also carries with it an understanding that victims deserve or require their own victimization (Waller, 2002: 249).

One need not look solely at psychological explanations. Alternatively, the tendency to "blame the victims" may also be conceived as a discursive practice. Indeed, the belief in a just world is itself a discourse, one that is promoted by various institutions to legitimize questionable policies and practices. Consequently, Waller (2002: 252) writes that a

> strong belief in a just world is associated with [a] rigid application of social rules and belief in the importance of convention, as opposed to empathy and concern with human welfare. How do we explain, for instance, the plight of the poor and homeless? Those who display a strong belief in a just world are most likely to blame the poor and homeless for their own suffering. Similarly, some find it more comfortable to believe that battered spouses must have provoked their beatings; that sick people are responsible for their illness; that persons involved in a traffic accident must

have been driving carelessly; that victims of theft surely brought it on themselves by not taking adequate security precautions.

The basis of just-world beliefs are many and varied. For the most part, however, we are simply socialized into such a belief. As children, we are taught that good behavior—telling the truth, cleaning your room, doing your homework—is rewarded, while bad behavior—lying, stealing, teasing your little sister—is punished. The family, consequently, is a major component in our socialization of what is just and unjust. Other institutions, including the media, religion, and academia, however, also provide salient lessons.

The consequences of a just-world belief are foundational to exclusionary practices, the discipline of bodies, and the regulation of populations. Such a belief permits a level of indifference to—and thus a lack of engagement with—the plight of others. Hence, members of the ingroup may not actually *perceive* the oppression of outgroup members as an act of oppression. Pol Pot, for example, genuinely believed that the genocidal regime he oversaw in Cambodia was justified; those who were killed were deserving of their fate. Consequently, interventions on behalf of the ingroup members is not warranted, so strong is the belief that the dehumanized, excluded Others are responsible for their own conditions.

In summary, then, it is possible to more clearly articulate my retheorized (and respatialized) population geography: Through an engagement with specific case studies of how bodies are disciplined and populations are regulated through a control of space, population geographers may be better positioned to intervene in the struggle against spatial and moral exclusionary practices that serve to categorize, discriminate, oppress, and, ultimately murder those who are perceived to be Others. In so doing we will necessarily contribute to the ongoing efforts to challenge a conservative culture of impunity that condones the existence of societal injustices and violence, including war and genocide.

WHY I WRITE

If we are to envision a less violent world, we must first understand how violent the world is. To this end, Jonathon Glover (2000: 406) explains that "it is necessary to see the size and urgency of the problem." He continues:

> For those of us whose everyday life is in relatively calm and sheltered places, the horrors of Rwanda or Bosnia or Kosovo seem unreal. The atrocities can be put out of mind. The television news reports torture or a massacre and we feel relief when it moves on to political scandals or sports. We bystanders look away. Repressing each atrocity maintains the illusion that the world is fundamentally a tolerable place. Yet it is almost certain that, as you read this sentence, in some places people are being killed and in others people are being tortured.

To do nothing is to cultivate a culture of impunity. Consequently, a retheorized population geography must empirically and theoretically engage with the historical and contemporary disciplining and regulation of people and populations through the management, administration, and control of space. Ethical, and not simply empirical, questions must be asked as to the beneficent or maleficent exercise of biopower in particular contexts. As McKendrick (2001: 466) warns, there is the ever-present danger in the population geographies of mathematical models that populations are dehumanized by being reduced to numbers. Such ethical considerations may (though not exclusively) follow Young's (1990: 37) conception that social justice concerns the "degree to which a society contains and supports the institutional conditions necessary for the realization of positive values. To affect the promotion of these values, however, it is necessary to critique and overturn those institutions that perpetuate *injustice*, composed of two forms of disabling constraints: oppression and domination" (p. 39). Both are intimately associated with the violence perpetrated against bodies and populations.

Findlay (2003) is absolutely correct when he states that population and demographic issues are at the center of much work in academia. How is it possible to talk of war or genocide without talking about people? The question is: What do we do? As academics? As geographers? As population geographers? The nearly two-decade call for a retheorized population geography is not fundamentally a methodological problem. Rather, I read the ongoing debates as an ethical dilemma and a normative question about what we should do and why. Concurrently, apart from the question of *how* to retheorize population geography, we need to reconsider the reasons *for* a retheorization. Are population geographers (myself included) fundamentally concerned with the survival of population geography as an institution? Is the health of our field measured—quantitatively—by membership in the Population Specialty Group, submission of articles to leading journals, or subscriptions to *Population, Space and Place*? Are we concerned with our own perceived "marginalization" within human geography specifically, geography in general, and the social sciences more broadly? If these are the underlying reasons for a retheorized population geography, then I personally would not be saddened by its demise.

A retheorized population geography is required, however, so that we as conscientious scholars and teachers may work toward a more humane and just society through the elimination of structural injustices. Brian Barry (2005: 3), a political philosopher, asks why we need to develop a theory of social justice. He writes: "In the poorest countries, people do not need a theory to tell them that there is something wrong with a world in which their children are dying from malnutrition or diseases that could be prevented by relatively inexpensive public health measures." Most people would agree that these preventable deaths are unfortunate; few, though, would agree as to the cause of these conditions, or their own obligations and responsibilities to ameliorate these deaths. In short, many of us would contribute to an ongoing culture of impunity.

When faced with practices of moral exclusion, we need to confront our own level of engagement. The time is now. As David Sibley (1995: 184) somewhat optimistically declares, the "social sciences, and human geography in particular, might now be better equipped to challenge xenophobia, racism and other exclusionary tendencies because of a greater intellectual awareness of difference." Throughout the course of *War, Violence, and Population* I do not cover the typical subject matter found in traditional and conventional population geography texts. My concerns, rather, coalesce around topics such as state-sanctioned violence, the deliberate targeting and killing of civilians in war, and war-related rapes. These topics are, on the one hand, generally neglected in the study of population but, on the other hand, are intimately associated with Foucault's anatomopolitics of the body and biopolitics—in other words, biopower. In the pages that follow I begin to chart such a course. My position, following Robert Young (2003: 7), is that a retheorization is necessary in order to "change the way people think, the way they behave, to produce a more just and equitable relation between the different peoples of the world." In the chapters that follow I advocate one particular approach, one that is heavily indebted to poststructuralism and postcolonialism. What I envision is unlike any other population geography text or approach. Through three specific examples of mass violence and genocide—Vietnam, Cambodia, and Rwanda—I highlight the discipline of bodies and the regulation of populations through the production and control of space. Throughout these studies I emphasize the production of knowledge-claims that legitimize and justify the perpetuation of violence through the marginalization of bodies and populations. In so doing, I focus mostly, though not exclusively, on violence, genocide, and war. My reason is simple. Population geography has paid insufficient attention to the structural forms of social injustice and violence—and most especially those related to war and genocide—enacted on bodies and populations. As Dith Pran (1997: x), the survivor of Cambodia's holocaust whose life was portrayed in the film *The Killing Fields* (Joffé, 1984), writes, "The dead are crying out for justice. Their voices must be heard. It is the responsibility of the survivors to speak out for those who are unable to speak.... " It is our responsibility as well.

2

BIOPOWER IN VIETNAM

Michael Clodfelter, an author and historian, is also a veteran of the Vietnam War. In his book *Mad Minutes and Vietnam Months*, Clodfelter (1988) captures the dehumanizing aspects of war and the immorality of violently induced mortality. After one firefight, for example, Clodfelter (p. 105) describes his reaction to viewing the bodies of two young Vietnamese soldiers:

> Both wore ironic expressions of contentment on their young faces. Though caking, scarlet pockets of bullet wounds and vacantly staring eyes were the only indications that these men were dead instead of dreaming, they already seemed somehow less human to me. I could not allow myself the awareness then that I could have easily been lying there in my death posture; my life's experiences, hopes, memories, all suddenly terminated as were those of the young men whom I could not now grace with the quality of humanity for fear of its implications of my own mortality.

Elsewhere, Clodfelter (1995: 121) describes the registration of death: the body counts. "Nineteen bodies were found in expressions of death in their vast green sarcophagus," he writes. "The only acknowledgment of our execution of those men would be an entry in the neat, fine print of official battle reports, the military's record book that neither bled nor carried the stench of death." In stark detail, Clodfelter writes of the Othering of war, of what the Nobel laureate Wole Soyinka describes as a "spiral of antihumanism." Clodfelter recalls, from his combat experiences, that "violent death still brought grief when a friend fell, but the death of a Vietnamese, any Vietnamese, not just the enemy, was looked upon with no more pity than a hunter gives his prey.... " For Clodfelter, "Killing a dink had become different from killing a human being, and even if a bit of remorse remained, war excused and vindicated killing and exonerated the souls of men who murdered but yet refused to consider themselves as murderers." Acknowledging the downward slide to antihumanism, and the existence of a culture of impunity, Clodfelter (p. 149) concludes that "war was working insane logic on us. We were learning to deny the enemy's humanity, and because it was so difficult to distinguish the enemy from those who merely hated us, it had become easier to kill both."

The political geographer Colin Flint (2005: 3) asks "What is war?" His question has occupied the attention of political scientists, political geographers, and philosophers. Less so have population geographers confronted so starkly the question of war, and yet I maintain that war *should* be fundamental to the study of population. Acknowledging the many "forms" of war, Flint, for example, argues that one aspect of war is universal across space and time. War, Flint concludes, is tyranny. He elaborates (p. 3) that this statement refers to the "processes by which people who did not initiate war become cogs in a fighting machine mobilized to defend territory, values, and collective identities from aggression." Furthermore, for Flint, geography provides a number of themes through which war may be approached. These include, among others, territoriality, borders, place, and scale. Ultimately, Flint (p. 6) proposes that war "is a political process that has as its purpose the control of territory to enable subsequent projections of power."

This is all very good, but we should also consider the demographics of war, and especially a corporatist, industrial form of warfare as it has evolved throughout the 20th century (cf. Adas, 2006; Hossein-Zadeh, 2006). The control of territory—frequently a crucial aspect of military strategy—arises from the discipline of bodies and the control of populations. This control is often predicated on the capture or killing of large numbers of people. Indeed, Arthur Westing (1982: 261) notes that of the hundreds of wars that have ravaged the globe in the 20th century, 45 of these conflicts can be considered "high fatality," defined as contributing to over 30,000 fatalities. The impact of these wars can be further grasped by considering global population trends. In 1900 the world's population stood at approximately 1.6 billion persons; eight decades later the population surpassed 4.7 billion. In the interim, Westing (1980: 1982) concludes, approximately 86 million fatalities resulted from these high-fatality wars. In other words, these wars resulted in a premature death for 1.4 percent of all peoples living during the period.

Such catastrophic loss of life has precipitated much interest in the notion of "just" wars (Walzer, 1977). Within population geography, however, minimal attention has focused on the *population geographies* of warfare. To be sure, there are numerous accounts of the demographic losses attributable to wars—although many of these studies are conducted by nongeographers, and certainly not by population geographers (Carlton-Ford, Hamill, and Houston, 2000; Heuveline, 1998; Hirschman, Preston, and Loi, 1995; Horne, 2002; Reza et al., 2001; Westing, 1980, 1982; Winter, 1998).

An engagement with warfare by population geographers will contribute to an antiwar ontology and thus to the building of peace through education. As the historian Howard Zinn (2005: 37) writes, the idea of a just war is a flawed belief. He explains that "a cause may be just, an injustice may have taken place, but that doesn't mean that the use of war to remedy that injustice is itself just." Zinn (p. 38) is blunt in his assessment: "War ... is the massive and indiscriminate killing of human beings." And Zinn's qualifier "indiscriminate" is as deliberate as are the deaths of which he writes. The majority of war-related deaths, especially throughout the 20th century, have been civilians. Of those who perished in the wars in Vietnam, Afghanistan, and Iraq, for example, over 90 percent were civilians. And the trend in increased civilian deaths has not been accidental. Indeed, the indiscriminate targeting of "enemy" populations has resulted from a combination of changing political–military strategies and technological advances in the conduct of war. This is seen most clearly in the increased use of aerial bombardment. As Horne (2002: 482) finds, from 1915 onward, airship and bomber raids on cities and countrysides brought about an awareness of the potential of air warfare as a strategic arm that could bring combat directly to enemy populations. During World War II, as a case in point, the government of Nazi Germany authorized the bombing of civilian targets. In response, Britain embarked on its own strategic bombing campaign. With the entry of the United States into the war, American forces conducted intensive bombing campaigns over the skies of Europe and Japan. In total, aerial bombardments during World War II claimed over 1 million civilian lives throughout Europe and Japan.

Following World War II, military strategies continued to target civilian populations. In many respects, no other conflict symbolizes the wanton disregard for human life as the American-led war on Vietnam (1954–1975). During this conflict American officials embarked on a systematic campaign to discipline bodies and regulate populations for political–industrial purposes. As Clodfelter (1995: 236) writes, "A great many of the civilian victims of American arms died as a result of the way the Americans chose to wage war." It was about killing bodies in an attempt to regulate populations. Men like Robert McNamara and Walt Rostow, for all their sophisticated models, theories, and statistics, were woefully ignorant of, or simply uncaring about, the local conditions and peoples of Vietnam. And men like President Richard M. Nixon, Henry Kissinger, and General William Westmoreland were cavalier toward humanity in their pursuit of realpolitik. Indeed, it was Westmoreland who explained, in Peter Davis's Oscar-winning documentary *Hearts and Minds* (1974), that "the Oriental doesn't put the same high price on life as does a Westerner. Life is plentiful. Life is cheap in the Orient." Such a callous disregard for the value of human life epitomizes the dehumanizing practices that accompany warfare.

Violent acts and atrocities, of course, occurred on both sides during the war. This in no way excuses the violence perpetrated by the Communist Democratic Republic of Vietnam (DRV) and their South Vietnamese compatriots, the National Liberation Front (NLF). However, two things stand out. First, the United States and its allies invaded and occupied Vietnam as that country attempted to liberate itself from French colonial rule. In mapping their own imaginative geography, American policymakers attempted to transform a colonial war into a civil war through the creation of South Vietnam. Concurrently, American military strategists, politicians, and civilian advisors (with few exceptions) conducted a war founded on explicit strategies to kill Vietnamese regardless of any perceived "innocence."

Jonathan Neale (2003: 77) maintains that America was a corporate industrial power and it fought a corporate industrial war. New and "improved" methods were devised to kill *people*—not soldiers, not guerrilla fighters—but *people*: Vietnamese people. Scientists refined the use of cluster bombs and napalm; researchers studied the most effective way to explode human flesh. The efficiency and efficacy of their scholarship was measured in lives. In Vietnam, the war claimed an estimated one to three million persons. These grim statistics alone do not fully capture the devastation. Clodfelter (1995: 257) further reports that in South Vietnam alone, by 1975, there were 83,000 amputees, 8,000 paraplegics, 30,000 blinded, 10,000 deafened, and 50,000 other disabled persons. To these figures we can add approximately 800,000 orphans.

Part and parcel of the loss of life is the environmental destruction meted on Vietnam. Population geographers and other social scientists have long addressed the interconnections of population and the environment. Often, these discussions have highlighted the deleterious effects on the environment resultant from human activities. To this end, scholars have debated the root causes of various ecological problems, such as global warming, deforestation, and the pollution of our atmosphere, oceans, rivers, and soils. Related to these discussions are concerns over the supply of food for human populations. As early as the 18th century, for example, Thomas Malthus questioned the balance between population size and the availability of food. Consequently, social scientists have examined, among other things, trends in food production, the geographic distribution of food supplies, and the ability to increase yields on cultivated lands. Missing from most of these accounts, however, is the *deliberate* destruction of both the environment and food supplies as a means of controlling populations. Indeed, a reconstituted population geography must engage more explicitly with the topic of environmental warfare. Defined by Paul Cecil (1986: 3) as the "destruction of housing, forced relocations of populations, destruction of food supplies, elimination of concealment and forest sanctuary, and driving the enemy into inhospitable terrain unsuitable to agricultural support," environmental warfare is inseparable from the traditional domains of population geography. The American-led military campaign in Vietnam included napalm, defoliants, wetland drainage, crop destruction, and a bombing campaign of "historic intensity"; in all, these techniques of power helped "create a continuing legacy of ecological and health problems" that plagues Vietnam to this day (Cecil, 1986).

In this chapter I present not a history of the Vietnam War, but rather a population geography of the war. My intent is not to highlight the firepower, but rather to emphasize the biopower involved in the military campaigns of the war, and to encourage others to think critically about population issues in the context of war.

THE CONTEXT OF THE VIETNAM WAR

Accessibility to the lucrative China trade was the primary lure. Vietnam was viewed as a means to that end. Beginning in 1859 Vietnamese sovereignty was steadily reduced by French colonial efforts. In that year a French naval expedition seized Saigon and within 3 years the Vietnamese emperor, Tu Duc, conceded to the French Saigon and three surrounding provinces. France initially was attracted to Vietnam because of the presence, in the north, of the Red River. French authorities hoped that the river would lead directly to the heart of China and its attendant riches. Over time it became clear that the Red River was not the riverine path to riches. Vietnam, nevertheless, contained valuable mineral deposits and other agricultural products for export and profit.

By the end of the 19th century France had acquired all of Vietnam. Vietnam disappeared off the map and was replaced by an imaginative geography called *Indochina*. Administratively, the former Vietnam was divided into three parts. Cochin China, located in the far south and centered on Saigon, was ruled as a French colony; Annam, the central region, based at Hue, and Tonkin, in the north, centered on Hanoi, were both officially "protectorates," but in actuality were ruled as colonies. To these three divisions were added neighboring Laos and Cambodia.

For the first four decades of the 20th century France governed Indochina. Throughout these years, resistance to French rule was widespread but sporadic, and did not solidify until the 1920s (SarDesai, 2005). A number of popular movements emerged, many of which were religious-based. Still other movements were modeled after revolutionary parties outside of Indochina. In 1927, for example, the Viet Nam Quoc Dan Dang (VNQDD) was established, based on China's Kuomintang. Most significant, however, was the foundation in 1930 of the Indochina Communist Party (ICP). Formed by a young nationalist named Ho Chi Minh, the ICP was not, as yet, a threat to French colonial rule.

During World War II Indochina was occupied by the Japanese. However, a Japanese agreement with the Vichy regime in France permitted French colonial authorities to remain in power until the waning days of the war. As was the case throughout Southeast Asia, the defeat of French forces by the Japanese added impetus to the growing nationalist movements within Indochina.

In 1941 the Vietminh (Viet Nam Doc Lap Dong Minh, or League for the Independence of Vietnam) had been established as a front organization for the ICP. Throughout the war the Vietminh—frequently with the help of American and other allied forces—waged a guerrilla campaign against the Japanese. Following Japan's surrender, members of the Vietminh assumed that they would take control of the government.

The principle wartime allies of the United States, Britain and the Soviet Union, considered events in Southeast Asia secondary to the defeat of the Axis powers. Nevertheless, as the war progressed, the Allied powers, including France and the nationalist government of Chiang Kai-shek in China, began to develop plans for the future of Southeast Asia. Churchill, for example, insisted that France should keep its colonies in Indochina; he was dedicated to retaining the British Empire, and was worried that Indochinese independence from France would strengthen the case for Indian and African independence from Britain (Neale, 2003: 25). In contrast, American officials desired a more open strategy, one that would facilitate greater economic integration of the region into U.S. plans. The American position on postwar Indochina initially reflected President Roosevelt's antipathy to renewed European colonialism. Indeed, Roosevelt hoped to establish a liberal capitalist world system based on the principle of equal commercial opportunity (Hearden, 2005: 22). Colonialism was anathema to such a vision. Roosevelt preferred instead the establishment of trusteeships for colonial areas. In 1943, for example, Roosevelt mused that France had "milked it [Indochina] for one hundred years" and had left its people "worse off than they were at the beginning" (Karnow, 1983: 136).

Following the defeat of Japan, and pursuant to the Potsdam Agreements of July 1945, British troops occupied Vietnam south of the 16th parallel while Chinese Nationalist forces occupied the lands north of the partition line. The French were initially excluded from the postwar occupation. However, the French were committed to restoring their power over all of Indochina. By February 28, 1946, the French did secure, through the Franco–Chinese Accords, a Chinese withdrawal from the north in return for yielding concessions in China. French officials subsequently reached an agreement with British officials that acknowledged France's position in southern Vietnam.

Vietnamese forces, however, continued to push for independence. On September 2, 1945, Ho Chi Minh declared the end of French rule, the reunification of Tonkin, Annam, and Cochin China, and the formation of the Democratic Republic of Vietnam (DRV). Citing the American Declaration of Independence and the French Revolution's Declaration of the Rights of Man, Ho believed that he could muster support from the United States for a free and independent Vietnam. However, his appeals to American officials went unheeded. Publicly, American policymakers spoke about high moral principles and ideals. In practice, however, economic considerations—and especially those favorable to the United States—most often outweighed the rhetoric of liberty, democracy, and freedom. American officials asserted, for example, that communist control of Indochina threatened 70 percent of the world's natural rubber and 50 percent of the world's tin supply (Schulzinger, 1997: 54).

On March 6, 1946, a Preliminary Convention was signed in Hanoi. The French promised to recognize the government of the DRV as a free state within the French Union. Vietnam, consequently, would have its own parliament, army, and finances, and would be part of an Indochinese Federation that included Cambodia and Laos. A referendum, furthermore, was scheduled in three parts (Tonkin, Annam, and Cochin China) to determine the final political status of Vietnam. This arrangement, however, preserved a French presence and left unclear the question of whether Vietnam would remain a single country or possible three republics (Schulzinger, 1997: 26). Ho, for his part, desired a Vietnam that reunited Cochin China, Annam, and Tonkin and adamantly opposed the severing of Cochin China from the greater Vietnamese state. With no apparent diplomatic recourse possible, the Vietminh turned to armed conflict. On December 19, 1946, the Franco–Vietminh war began. Lasting 8 years, the conflict resulted in 172,708 casualties for the French and their allies; Vietminh losses were probably three times as high. An estimated 150,000 Vietnamese civilians were killed throughout the conflict (Tucker, 1999: 78).

Cold war ideologies hardened throughout the Indochinese conflict. In January 1950 both the Union of Soviet Socialist Republics (USSR) and the newly formed People's Republic of China (PRC) recognized Ho's DRV. In response, the United States, in part as a result of the defeat of Chiang Kai-shek's nationalist forces in China, recognized the hastily established puppet government of Bao Dai in South Vietnam the following month. In so doing, the Truman administration was able to immediately provide military and economic assistance to the State of Vietnam through French channels. By the spring of 1950 the United States began a policy of direct political, economic, and military support. Gradually, the United States assumed the lion's share of the financial and military burdens of supporting French colonialism in Vietnam. By 1953, the United States was supplying most of the French arms and ammunition and was paying about two-thirds of the cost of the war (Neale, 2003: 61).

THE DEMOGRAPHICS OF STATE BUILDING

By the spring of 1953 it was clear to most observers that a French military victory was a chimera. Moreover, concerns grew among the great powers that the Indochinese conflict might rapidly spiral out of control. The United States, the Soviet Union, Great Britain, and France decided that a diplomatic solution to the war was necessary. An international convention was held in Geneva between May 8 and July 21, 1954, to determine the fate of Indochina. In attendance were delegates from Great Britain, the United States, the Soviet Union, the People's Republic of China, France, India, Laos, Cambodia, the (French-backed) State of Vietnam, and the (Communist) Democratic Republic of Vietnam. Significantly, the outcome of the Geneva Convention highlights the salience of population geography for international politics.

Following the Geneva Accords, two military zones were established and administered by two civilian governments. To the north was the DRV and to the south the State of Vietnam Among the various conditions of the accords was a cease-fire throughout Vietnam, to be accompanied by troop withdrawals of French forces from the north and Vietminh forces from the south. Most importantly, free elections were scheduled for 1956, with the goal of reunification of northern and southern Vietnam. The United States declined to sign the accords but did, in principle, agree with the outcome.

Convinced that the fall of Vietnam to communism would lead to the loss of all of Southeast Asia, the administration of President

Dwight Eisenhower in late 1954 began to create in southern Vietnam a state that could stand as a bulwark against communist expansion and serve as a proving ground for democracy in Asia (Herring, 1996: 47). It was hoped that the 2-year interim period—until the scheduled 1956 elections could be held—would provide time to build a viable noncommunist government, replete with a self-sufficient military force, in southern Vietnam.

South Vietnam, however, was ill-defined from the start. On paper, it was ruled by Emperor Bao Dai—the last emperor of Annam who had served both the French and the Japanese—and Prime Minister Ngo Dinh Diem. A Catholic, Diem enjoyed the support of many high-ranking American officials, including Chief Justice of the Supreme Court William Douglas and Senators John F. Kennedy and Mike Mansfield. Diem convinced these officials, along with others, that he alone was the only viable nationalist alternative who could withstand the onslaught of communist aggression.

America's strategy toward Vietnam, and its initial support of Diem, constitutes a tragic example of how policymakers fell into a "territorial trap." According to John Agnew and Stuart Corbridge (1995: 83–84), policymakers commonly make the erroneous assumption that territorial states constitute the geographical essence of international relations. More specifically, state territories are frequently reified as set or fixed units of sovereign space, and these states are viewed as existing prior to and as a container of society. Within the context of Vietnam, military planners and civilian advisors—having "constructed" the State of Vietnam—continuously viewed the state as being a fixed territorial entity. Through such a metageographical construct, deliberate military strategies were set in motion that dictated the course of the war. Such geographic myopia would have a devastating effect on the population and environment of Vietnam.

An early example of this thinking is found in America's demographic accounting of the DRV (North Vietnam) and the State of Vietnam (later renamed the Republic of Vietnam). Following the signing of the Geneva Accords, and the mandate for *statewide* elections to be held in 1956, American officials were well aware of population differences between the two entities. Given the more populous North, Ho's government was believed to have a distinct demographic advantage in determining the outcome of *national* elections. One individual determined to change this situation was Colonel Edward Lansdale, a noted authority on counterinsurgency techniques. For Lansdale, an early determinant of America's strategy was found within the Geneva Accords: "any civilians ... who wish to go and live in the zone assigned to the other party shall be permitted and helped to do so" (quoted in Currey, 1988: 155).

Lansdale had recently arrived in South Vietnam as chief of the Military Assistance and Advisory Group (MAAG). A graduate of the University of California at Los Angeles, Lansdale had served as both a U.S. Air Force officer and an agent for the Central Intelligence Agency. His initial assignment in Vietnam was to plan, coordinate, and execute a psychological warfare campaign in North Vietnam. He drew on past personal experiences, including the conduct of counterinsurgency operations in the Philippines during the so-called Huk Rebellion. In the Philippines, American officials worked to uphold the landed elite within the Philippines, and to engage and support forces to suppress the peasants. Lansdale was critical in constructing the rebellion as communist-led (it was, in fact, an agrarian uprising dating to the 1930s; see Tyner, 2007). In March 1946 Lansdale alleged to his superiors that the Hukbalahap leaders were "Communist-inspired" and "like all true disciples of Karl Marx" believed

> fully in revolution instead of evolution. They have made their boast that once their membership reaches 500,000 their revolution will start. Meanwhile, in the provinces of Pampanga, Nueva Ecija, Tarlac, Bulacan, and Pangasinan, they are establishing or have established a reign of terror. So ironclad is their grip and so feared is their power that the peasants dare not oppose them in many localities. Upon liberation, their members were about 50,000; sources now report some 150,000 tribute-paying members.... [The rebellion is now organized] into trigger men, castor oil boys, and just big strong ... ruffians to keep the more meek in line. (quoted in Kerkvliet, 1977: 147)

After having suppressed the rebellion in the Philippines, Lansdale was asked to replicate his success in Vietnam. His new assignment was to stimulate a refugee exodus of the Vietnamese from the North to the South (Maclear, 1981). Consequently, a pivotal aspect of Lansdale's approach was a massive population relocation strategy.

Lansdale's strategy can best be described as one of state-induced terror. To construct and facilitate a massive refugee flow, one that could significantly alter the demographic balance of Vietnam, Lansdale required a program to portray the DRV as an untenable place to live. Initially, he employed rumor campaigns. His team distributed leaflets in North Vietnam, spreading disinformation about new economic and monetary regulations. This helped cause panic among many affluent residents. Rumors were also spread of rampaging Chinese communist troops who would occupy the North and rape the women (Young, 1991: 45); other rumors included the sentiment that Christ had moved south. In addition, Lansdale hired astrologers who predicted imminent disasters certain to befall Vietminh leaders and who forecast a long period of prosperous unity for those in the South (Currey, 1988: 158).

It is one thing to strike fear in a populace and to encourage people to flee their homes. It is quite another to physically carry out such plans. To this end, and encouraged by the Catholic hierarchy, entire parishes were carried south on American ships. Within weeks approximately 850,000 Vietnamese began the trek south. Most were Catholics and/or small landowners (Maclear, 1981: 51). Subsequently, highly publicized accounts of refugee flows were used to support and legitimize America's growing involvement in Vietnam. Officials, for example, utilized the fabricated refugee flow as an indicator of the threat of communism (these lessons would be applied again during America's war against the Sandanistas in Nicaragua during the 1980s). An editorial appearing in the journal *America*, for example, explained that 1.2 million Catholics lived in the area north of the 17th parallel, which was to be sealed off by another "Iron Curtain." The same editorial stated that the migrants would play a "major role in the area south of the 17th parallel, if that part of Vietnam which still remains free is to be strengthened against Communist infiltration." The American Friends for Vietnam, a lobbying group, used the plight of the refugees to garner support for Diem's government and to denounce the activities of Ho Chi Minh. As Young (1991: 45) concludes, the usefulness of the refugee population did not end with their much-photographed arrival in the South. Photo-spreads of confused, tired women and children appeared in the *New York Times Magazine* and other highly visible outlets.

Perhaps not surprisingly, given the cold war political climate, the scheduled 1956 elections for the possible national reunification of Vietnam were not held—a decision originating with Diem and backed by his American supporters. Instead, Diem called for a national (meaning southern) referendum to determine whether the ineffective Bao Dai would remain as emperor or if Diem himself would lead the republic. Diem, not surprisingly given the level of corruption in his government, won 98 percent of the vote. Bao Dai was removed from power and the Republic of Vietnam (RVN) was established on October 26, 1956, with Diem as president.

In light of Diem's political maneuvering, Ho permitted the southern communists to engage in limited military actions. This decision paved the way for the formation, on December 20, 1960, of the National Liberation Front (NLF) of South Vietnam. The purpose of the NLF—derisively termed "Viet Cong" by Diem—was to provoke a general uprising and to bring about a communist revolution in the South.

The NLF was a semiautonomous organization. Despite claims to the contrary, notably by American officials such as Rostow, the NLF was neither a puppet of the Soviet Union nor of the DRV. Rather, "the founders of the Front were independent professionals, architects, lawyers, doctors, school teachers, along with members of the Communist Party, Buddhists, and one or two Catholics. They framed a set of demands that would appeal to all sectors of southern society that had been hurt by the Diem regime" (Young, 1991: 70). Both politically and militarily, they worked toward the eventual reunification of Vietnam.

POPULATION AND THE ROSTOW DOCTRINE OF WAR

> I suddenly thought of my dear ones in both parts of the country,
> And told myself, Death is so simple! We can only wait for bombs and artillery shells to rain down and tear the small forest apart.
> —DANG THUY TRAM[1]

America's overt military involvement in Vietnam was gradual, reflecting an ignorance and uncertainty over policy. From the signing of the Geneva Accords in 1954 to 1960 only a few hundred military advisors of the U.S. Military Assistance Advisory Group (USMAAG) were stationed in South Vietnam. The election of Kennedy to the White House, however, paved the way for an enlarged U.S. commitment to Vietnam and the greater Southeast Asia region. In many respects, the Kennedy administration "set the tone for the beginning of a bold American policy" (Hearden, 2005: 67). Schulzinger (1997: 97) concurs, noting that "Kennedy, along with most foreign affairs experts of the late 1950s and early 1960s, believed that the Cold War was a global struggle: events were interconnected, and weakness in the face of communist adversaries' moves encouraged aggression elsewhere." Moreover, "Kennedy and his principal foreign affairs advisers considered the communist–nationalist insurrection in South Vietnam part of this global competition."

Kennedy entered the White House with a cadre of intellectuals who were determined to advance their own personal theories, models, and ambitions as much as they would American foreign policy. His advisors were not politicians per se, but rather corporate executives and leaders from the realms of academia and finance. Robert McNamara, as secretary of defense, was one such individual. McNamara began his professional career as a professor at the Harvard Business School. Later, during World War II, he was recruited to work in the Statistical Control Office (SCO), under General Curtis LeMay, of the U.S. Army Air Corps. In that position McNamara utilized a suite of mathematical models to plan the logistics of bombing raids in German and, later, Japan (Edwards, 1996).

Following the war McNamara enlisted nine of his coworkers to apply their quantitative skills to industrial productivity. These former SCO analysts were employed at Ford Motor Company and subsequently introduced various military techniques into business management. It was at Ford that McNamara—named president in 1960—and his associates became known as the "whiz kids." Edwards (1996: 126) explains that "like many other intellectually oriented managers of the 1950s, McNamara found mathematical modeling techniques far superior to traditional wisdom or intuitive approaches to management based on shop-floor experience." He would bring this same approach to the Defense Department.

As former president of Ford Motors, McNamara stressed efficiency in his management of foreign policy. Dazzled by numbers, computers, and statistics, McNamara was part of a quantitative revolution in foreign policy. Neale (2003: 89) writes that McNamara "ran the war like the Ford Motor Company. You had the capital, you had the hardware, and you had the men—they were just labor." Capturing this element of the conduct of war, Clodfelter (1988: 91) laments his experiences as a combat soldier: "As the value of Vietnamese life went down in your estimation, so too did the realizations start to sink in that your body and your life was really of very little importance to the men and the machines who ran the war...."

At the Department of Defense, McNamara—along with RAND economist Charles Hitch—established the Office of Systems Analysis (OSA). Hitch subsequently chose another RAND economist, Alain Enthoven, to direct the OSA. (In 1971 Enthoven and another OSA employee, K. Wayne Smith, wrote a book on the activities of the OSA.) In time, this group of Pentagon analysts would be christened the "whiz kids," like McNamara's team at Ford Motor Company.

The OSA, a predominantly civilian group, was created to work full-time on military-related projects defined and delineated by McNamara. Among its various functions was the analysis and review of quantitative requirements in the areas of force structures (for example, troop deployments), weapons systems (for example, bombs, torpedoes, ships, ammunition), transportation, and information and communication systems (Enthoven and Smith, 1971: 77). In addition, members of the OSA prepared cost-effective studies on these areas, all with the aim of providing empirical data to support McNamara's assessment of the war's progress.

The whiz kids ran the OSA like the business managers and economists they were. As a whole, the OSA rejected both experience and history as guides, believing instead in the infallibility of analytical techniques and computer-generated "facts." During the early years of military buildup, McNamara and his aides "churned out situation reports and position papers based on the reels and reels of computerized data that had been processed on their mainframes" (Adas, 2006: 295). Adas (p. 295) continues by noting that McNamara's newly created OSA "performed cost–benefit analyses for tasks as diverse as weapons procurement, streamlining the defense bureaucracy, and responding to the volatile situation in Vietnam. When they argued for widening the war, they prided themselves on using scientific procedures and verifiable (that is, wherever possible, statistical) data, which they believed made their decisions far more objective than the recommendations of the critics of escalation." When other officials questioned America's increasing involvement in Vietnam, McNamara and his analysts deflected such concerns with "a surfeit of statistics and elaborate computer projections."

The geographic knowledge produced by the OSA and other units was decidedly biased in favor of quantitative mathematical understanding. Alain Enthoven, for example, could not conceive of a meaningful way to factor historical experience (which could not be quantified) into planning for high-tech military forces (Adas, 2006: 294–295). In his defense of computer modeling, Enthoven explained that "computers are replacing military judgement" and that "computers are running the wars of the future" (quoted in Edwards, 1996: 133). Adas (2006: 295) explains further that "in the buildup to what in effect was the recolonization of Vietnam in the mid-1960s, none of the many government agencies involved undertook systematic investigations of local social systems, the Saigon regime, or even the history of the Vietnamese civil war." He continues by pointing out that "as the sorry history of American interventions in Vietnam would make clear, social science programs and cost–benefit analyses could not compensate for the policymakers' woeful ignorance of the history of the refined and deeply rooted societies and cultures of Indochina" (p. 296).

McNamara and his whiz kids were managers; they were not creators. As Milne (2007: 186) explains, McNamara was a brilliant manager of facts and data, but no innovator. He took his ideas from others, subjected them to a searching quantitative critique, and if the numbers worked, he made his decision. It was left to others to provide a compelling rationale for escalation in Vietnam and a blueprint for victory (Milne, 2007: 173; see also Milne, 2008).

Among the many analysts formulating ideas and providing the theories of how America should respond to the communist threat in Vietnam, none stood out more than Walt Whitman Rostow. Geography students have long been familiar with *some* ideas of Rostow, namely, his five-stage model of economic growth. Fewer students, however, are aware of the remarkable contributions he made toward the destruction of the Vietnamese people. Indeed, David Milne (2007: 169) describes Rostow as "the most aggressive civilian member of the John F. Kennedy and Lyndon B. Johnson administration." The career of Rostow, especially as a civilian advisor, vividly illustrates the confluence of geographic knowledge and military pursuits. Furthermore, Rostow embodies the many U.S. policymakers who viewed Vietnam as

> a superb arena in which to test American approaches to development and to demonstrate the advantages of capitalist democracy over communist alternatives. No other contested site in the "Third World" seemed better suited to impress upon the global community America's technological superiority over its communist rivals and thus its incomparable capacity to deliver economic and technical assistance to developing countries. (Adas, 2006: 289)

For Rostow and like-minded presidential advisors, in the early stages of U.S. involvement, "American-style development was more than just a way to inoculate emerging societies against the 'disease' of communism. It was also the key to the American mission of fostering industrialization and democracy in developing nations without disrupting global financial institutions and trade networks" (Adas, 2006: 303).

Born of a Russian immigrant father and an American-born mother, Rostow grew up in New Haven, Connecticut. His father, a metallurgical engineer, was both an idealist and a socialist and, ironically, named his children after the socialist visionaries Walt Whitman, Eugene Debs, and Ralph Waldo Emerson (Pearce, 2001: 12). As Walt Rostow grew and matured, he developed into the antithesis of his father's heroes. Indeed, Rostow was a military hawk and ardent cold warrior, one who promoted the use of massive military firepower even as American presidents and other planners counseled moderation.

Academically, Rostow received both a BA and a PhD (1940) in economics from Yale; he later was granted MAs from Oxford and Cambridge in 1946 and 1949, respectively. For a brief period (1940–1941) Rostow taught economics at Columbia University. With the onset of World War II, however, Rostow enlisted for military service. Serving in the Office of Strategic Services, Rostow worked with the British Air Ministry, helping to select bombing targets in Europe. Pearce (2001: 12) contends that "Rostow's time in the military was formative in directing him toward a career in government service, economic diplomacy, and policy planning." Indeed, Rostow would later serve as McGeorge Bundy's deputy at the National Security Council (January–November

1961), as chairman of the Policy Planning Council at the State Department (November 1961–March 1966), and as President Johnson's national security advisor (April 1966–January 1969).

After World War II, Rostow assumed a 1-year post in the State Department as assistant chief of the German–Austrian Economic Division. In this position Rostow contributed to the development of Germany's economic reconstruction. He later returned to academia in 1946 as professor of American history at Oxford and, eventually, the Massachusetts Institute of Technology (MIT). While at MIT Rostow cofounded, with his friend Max Millikan, the Center for International Studies (CENIS). This academic institution was funded by both the Ford and Rockefeller Foundations, as well as by the CIA.

Between 1958 and 1959, while on a sabbatical from CENIS and visiting Cambridge, England, Rostow delivered a series of eight lectures that would form the basis of his highly influential 1960 book *The Stages of Economic Growth: A Non-Communist Manifesto*. In what would become known as the "Rostow doctrine," Rostow developed the idea that all nations pass through five stages of economic growth. And true to form, Rostow emphasized that communism was not the final stage of economic development. Communism, for Rostow, was merely (albeit dangerously) a "disease" that impairs economic growth.

In the beginning, Rostow argued, there existed *traditional societies*. In this stage, societies were primitive and characterized by rigid social structures. The economies of traditional societies were dominated by subsistence agriculture. These societies, moreover, were resistant to technological innovation, thus exhibiting an ideological antipathy toward modernization. At some point, however, societies evolve into Rostow's second stage, as evidenced by the prevalence of key *preconditions* for takeoff. During this stage, certain leaders in the society moved the nation toward greater economic flexibility, openness, and diversification. The reasons why some societies moved into the second stage were varied; Rostow suggested, among others factors, national prestige and personal profit. Having begun the path toward modernization, societies were then presumed to enter into a third *takeoff* stage. Here, the society demonstrates its full embrace of modernization. Growth is commonplace and expected by the population. The fourth is marked by a *drive to maturity*. At this point, technology is widespread and industrial production is highly diversified. Lastly, societies complete their stages of economic growth when they arrive at a point Rostow termed the *age of high mass consumption*.

In the development of his model, Rostow argued that all nations passed naturally through these same phases of development. One consequence was that his arguments convinced U.S. policymakers to homogenize their methods of economic interventionism in the third world (Pearce, 2001: 77). A second consequence was that Rostow's thesis formed the basis of the Rostow doctrine, an ideology that proved highly influential—and misguided—in America's conduct of the Vietnam War. Through CENIS, Rostow "began a phase of his academic and political life in which his theory of the stages of economic growth would be disseminated throughout the foreign aid policy community" (Pearce, 2001: 13). It was through CENIS, likewise, that Rostow was able to serve as foreign policy advisor in the administrations of Eisenhower, Kennedy, and Johnson.

As Milne (2007: 170) identifies, "Rostow's 'stages of growth' were little more than Marx's dynamic of historical materialism with a happier, capitalist ending" in that his model was similarly informed by economic determinism. Central to Rostow's thesis and his whole doctrine was a series of presuppositions. First, he maintained that the driving force of history was the aspiration of poorer countries to attain the levels of wealth enjoyed by those in the West. Second, he believed that the leaders of nations view the health of their economies as their overwhelming preoccupation in peace and war. Consequently, any threat to a nation's economy would constitute coercion of the highest order (Milne, 2007: 171). Falling into his own territorial trap, Rostow argued that the NLF insurgency in South Vietnam (supposedly a sovereign state) was manipulated by North Vietnam (the "enemy" sovereign state). Plainly put, therefore, the Rostow doctrine held that if the United States bombed—or even threatened to bomb—the North, then the leaders of North Vietnam would be compelled to relinquish their support of the southern insurgency. Moreover, given that the North's resources and military personnel would be tied up protecting the North's industrial economic base, North Vietnam would be in no position to provide any assistance to the NLF forces in the South.

Rostow's rationale, of course, assumed that the priorities of North Vietnam's leaders, such as Ho Chi Minh, were the same as his own, namely, that the pursuit of economic growth was the overwhelming consideration in peace and war (Milne, 2007: 171). Rostow, however, was not a military strategist—although he viewed himself as one. He failed to consider the historical development of Vietnam, as well as the complex and dynamic geopolitical relationships between China, Vietnam, and the Soviet Union. Perhaps most damning, however, was his failure to adequately consider the cultural and national nuances of the Vietnamese people.

Such geographic ignorance is not wholly unexpected from Rostow. His stages-of-growth model was built on his reading of British industrialism, which he assumed served as the model for all other societies. Moreover, as Marilyn Young (1991: 77) suggests, Rostow was "an economic and anti-Communist polemicist" who offered the third world a "non-Communist manifesto" as a guide to its development. Rostow was staunchly opposed to communism and argued that material deprivation (poverty) made individuals more receptive to communism. Therefore, economic growth was seen as a weapon against communism. More specifically, American economic growth and its subsequent promotion of growth in the third world was viewed as a corrective to the seductions of communism. Tragically, however, while wedded to development strategies dependent on market expansion, U.S. policymakers such as Rostow "overlooked the extent to which most Vietnamese associated capitalism with colonial exploitation" (Adas, 2006: 298).

There is an additional component of the Rostow thesis/doctrine that bears mentioning, one that is thoroughly connected to the population geography of the Vietnam War. Within his *Stages of Economic Growth*, Rostow provides a lengthy discussion on the place of war in modern history. He identifies three kinds of war, namely, colonial wars, wars of regional aggression, and wars over the Eurasian balance. These latter wars, interestingly, harken to the "heartland thesis" advocated by British geopolitician Halford Mackinder. What I find most intriguing about Rostow's discussion of war within the context of economic growth and development, however, is his understanding of sovereignty. This concept, of course, dates to the 17th century and the Treaty of Westphalia. Understood as the crucial element in the formation of the nation-state concept, sovereignty over territorial space in a world fragmented into other, discrete territorial states is presumed to give the state its most powerful justification (Agnew and Corbridge, 1995). Indeed, as Agnew and Corbridge (p. 84) argue, "Without [sovereignty] a state would be just another organization. Its claim to sovereignty is what distinguishes the state."

Earlier I indicated the territorial trap of assuming the existence of North and South Vietnam as being fixed, sovereign states. Here I introduce Rostow's conception of sovereignty. For Rostow, this political concept was born in traditional societies; current understandings of sovereignty are thus inherited from earlier, precapitalist societies. This, he claims, is a simple historical fact. More specifically, however, Rostow (1960: 107; emphasis added) explains that "Nation sovereignty means that nations retain the ultimate right—a right sanctioned by law, custom, and what decent men judge to be *legitimacy—the right to kill people of other nations in defense or pursuit of what they judge to be their national interest.*" To the extent that Rostow was, in Milne's (2007: 186) words, "the prophet of American victory in the Vietnam War," we must continually remind ourselves that the Rostow doctrine was undergirded by a basic premise: that killing is an acceptable strategy for states in the pursuit of national goals and objectives.

ROSTOW'S AIR CAMPAIGN OF TERROR

> Still, the airplanes scream overhead, a series of bombs raining down with each pass, the explosions deafening.... Who is burned in that fire and smoke? In those heaven-shaking explosions, whose bodies are annihilated in the bomb craters? The old lady sitting by me stares at the hamlet and says, 'That's where Hung's mother-in-law lives.
> —Dang Thuy Tram[2]

Throughout December 1960 and January 1961 Lansdale toured Vietnam. His travels, however, were not to visit historic sites nor to enjoy new cuisines. Rather, his objective was to assess the current political climate of Vietnam and to provide recommendations for Kennedy. Based on his experiences, Lansdale prepared a bleak assessment on the viability of the Diem government. Ever vigilant, and determined to shape the course of events, Rostow presented Lansdale's report to Kennedy. Initially, however, Kennedy was preoccupied with events elsewhere in the world (for example, Cuba, Europe), but at Rostow's insistence, he took a closer look. Lansdale's warning struck a cord; Kennedy, ever sensitive to the charges that brought another president down—specifically, Truman having "lost" China to the communist sphere—made a decision. And Rostow, working at the National Security Council, assumed point on the Vietnam problem.

Over the next few months Rostow issued repeated memoranda advocating a vigorous military response to defend South Vietnam. Initially, his ideas were in line with other conventional counterinsurgency approaches advocated by advisors such as Lansdale. Early on, as the war was escalating, Rostow told Kennedy that "it is somehow wrong to be developing these capabilities [helicopters and the newly created Green Berets] but not applying them in a crucial theater" (quoted in Herring, 1996: 87). In time, however, Rostow began to more clearly apply his own economic reading of history to the deteriorating situation in Vietnam. No longer did Rostow support a campaign of pacification (see below); instead, he promoted a more aggressive campaign that centered on air power.

Concerned with raising troop levels, in October 1961 Kennedy dispatched his special military advisor Maxwell Taylor, along with Rostow, to gauge conditions in South Vietnam. Not unexpectedly, they confirmed the pessimistic reports concerning the Diem government that Kennedy was receiving. According to the Taylor–Rostow report, the Diem government was weak and ineffective; morale among South Vietnamese troops was low; and the peasants were increasingly supporting the communist insurgents. Rostow, however, developed his own theory of why communism held appeal in the South. He maintained that the Vietnamese people had been suddenly confronted with "modernization"; as malleable, naive, and restive children, they were confused and unsure of what to do. Rostow conveniently downplayed any talk of nationalism, colonialism, or economic exploitation and oppression (Milne, 2007: 179).

Taylor and Rostow recommended a significant expansion of American aid, equipment, and advisors, including the sending of approximately 8,000 ground forces. Only with a more overt American presence, they argued, could U.S. objectives be realized in South Vietnam. Rostow, however, also presented another recommendation, based on his own doctrine, that the United States should bomb, or at least threaten to bomb, North Vietnam. He was ever more convinced that a threat to the North's industrial base was the key to victory. He would later advocate bombing the dikes of North Vietnam and the principle cities of Hanoi and Haiphong, as well as invading Laos and North Vietnam. How far these ideas at the time would be carried out remains unclear; the obstinate Rostow gradually fell out of favor within the White House and he was reassigned to the Policy Planning Council at the State Department (Milne, 2007: 183). Kennedy did, however, secretly deploy additional advisors; by October 1963 there were over 16,000 Americans serving in South Vietnam.

As events seemed to *draw* the United States inexorably into war—in reality, of course, individuals such as Rostow *led* the United States into war—Johnson, having assumed the office of the presidency following Kennedy's assassination, was faced with limited options. By 1964 Vietnam had become a symbol of American foreign policy. It was claimed by the highest echelons of U.S. policymakers that America's ability to influence, if not dominate, the global world order hinged on the stance taken in Vietnam. How to proceed was less clear.

The joint chiefs of staff (JCS) advocated an aggressive military response to the continued NLF insurgency in South Vietnam. Curtis E. LeMay, the Air Force chief of staff, for example, supported a no-holds-barred use of airborne force. His "data" suggested that a punishing series of attacks against the North would compel the communists to give up all assistance to the NLF and agree to the existence of a sovereign (and pro-Western) Republic of Vietnam. To this end, LeMay had his staff draw up a list of 94 targets in the North. He estimated that all targets could be destroyed within 16 days. Conversely, Rostow, initially, disagreed with the heavy-handed tactics of LeMay. For Rostow, simply the threat of an aerial bombardment of the North would be sufficient. In an elaboration of his thesis, Rostow surmised that any threat to a nation's economy would prove decisive in itself (Milne, 2007: 184).

Johnson had a difficult choice to make. The year 1964 was an election year and Johnson was concerned about public reaction. To the sitting president, LeMay's plan seemed frightening. Rostow's plan, in comparison, was more palatable, politically speaking. Such reasoning led Johnson, on March 17, 1964, to approved National Security Action Memorandum 288, which reaffirmed the U.S. commitment to the existence of South Vietnam. The objective, at this point, was to "win the war in the South" and not to "liberate" the North. The strategy, as it developed, and consistent with the Rostow doctrine, was to destroy military bases, supply depots, and infiltration routes in southern Vietnam, while conducting punishing air attacks against the North's industrial base. Northern targets, in particular, would include industrial sites, and especially the petroleum-production facilities located in and around the Hanoi–Haiphong region. According to Adas (2006: 325), "Rostow's faith in air power had been instilled by his service in the air force during the Second World War." Rostow, in his analysis, consciously drew comparisons between the Allied bombings in World War II and Vietnam. Both a recognized and self-proclaimed expert on development, Rostow maintained that "a carefully calibrated escalation of precision bombing against North Vietnam would at some (undetermined) time force its leaders to give up the expansionist designs that motivated their support for the insurgency in the South." Rostow (quoted in Young, 1991: 122–123) explained that "Ho has an industrial complex to protect; he is no longer a guerrilla fighter with nothing to lose." Such devastation would, in theory, compel Ho Chi Minh to agree to the existence of a noncommunist Republic of Vietnam.

Sustained bombing campaigns of the North began in mid-February 1965 with Operation Rolling Thunder. In April alone U.S. and South Vietnamese air force and navy planes flew 3,600 sorties against fuel depots, bridges, munitions factories, and power plants in the North. Rostow, by the end of May, argued that total victory was possible—indeed, that it was nearer than anyone could imagine (Kolko, 1994: 166).

Repeated sorties, however, failed to deliver the expected results. And as each phase of the bombing failed to produce the results predicted by Rostow's doctrine, Johnson gradually expanded the list of targets and the number of strikes throughout Vietnam. Sorties against North Vietnam increased from 25,000 in 1965, to 79,000 in 1966, and to 108,000 in 1967; bomb tonnage increased from 63,000 to 136,000 to 226,000 over the same period (Herring, 1996: 161). By the end of the war, the United States and its allies would drop nearly 8 million tons of bombs on Vietnam and its neighbors—more than twice the tonnage dropped by the Allies in all of World War II (Tucker, 1999).

Casualty rates likewise continued to spiral upward. Vietnamese civilian and military casualties nearly doubled from 13,000 in 1965 to approximately 24,000 in 1966 (Schulzinger, 1997: 213). In 1967 alone, the CIA estimated that Vietnamese casualties ran as high as 2,800 per month; the figures, the CIA admitted, where heavily weighted with civilians (Herring, 1996: 162).

Aside from the cost of life, the near-indiscriminate bombing of a country was not cheap either. According to Herring (1996: 165), the direct cost of the air war in Vietnam, including operation of the aircraft, munitions, and replacement of planes, was estimated at more than US$1.7 billion during 1965 and 1966. Studies indicated that for each $1 of damage inflicted on North Vietnam, the United States spent $9.60. And the money—from the point of view of men like Rostow and Johnson—was not being well spent. Despite its costs and severity, the air campaign was not effective. Most of North Vietnam's military targets were destroyed by 1967 and yet, contrary to Rostow's belief, the North Vietnamese leaders refused to capitulate. Indeed, many reports contradicted Rostow's hawkish strategy. Early reports prepared by a joint CIA–Defense Department team, for example, indicated that the bombing campaigns had produced only minimal results; this was not surprising, the report concluded, given that only about 12 percent of North Vietnam's economy could be considered "industrial"; the DRV, unlike Germany, was primarily a rural, agrarian-based economy (Schulzinger, 1997: 207). Furthermore, the continued bombings did nothing to prevent the North's support of the NLF. In fact, official American estimates concluded that infiltration increased from about 35,000 men in 1965 to as many as 90,000 men in 1967 (Herring, 1996: 165).

Up to this point, North Vietnam failed to follow Rostow's theory. Events were refusing to conform to his thesis that limited bombing and the threat of more to come would compel the north to cease its aggression. So Rostow gradually shifted to the JCS position that destruction—not diplomacy backed by threats—was the crucial determinant for American victory (Milne, 2007: 188). Faced with diminishing returns, the air campaign steadily resulted in the wanton and indiscriminate killing of Vietnamese.

Research and development teams in the United States were ready to provide the military with new and improved means of killing bodies. As Krepon (1974: 595) notes, "In design and in its practical deployment, the most indiscriminate antipersonnel weapon used in the Vietnam War was almost certainly the so-called Cluster Bomb Unit (CBU)." In military parlance, cluster bombs are usually described as "flak suppression" weapons. These munitions are supposedly used against antiaircraft artillery installations to protect pilots flying over to bomb other targets. However, cluster bombs are also described as "area denial munitions" and "antipersonnel weapons"; they are, in fact, fragmentation munitions that are effective primarily or solely against human beings.

Fragmentation bombs were initially developed during World War II and later improved during the Korean War. Early munitions were rather unsophisticated, however, and scientists working at the Development Center at China Lake, California, and at Eglin Air Force Base, Florida, made substantial progress in terms of *controlled* fragmentation (Krepon, 1974: 597). The principle behind fragmentation bombs is fairly straightforward. When an explosive inside a metal case is detonated, the explosive is rapidly converted to a hot gas. Under the pressure of the expanding gas, the bomb's outer case swells momentarily and then ruptures. The fragments of the case are propelled outward at a very high velocity, shredding any objects in their path. This is known as "natural" fragmentation. Military strategists during and after World War II recognized the sporadic and inefficient use of natural fragmentation. The explosion of World War II artillery shells, for example, produced a range of fragments, some large, but others so small that they were generally ineffective in maiming or killing the enemy. Consequently, scientists began to work on ways to narrow the range of fragments to be most effective. It was determined, for example, that fragments weighing less than 1 gram could cause severe wounds if they struck a human body with sufficient force (Prokosch, 1976: 345).

"Controlled" fragmentation bombs, as the name implies, attempt to reduce the random factor in the dispersal of casing fragments. Scientists discovered news ways in which the size and shape of fragments can be predetermined by scoring or grooving the case. In addition, scientists developed new means of affecting the areal coverage of fragmentation. Depending on the dispensing system, as well as the height of detonation, bombs could be designed to disperse fragments in various patterns: oval, linear, or figure eights. A more lethal discovery, however, was the insertion of preformed fragments within the case. This is the basis of the modern cluster bomb.

Today's cluster bombs, in general, consist of metal cases containing approximately 640–670 bomblets, known as bomb live units (BLUs). Each BLU, roughly the size of a tennis ball and weighing on the order of 1 pound, contains approximately 300 metal fragments. Dropped from a fighter or bomber aircraft, the dispenser splits apart, releasing its contents. The small bomblets are grooved in such a way as to fragment before, during, or after impact, depending on the fuse employed. The casing of the BLU, likewise, is designed to fragment into small pieces. If all of the bomblets detonate from a single CBU, some 200,000 metallic fragments are propelled outward.

By the end of the Vietnam War, the U.S. Air Force was believed to have 30 varieties of CBUs, although the CBU-24 was the most widely used cluster bomb in Vietnam. Nicknamed "guavas" by the North Vietnamese, CBU-24s contained more fragments than earlier series; these also provided greater areal coverage. Aside from metal pellets, other cluster bombs were filled with napalm, land mines, sarin nerve gas, or nail-like fleschettes. The WDU-4, for example, contained 6,000 barbed metal darts that could literally nail victims to the ground. Fiberglass flechettes were also used. Fiberglass shrapnel, it was discovered, was invisible to x-rays and thus was harder and more painful to remove (Neale, 2003: 78).

The killing range of CBUs was (and remains) remarkable. Estimates made by observers in Vietnam suggest that a single CBU dropped in a linear pattern and detonated at an altitude of 600 feet was able to disperse its fragments so as to kill or wound people at an effective range of 300 meters by 1,000 meters. Other estimates suggest that a single fighter aircraft carrying CBUs could cover an area anywhere from 1 to 15 square kilometers. The ordnance package for a single F4 Phantom jet, it should be noted, included eight CBUs or, with special racks, as many as 15–20 (Krepon, 1974: 598).

The shower of fragments may be effective against light military targets (as a flak suppressant) but, for the most part, the CBU is effectively only against human beings (Krepon, 1974: 596). In fact, most of the barbed metal darts or fiberglass arrows would be highly ineffective against antiaircraft installations. And even the hundreds of steel balls contained in the CBU-24 were too small to perforate steel or concrete (Prokosch, 1976: 341). CBUs were therefore used principally to kill people and to instill terror in the populace. Consider, for example, the CBU-29, also widely employed in Vietnam. This cluster bomb contained bomblets that had random delay fuses that would explode sometime *after* the initial attack (Prokosch, p. 344). These were clearly not designed as flak suppressants, nor as weapons against attacking armies. Rather, these were designed expressly to kill people, indiscriminately, at random times. Studies conducted during the war found that death rates from pellet bombs were highest among women and children (Prokosch, p. 342).

And how did people die? When a high-velocity projectile, such as a steel pellet from a CBU, passes through the body, it pushes aside the soft tissues in its immediate path. These tissues, in turn, impart velocity to tissues further away. A "temporary" cavity, several times the size of the wound track, is formed. This expansion of the cavity crushes tissues and organs, fractures bone, and damages nerves. Within a fraction of a second the cavity closes, but the damage has been done. The controlled fragmentation device literally explodes—through sheer force—within the body (Prokosch, 1976: 349). Many scientists contributed to detailed understandings and relationships between bombs and bodies. Wartime studies of the mathematical relationship of wounding, for example, concluded that the volume of the temporary cavity is directly proportional to the amount of kinetic energy lost by a missile as it passes through the body. A general rule of thumb among weapons designers is that the severity of the wound is proportional to the kinetic energy lost in the body by the wounding missile (Prokosch, p. 350).

The use of CBUs within the Vietnam War were part and parcel of the punishment that advisors such as Rostow and LeMay sought to inflict. Throughout the war CBUs were used primarily in North Vietnam and against the trail complexes in eastern Laos. CBUs were also employed in B-52 raids against supply areas and suspected NLF strongholds in the south. It was estimated that by 1973 approximately 29 percent of the U.S. Air Force's procurement budget went to purchase controlled fragmentation munitions (Krepon, 1974: 604). Overall, approximately 285 million submunitions were dropped on Cambodia, Vietnam, and Laos during the war.

Despite the use of cluster bombs and other munitions, the North Vietnamese refused to conform with the Rostow doctrine. Even within the Johnson administration, a number of analysts began to express reservations. By the fall of 1967, for example, McNamara—who would resign in November—abandoned hope that the war could be won simply through intensive and sustained bombing campaigns. His changed position, however, stood in stark contrast to that of Rostow, Taylor, and the new secretary of defense, Clark Clifford, who replaced McNamara.

These individuals opposed any thought of withdrawal from Vietnam and, indeed, advocated for an expansion of the war into neighboring Cambodia (Schulzinger, 1997). For hawks such as Rostow, therefore, the presidential victory of Richard M. Nixon in 1968 was heaven-sent. For the Vietnamese—and the Cambodians—the election was grievous. Nixon's primary concern—one that echoed that of his newly appointed national security advisor Henry Kissinger—was to end the war while retaining American credibility in Southeast Asia. The goal was, first, to retain America's prestige, and second, perhaps, to still pull victory from the jaws of defeat. Consequently, Nixon sought to expand the conflict to "win" the peace. This would translate into an intensified effort not to capture territory, but to inflict maximum damage on the Vietnamese population.

(DE)POPULATION FORECASTING

> What joy can there be when daily sufferings and death still weigh heavily on our lives? Just yesterday, in a mopping-up operation, the enemy killed five people. Every afternoon they bomb the hamlets.
> —Dang Thuy Tram[3]

The Vietnam War has been described as a war without fronts. It was a war without territorial objectives: no capitals to capture, no areas to secure. Consequently, other indicators were required to mark the war's progress. As such, the Vietnam War became a war of population geography.

It is commonplace for any population (geography) text book to begin with a discussion of the "basic demographic equation." Gary Peters and Robert Larkin (1999: 9), for example, explain that "the most fundamental characteristic of any population is its size. An area's population may be increased either by a birth within the area or by the migration into the area of a person from another area. Similarly, the population may be decreased either by the death of someone within the area or by the migration of someone from the area out to another area."

Such demographic logic enters into the strategies of warfare. Indeed, the above definition may be rewritten as: An enemy's population may be increased either by births or by the addition of new recruits, either from the area or beyond. Likewise, the enemy's population may be decreased either by the death of enemy populations or the removal of enemies (for example, via prisoner of war camps). Such a demographic reductive understanding of war prompts two principle techniques of warfare: (1) deny the enemy an ability to reproduce its numbers—either through the control of fertility or of recruitment strategies—and (2) kill off the enemy faster than the enemy is able to reproduce itself.

Never was a war so clearly a technique of depopulation as was the war in Vietnam.

Johnson's strategic aim was to simply compel North Vietnam to agree to the existence of South Vietnam. Johnson and Westmoreland's strategy, therefore, following the Rostow doctrine, was based on the central assumption that if the northern communists sustained enough military punishment they would relent. Consequently, American advisors continuously sought the "Holy Grail," the breaking point of North Vietnam.

Military strategists and civilian planners recognized that bombing campaigns were not sufficient in themselves. General William Westmoreland, for example, was firmly convinced of the benefits of a "big war" approach. He advocated a strategy designed to tempt the Vietnamese forces into "big unit" confrontations that would play into American strengths. Underpinning his approach to the conflict, Westmoreland advocated attrition warfare, based on the demographic assumption that the communists could not sustain large-unit fighting. He believed that although the DRV might constantly rebuild their military units with fresh recruits, these newer soldiers would progressively be less adequately trained and hence easier to defeat on the battlefield. Given America's technological and industrial superiority, Westmoreland assumed that the United States could inflict intolerable losses on the enemy while keeping its own losses within acceptable bounds (Herring, 1996: 171). The American strategy, as Neale (2003: 85) bluntly states, was to kill the Vietnamese until they gave up.

A crucial component of Westmoreland's attrition strategy was to locate and eliminate NLF and North Vietnamese Army (NVA) regular units (Herring, 1996: 166). In time, this approach would be known as "search and destroy."[4] This grim phrase, coined in 1965 by Westmoreland's own staff, referred to specific missions aimed at flushing the enemy out of hiding. Contrary to popular belief, the term (at least initially) did not mean "aimless searches in the jungle and random destruction of villages and property." Rather, the general had directed his advisors to find "expressive terms" to serve as a common terminology among the South Vietnamese and their American advisors. This term, in particular, indicated "operations to hold, fix in place, fight and destroy ... enemy forces and their base areas and supply caches" (Young, 1991: 163).

By saturating the Vietnamese countryside with patrols of American ground forces on search and destroy (S&D) missions, military strategists hoped to entice NLF and NVA forces into set-piece battles, whereby American firepower could then be brought to bear. One such operation was code-named MASHER/White Wing. It was conducted in late January 1966 in Binh Dinh province, an area considered to be an NLF stronghold. The operation itself consisted of combined amphibious and airborne assaults; approximately 20,000 ARVN (Army of the Republic of Vietnam), South Korean, and American troops were involved. By the end of the first week, an estimated 600 "enemy bodies" and 119 "allied bodies" were killed; no one bothered to count the civilians who perished, although 15 hamlets were destroyed in the fighting (Young, 1991: 163). Following the operation, American and allied forces departed. Nothing permanent was achieved; it was simply an operation to kill the enemy and move on. David Halberstam, writing in 1967, captured the dehumanizing essence of a war of attrition: "You simply grind out a terribly punishing war, year after year, using that immense American firepower, crushing the enemy and a good deal of the population, until finally there has been so much death and destruction that the enemy will stumble out of the forest, as stunned and numb as the rest of the Vietnamese population" (quoted in Mueller, 1980: 503).

Westmoreland's approach to war was a textbook example of the demography of violence. Sustained and (often) indiscriminate killings should, according to individuals like Westmoreland, produce one of the following responses. First, it was assumed (or hoped) that the enemy forces would lose more people than they could replace. Second, Westmoreland and his aides maintained that high death tolls would demoralize the enemy, therefore forcing them to sue for peace. And third, it was believed that such an aggressive campaign would buy time for South Vietnam to consolidate its power and military capabilities (Appy, 1993). As throughout the war, however, North Vietnamese forces refused to comply with American planning. Both the NLF and the NVA, by and large, refused to commit large units in battle—unless it was a battle of their own choosing. U.S. forces, consequently, were unable to police the entire country. Such a context required a steadily increasing commitment of American ground forces: 450,000 by the end of 1966, over 500,000 by 1967.

S&D operations included two other techniques: "clearing" operations, in which large enemy units were driven from populated areas in preparation for pacification of the area; and "securing" operations, undertaken to protect "friendly" Vietnamese, wipe out remaining local guerrillas, and "uproot" the enemy's secret political infrastructure (Young, 1991: 162–163). Many such missions were supplemented with advances in sophisticated technology. To locate an ever-elusive enemy, for example, the U.S. military used small, portable radar units and "people sniffers" that picked up the odor of human urine; IBM 1430 computers were also programmed to predict likely times and places of enemy attacks (Herring, 1996: 168).

In a war without front lines or territorial objectives, in a war of attrition where killing the enemy was the major goal, the "body count" became the preferred index of progress. Indeed, no measure of success was as important to the military command as the enemy body count (Appy, 1993: 156; Herring, 1996: 170). Cable (1991: 174) explains that "General Westmoreland and the Joint Chiefs, having defined the war in Vietnam as a struggle of attrition, would have been expected to focus upon the number of enemy killed and the ability of the North Vietnamese and Viet Cong to replace casualties as an excellent measure of the American progress toward victory." Cable (p. 174) concludes that although "only one of many statistical measures of results reported by military commands and intelligence agencies throughout the war, the body count and the exchange rates rose to the forefront as a result of the ever lengthening list of American dead through 1966."

The use of body counts—although a concept ingrained in our geographical imagination of the Vietnam War—did not originate with Vietnam. This grim statistic of mortality was widely employed in earlier conflicts, most notably the Korean War (Gartner and Myers, 1995). Under President Harry Truman's watch, for example, the U.S. Army adopted the body count as its dominant indicator of strategic assessment. And herein lies an interesting, albeit morbid, angle to population geography and war. The military campaigns in Korea and Vietnam were, in many respects, unlike those of World War II: no front lines, no capturing and securing of territory. Military conditions "did not lend themselves to traditional military measurement of ground warfare" (Gartner and Myers, 1995: 379). And yet military strategists required some means to measure success. Demographic accounting techniques provided one such measure. (De)population forecasts, in the guise of numbers of people killed, appeared to provide one rational and empirical method to gauge the success of a conflict.

With Vietnam, however, the use of body counts readily fit with McNamara's scientific management of the war. The Pentagon demanded statistics, deadly data that the whiz kids of McNamara were only too happy to provide. In some rear units of Saigon, officers would compile lists of cumulative kills on chalkboards (Neale, 2003: 85) and in Washington some of the most important pilot studies done by the OSA dealt with the strategy of attrition (Enthoven and Smith, 1971: 295). As James Gibson (1986: 124) explains:

> The production system with its precise reports of how many bodies were found on operations created the appearance of highly rational, scientific warfare. Body counts, weapons/kill ratios, charts of patrols conducted, helicopter and jet plane missions flown, and artillery rounds fired—all the indices of war production created at various command levels—presented Vietnam as a war managed by rational men basing their decisions on scientific knowledge. Statistics helped make war-managers appear legitimate to the American public.

Apart from gauging whether the war was being won or lost, these statistics were also instrumental in the actual conduct of the war. In particular, estimates of kill ratios influenced requests for additional troop buildups. Westmoreland, for example, promoted a ratio of 12 enemy soldiers killed for every American death; such thinking influenced the demand for troop buildups. After the battle for the Ia Drang Valley, for example, Westmoreland explained to the Pentagon that the buildup for the North Vietnamese was double that of the American forces; he required, therefore, additional U.S. troops (Schulzinger, 1997: 188).

Counting war dead, however, is not an easy demographic task. Soldiers are not census takers. It is one thing to engage in a firefight; it is quite another to have to traverse the battlefield in search of bodies. For one thing, not all bodies could be found. Furthermore, even if a dead body was found, it was not always possible to ascertain whether the corpse in front of you was, in fact, the enemy. A corpse was only evidence that *someone* had been killed. Enthoven and Smith (1971: 295), both of whom worked in the OSA, confirm that the concept of the body count did not mean that every enemy corpse was viewed by a foot patrol at close range and recorded. Rather, the "regulations provided only for counting 'males of fighting age' and others, male or female, known to have carried arms." Indeed, unless the body was found in association with a weapon, military equipment, or appropriate identification, it was impossible to be certain that he [or she] had been an enemy and not merely a civilian unfortunate enough to have been in the wrong place at the wrong time (Cable, 1991: 175).

The ever-present demand for empirical results, however, worked to produce favorable body counts. Officers, for example, were rewarded for producing high numbers (Schulzinger, 1997: 183). Competitions, likewise, were held between American units to produce the highest "box score" of enemy KIAs (killed in action) or the best "kill ratio" (defined as the most enemy killed in relation to American casualties) (Appy, 1993: 156). Enthoven and Smith (1971: 295) acknowledge that "errors could and did frequently creep in through double-counting, counting civilians (either bystanders or impressed porters), or counting graves, or through ignoring the rules because of the pressures to exaggerate enemy losses or the hazards of trying to count bodies while the enemy was still in the area." Herring (1996: 171) suggests that, given the heavy pressure to produce favorable body counts, casualty figures were probably inflated by as much as 30 percent.

Obtaining body counts was one thing; using these as empirical data was quite another. As Enthoven and Smith (1971: 295) caution, "The extreme emphasis on the body count as *the* measure of success led to various attempts to lend credence to the reported data." They explain that body counts, even if believed to be reliable, had to be tied to NLF and NVA replacement capabilities in order to be meaningful. In other words, did high body counts correspond to a decrease in the enemy's ability to reproduce soldiers? To make this assessment, Enthoven and Smith (p. 296) relate that "enemy manpower resources had to be estimated by census techniques and models applied to the North and South Vietnam populations, of which we knew very little."

The "war of attrition" coincided with Rostow's doctrine of a threat to the North's economic base. Both the air campaign and attrition were envisioned to punish the DRV, and thereby deny the NLF insurgents external support. Both strategies, however, failed to understand the Vietnamese situation—a fact that continues to mislead scholars of the conflict. Mueller (1980: 499), for example, argues that the war "was simply a matter of convincing the north that the war in the south was not worth the cost." He elaborates that "sufficiently punished, the Communists could reasonably be expected to relent, at least temporarily, in their effort to extend their area of control." Confronted with the loss of too many soldiers and resources, the North would be more vulnerable, and thus would give up their attempt to reunify the country and, ultimately, they would permit the existence of a pro-American state in the south. But herein lies a territorial trap that ensnared both American policymakers and subsequent historians. Mueller (1980: 499), for example, argues that the North Vietnamese were not fighting for the survival of their state (as were the Germans and Japanese in World War II). His sentiments effectively capture those of Rostow, Westmoreland, and others wherein American officials, by and large, believed that they were engaged in a civil war between the North and the South. However, the Vietnamese, from their perspective, viewed themselves as engaging in an anticolonial war against an illegal occupying force. From the North Vietnamese point of view, national survival was most certainly at stake. Mueller, however, falls into a territorial trap in that he presumes that both the DRV and the RVN were fixed, essentialized states, and that there was some primordial difference between the two.

Having fallen into a territorial trap, Mueller (like the military strategists of the Vietnam War) subsequently finds it easier to further dehumanize the Vietnamese in their "acceptance" of high casualty rates. Mueller (1980: 509; emphasis added) writes, for example, that "only occasionally in the last 160 years has a power absorbed battle deaths in an international war in the proportions *accepted* by the North Vietnamese." Mueller (p. 509) suggests that "American decision makers were on sound historical ground when they hoped and expected that, at some acceptable cost, they could break the 'will' of the North Vietnamese." Hence, he cautions that the argument is "not so much how the Americans could have made such a foolish miscalculation, but why the Vietnamese communists were willing to accept virtually unprecedented losses for the sake of a military goal that was far from central to their survival as a nation." But therein lies Mueller's own miscalculation. From the Vietnamese standpoint, particularly leaders such as Ho Chi Minh, the survival of a *unified* Vietnam was at stake.

And yet Mueller finds it easier, as did Westmoreland and other policymakers, to construct and accept an inherently cruel and fanatical enemy in the Vietnamese. Mueller describes the "enemy" as being "able to enforce upon itself an almost religious devotion to duty, sacrifice, loyalty, and fatalistic patience" (1980: 514). Note the underlying attitude, that the North Vietnamese accepted such losses. They could have refused by surrendering to the Americans. Hence, it is their own fault that so many people died. But let us rewrite Mueller's sentence: Only occasionally in the last 160 years has a military machine inflicted so many deaths in a war as did the United States in Vietnam. Viewed from this perspective, the United States unleashed an unprecedented killing campaign against people seeking to end colonial rule (first against the French, later against the United States) and to determine their own government structure.

POPULATION AND (THE DESTRUCTION OF) THE ENVIRONMENT (PART I)

> The war is extremely cruel. This morning, they bring me a wounded soldier. A phosphorous bomb has burned his entire body. An hour after being hit, he is still burning, smoke rising from his body. This is Khanh, a twenty-year-old man.... Nobody recognizes him as the cheerful, handsome man he once was. Today his smiling joyful black eyes have been reduced to two little holes—the yellowish eyelids are cooked. The reeking burn of phosphorous smoke still rises from his body. He looks as if he has been roasted in an oven.... His mother weeps. Her trembling hands touch her son's body; pieces of his skin fall off, curled up like crumbling sheets of rice cracker.
> —Dang Thuy Tram[5]

A few select images have come to symbolize the violence that was the Vietnam War. One thinks of Eddie Adams's 1969 photograph of a South

Vietnamese colonel executing an NLF prisoner on the streets of Saigon, or of Chick Harrity's 1973 photograph of a baby Vietnamese girl, Tran Thie Het Nhanny, lying in a cardboard box next to her brother, also on the streets of Saigon. Arguably, though, the most compelling horrific photograph of the Vietnam War was Nick Ut's shot of Kim Phuc, a 9-year-old Vietnamese girl running naked down a road near Trang Bang after a napalm attack. On June 8, 1972, Kim was a resident of Trang Bang when South Vietnamese planes dropped a napalm bomb on the village. As Kim attempted to flee the carnage with other villagers, her clothes were burnt off and she suffered third-degree burns over half her body. In the aftermath, she endured 17 operations over many years of burn therapy procedures. The story of Kim and of Ut's haunting photograph serves as a reminder of the suffering of innocents and innocence in times of war. Her body—or, more precisely, the burned flesh that she can never shed—also speaks of the dehumanizing corporatization of warfare as manifested in the development and deployment of napalm.

Napalm, as J. B. Neilands (1970: 213) bluntly attests, is "a purely American invention." Napalm was developed during World War II by Louis Fieser, a professor at Harvard University. As originally formulated, napalm was compounded from metallic soaps gelled with gasoline; it would later be reformulated (and called Napalm B) using 50 percent polystyrene mixed with gasoline and benzene. As a weapon, napalm is particularly insidious. It is a sticky, incendiary gel that burns flesh and bone. When used in bombs, the resultant explosion deoxygenates the air and creates large amounts of carbon monoxide, thus suffocating those who are in proximity of the bombing.

Napalm was first used in July 1944 to bomb a fuel depot in France. Napalm was also widely used in bombing attacks against Japanese cities—leading to untold civilian deaths in that country—and as a flammable liquid used in flamethrowers against Japanese soldiers throughout the Pacific theater of operations. Later, during the Korean War, napalm was widely employed; in the 3 years of overt military action across the Korean peninsula, over 32,000 tons of napalm was dropped (Neilands, 1970: 213).

Vietnam witnessed an escalation in the use of napalm. Throughout the conflict U.S. and South Vietnamese aircraft dropped 400,000 tons of napalm—constituting 10 percent of all munitions expended by fighter-bomber sorties during the war. This figure compares with the 14,000 tons dropped by American aircraft in World War II (Clodfelter, 1995: 236). According to various reports, American pilots were "given a square mile on a map and told to hit every hamlet within the area" with napalm bombs (Neilands, 1970: 213). Here is how one journalist who participated on a bombing mission over Vietnam described the experience:

> We flattened out over the target ... and I had a glimpse of three thatched huts burning along the edge of some water. Then I closed my eyes and could not open them again until we were several thousand feet up. Below, the trees and huts were blotted out by a cloud of nauseous black smoke.... On the second run I managed to hold my eyes open. As we pulled out through the smoke, I saw the second napalm bomb a couple of seconds after it had burst. A ball of brilliant flame was rolling out across more than 200 feet, swelling like a giant orange cauliflower.... I asked the commander about the target.... "Well, we don't rightly know for sure," he said.... "You can't rightly see much at those speeds.... But most times you can reckon that whatever moves in the Delta is V.C." (quoted in Neilands, 1970: 214)

Marilyn Young (1991: 130) likewise quotes an American pilot who profusely praised the benefits of white phosphorous:

> We sure are pleased with those backroom boys at Dow [Chemical]. The original product wasn't so hot—if the gooks were quick they could scape it off. So the boys started adding polystyrene—now it sticks like shit to a blanket. But then if the gooks jumped under water it stopped burning, so they started adding Willie Peter [WP—white phosphorous] so's to make it burn better. It'll even burn under water now. And one drop is enough, it'll keep on burning right down to the bone so they die anyway from phosphorous poisoning.

The use of napalm and other chemical and biological forms of warfare certainly predates America's involvement in Vietnam. Historical accounts indicate the use of chemical-based warfare as early as the Peloponnesian War when, in 428 B.C., the Spartans burned wood saturated with pitch and sulphur under the city wall of Plateae to create choking, poisonous chemical fumes. Over the next 2,500 years military strategists developed other, equally innovative biological or chemical techniques to incapacitate—if not outright kill—their enemies. Examples include the Roman's application of salt to sterilize the soils of the Carthaginians in 146 B.C., "provision" of diseased-infected blankets to Native Americans by British forces in 1763, and the destruction of buffalo herds during the late 19th-century Indian Wars in the United States (Cecil, 1986: 2–3).

It was not until World War I (1914–1918), however, that widespread usage of chemical and biological weapons occurred. Beginning in August 1914 French soldiers fired rifle-launched cartridges filled with an irritating and slightly suffocating chemical agent. Military planners on both sides of the conflict soon experimented with other agents and other delivery systems. By 1915 both the French and the German armies were regularly using cylinder-dispensed chlorine gas, along with phosgene, chlorine, and mustard gas. Although artillery-delivered chemical weapons eventually became the preferred method, other tactics included chemical hand grenades and trench mortars. By the end of the war, casualties resultant from chemical weapons totaled nearly 1.3 million, with more than 91,000 fatalities (Cecil, 1986: 4).

The horrors attendant upon chemical warfare led to the adoption of the 1925 Geneva Protocol, an measure that condemned the use of asphyxiating, poisonous, or other gases in the conduct of war (Neilands, 1970: 210–211). Such moral considerations as articulated in the Geneva Protocol, though, did not prevent continued experimentation with chemical weapons. The scientific development of such agents, along with the technologies to most effectively disseminate such weapons, proceeded. Successive U.S. governments, for example, consistently abided by the terms of the Geneva Protocol, although many officials in the State Department continued to read the protocol as "prohibiting only lethal gases" and thus not applicable to other forms of chemical agents (for example, "riot control" gases or herbicides) (p. 211). Consequently, military planners in the United States focused on three forms of spraying and dusting chemicals: lethal and nonlethal chemicals, screening smoke, and incendiaries. Nonlethal forms would, ostensibly, include herbicides used to remove forest cover in an attempt to deny the enemy areas of cover. Likewise, during the 1930s the U.S. Army

Air Corps developed the basic mechanisms, techniques, and tactics of aerial chemical delivery. Scientists also considered the effects of atmospheric convection, wind, and temperature on spraying techniques (Buckingham, 1982: 3).

Nor did the Geneva Protocol prevent the use of chemical weapons in warfare. Unconfirmed reports indicated the use of chemical and biological weapons during the Spanish Civil War as well as during the suppression of civil strife in northern China in the 1930s. Japan is also suspected of using chemical weapons against the Chinese in 1937 (Cecil, 1986). The first openly acknowledged use of these weapons, however, occurred in 1936 when the Italian air force delivered mustard gas in combat. Employed in Italy's annexation of Abyssinia, this usage constituted the first aerial-based act of chemical warfare. Although Italy's actions were morally condemned, strategists did note that it was an effective military technique (Buckingham, 1982: 3).

Lethal chemical sprays, according to Buckingham (1982), were apparently not used during World War II—though certainly many other equally destructive weapons were employed, not least of which was the nuclear bomb. Indeed, chemical weapons were viewed by some military officials as unethical. Admiral William Leahy, then serving as the U.S. chief of staff, considered poison gas to be a "barbarous weapon." When a proposal surfaced to employ biological weapons to destroy Japanese rice crops—a proposal foreshadowing the use of chemical agents in Vietnam—Leahy expressed the opinion that such a weapon "would violate every Christian ethic I have ever heard of and all of the known laws of war" (quoted in Neilands, 1970: 211).

Such moral condemnation was not widespread, however. Throughout the 1950s governments increasingly used chemical weapons as a means of warfare. The British military, for example, employed aerially sprayed herbicides in Malaya in an attempt to suppress a communist-based liberation movement. During this campaign the British used both helicopters and fixed-wing aircraft to eradicate food crops as part of a larger program designed to restrict food supplies which could be used, supposedly, to support insurgents (Buckingham, 1982: 5). Such a food-denial strategy, though, also had the effect of starving noninsurgents, that is, innocent civilians. The British ultimately abandoned this strategy when they recognized that food denial was counterproductive: the destruction of food crops did not distinguish between insurgents and friendly civilians, thus potentially driving more people to the enemy ranks (Cecil, 1986: 17).

Although this form of environmental warfare was abandoned by the British in Malaya, it formed the basis for American usage in Vietnam. In April 1961, as U.S. officials began to seriously contemplate the use of herbicides as a military strategy in Vietnam, Rostow forwarded a memo on Vietnam to Kennedy in which he proposed a high-level meeting to consider "gearing up" the whole Vietnam operation. Nine specific courses of action were considered, including a recommendation that a military hardware research and development team travel to Vietnam to work with the Military Assistance Advisory Group (MAAG) in exploring the usefulness of various techniques then available or currently under development. One such technique was aerial defoliation (Buckingham, 1982: 9–10).

In 1961 Johnson (then serving as vice president) established the joint United States/Vietnamese Combat Development and Test Center (CDTC) in Vietnam, under the direction of the Defense Department's Advanced Research Projects Agency (ARPA). The mandate of the CDTC was to develop new counterinsurgency methods and weapons. The use of herbicides as a defoliation strategy was high on the list for advancement (Cecil, 1986: 23). In fact, by July 1961 specific proposals were drafted that included the use of chemical plant killers.

The time from proposed use to actual use was very short. On August 10, 1961, the first defoliation test mission over South Vietnam was conducted when a South Vietnamese Air Force H-34 helicopter equipped with a HIDAL (Helicopter Insecticide Dispersal Apparatus, Liquid) spray system released the chemical dinoxol over crops in South Vietnam, just north of Kontum. Two weeks later the first fixed-wing spray mission was conducted, with additional tests conducted in Thailand and Cambodia (Buckingham, 1982: 11; Neilands, 1970). By November 30, 1961, Kennedy authorized the explicit use of defoliants.

Initially, the use of chemical or biological weapons was to be selective and carefully controlled—though not limited in geographic coverage. Some early proposals, for example, envisioned a defoliation campaign that would eradicate 31,250 square miles—approximately half of the entire country of South Vietnam (Buckingham, 1982: 15). Defoliants would be employed to destroy foliage to remove protective cover. Designated targets would include, for example, the clearance of key transportation routes. In part, reluctance on the part of Kennedy and his advisors stemmed not from a concern on the effects such a campaign would have on Vietnam or its people. Rather, concerns were expressed over the public image of chemical defoliants. McNamara, for example, preferred to disguise the defoliation campaign as purely a South Vietnamese operation. Lansdale, likewise, urged caution, reminding his colleagues that the North Koreans had charged the United States with using biological weapons during the Korean War. Any media leak would generate potential adverse publicity (Buckingham, pp. 26–27).

The overt and deliberate use of chemical warfare in Vietnam began in early January 1962.[6] Following a series of "familiarization" flights, chemical defoliants—conducted as part of Operation Ranch Hand—were released from Air Force C-123s on January 10, 1962. By the time Operation Ranch Hand was stopped—amid widespread criticism—9 years later, approximately 18 million gallons of chemicals had been sprayed on 20 percent of South Vietnam, with 4,747,587 acres of forest defoliated and 481,897 acres of cropland destroyed (Buckingham, 1982).

As the war escalated, so too did the indiscriminate use of herbicides and other chemicals. Beginning in late 1962 American military strategists began using defoliants not simply to clear jungles, but as techniques for food denial. One example is the defoliation of the 18,500-acre Boi Loi Woods. Located approximately 25 miles northwest of Saigon and 10 miles from the Cambodian border, the Boi Loi region was presumed to be a major and secure base of NLF forces. In addition, it was believed that about 100 acres of land were devoted to food crops for NLF troops. The operation, code-named Sherwood Forest, called for the use of defoliants to strip the leaves from trees, and subsequently to completely burn the forest. American advisors had first broached the idea in October 1964. On December 3 a formal request was made. Apart from exposing the potential insurgents, an additional benefit was identified: the defoliation campaign would force the civilian population to relocate to other settlements, thus denying their assistance to the communist insurgents.

The Boi Loi Woods were home to an estimated 6,000 people. Approximately 4,000 of these residents, described as "pacificistic," lived in three hamlets as farmers; another 2,000 people earned their living cutting firewood in the forest. After General Westmoreland called for a feasibility study to be conducted, operations and intelligence specialists recommended the destruction of the forest. Final approval was given by the U.S. Embassy on January 2, 1965. The U.S. Air Force, concomitantly, requested the Boi Loi Woods be designated a "free bomb" area.

Prior to the initial wave of destruction, leaflets were dropped and messages broadcast over loudspeakers urging the population to evacuate the area. Promises of financial assistance were also made to induce evacuation. Then, between January 18 and January 20 American fighter pilots conducted 139 sorties and dropped nearly 800 tons of bombs on the forest. Some munitions were targeting bombs; most, however, were area coverage bombs. Additionally, bombs with time-delay fuses were employed. Refugees later reported that these bombs were very effective in inducing fear because they exploded at times when no aircraft were present. Lastly, riot gas was dispersed as an added incentive for the people to flee. After 2 days of an intense terror campaign, only 2,182 refugees left the Boi Loi Woods (Buckinham, 1982; Cecil, 1986).

Beginning on January 22 and lasting till February 18, the main defoliation campaign of Boi Loi was waged. Over 100 sorties delivered 83,000 gallons of herbicides on the woods. An additional 316 sorties dropped more than 372 bombs and fired 85,000 rounds of ammunition. Six weeks later American pilots attempted to ignite the woods through the dumping of thousands of gallons of diesel fuel, followed by the delivery of napalm and incendiary cluster bombs. Ironically, the attempt to completely burn the woods proved unsuccessful as monsoon rains extinguished the conflagration.

As the war progressed, the public relations fears of McNamara were slowly realized. It was widely reported, for example, that poisons that were banned in the United States were widely used on the Vietnamese population and environment. In the fall of 1969 it was reported that Agent Orange would no longer be used domestically in the United States, as studies by the Bionetics Research Laboratory indicated that the agent was teratogenic and that the offspring of laboratory animals fed 2,4,5-T showed 100 percent birth defects. U.S. officials immediately stated that the restriction would *not* apply to the use of 2,4,5-T in Vietnam. Furthermore, during the summer of 1969 a number of newspapers in Saigon disclosed a sharp rise in birth defects and linked this occurrence to the prevalence of defoliation campaigns. The newspapers were immediately shut down by the South Vietnamese government (Neilands, 1970: 221).

Within the United States, the public outcry continued to mount. A *Washington Post* editorial "called into question the wisdom of such agents, and the sort of unselective and nondiscriminatory warfare." Moreover, the editorial cautioned that "the employment of the devices of chemical warfare even in enemy country where the inevitable hardships fall upon the enemy's civilian population is open to all sort of ethical doubts. Their employment in a civil war, where the consequences are visited upon a civilian population we are trying to defend, is folly compounded" (quoted in Buckingham, 1982: 94).

Critics of the operation were supported in their condemnation through the actions of a number of academics. Especially notable were the efforts of the scientists associated with the American Association for the Advancement of Science (AAAS). In December 1969 Harvard biologist Matthew S. Meselson presented the preliminary findings of a fact-finding report at the annual convention of the AAAS. Meselson was, at the time, head of the AAAS Herbicide Assessment Commission, tasked with investigating the military use of herbicides in Vietnam. Between August and September 1970 Meselson and other commission members conducted on-site inspections in South Vietnam; to these field surveys were added interviews held with various experts, military planners, and other officials engaged in the ongoing herbicidal campaign in Vietnam. The AAAS findings, subsequently printed in journals and reports, were disturbing at the time, and remain so today. Meselson and his colleagues determined that by 1970 "about one-seventh of the land area of South Vietnam—equivalent in size to the state of Massachusetts—had been treated with herbicides" (Boffey, 1971: 44). Most chemical applications were delivered via "low-flying C-123 cargo aircraft that made more than 19,000 individual spray flights between 1962 and 1969"; about "90 percent of the herbicide was dropped on forest land and about 10 percent on crop land" (p. 44).

The destruction uncovered by numerous scientific teams was found to be widespread, wreaking significant damage to the forest and agricultural ecosystems. In 1969, for example, Drs. E. W. Pfeiffer and G. Orians, working under the joint auspices of the Society for Social Responsibility in Science and McGraw-Hill Publications, conducted a survey on the environmental damage accruing to South Vietnam. In their tours of defoliated areas throughout South Vietnam, they discovered no insectivorous or frigivorous birds and only a few fish-eating birds (Neilands, 1970: 223).

The destruction of Vietnam's forests would reverberate throughout South Vietnam. The AAAS team, for example, identified the "total annihilation" of mangrove forests throughout the coastal regions of South Vietnam. Moreover, early assessments—confirmed years later—indicated that the rejuvenation of the forests would take decades. Tropical hardwood forests were equally devastated. Meselson's team estimated that "more than half of the forest in three provinces" were "very severely damaged." Arthur Westing, the team's forestry expert, "concluded that about 35 percent of South Vietnam's 14 million acres of dense forest [had] been sprayed one or more times and that, as a result, 6.2 billion board feet of merchantable timber [had] thus far been killed by herbicides." This amounted to South Vietnam's entire domestic timber needs, based on then-current demand, for the next three decades. The economic effects, furthermore, would be astronomical. Westing determined that the lost timber represented approximately US$500 million in stumpage taxes that would have accrued to the South Vietnamese government (Westing, 1971, 1975). Apparently the potential revenue from forestry did not factor into Rostow's development scheme for South Vietnam. Additional studies reported that Operation Ranch Hand had a devastating effect on the economy of South Vietnam; in one year, for example, rubber production fell by 30 percent. Jack fruit, mango, manioc, and guava production was likewise reduced through herbicidal campaigns (Neilands, 1970: 223).

The AAAS scientists concluded also that the destruction of some "2000 square kilometers of land" entailed "destruction of enough food to feed 600,000 persons for a year" (Boffey, 1971: 45). Moreover, the destruction had been especially pronounced in the food-scarce Central Highlands, populated by an indigenous people known as the Montagnards. Related studies indicated that the destruction of food reserves by defoliation chiefly afflicted the aged and the infirm, pregnant and lactating women, and children under 5 years of age (Neilands, 1970: 220).

Apart from the physical destruction of the cropland, the AAAS team found contradictions between "reality" and military "assessments" of the herbicidal program. Operations in Quang Ngai province were singled out for discussion. According to military officials, this region was (1) virtually uninhabited—defined as less than eight persons per square kilometer; (2) recently expanded in size of cultivation; and (3) exhibiting signs of terracing as a rice-growing strategy. According to military authorities, these factors amounted to one conclusion: increased village support for the provision of foodstuffs to the enemy. Indeed, it was this form of reasoning that supported the Strategic Hamlet Program. In essence, military officials argued that the region was occupied by a small number of Montagnards; however, the cultivated area was considered to be much larger than needed to support the small population. This, to the military planners, indicated the presence of "the enemy." Furthermore, it was claimed that Montagnards did not practice terracing—supposedly further evidence of an enemy presence (Boffey, 1971: 45).

Meselson and his colleagues reached a different conclusion. Aerial photographs taken by the AAAS team, combined with a map issued in 1965, indicated the presence of more than 900 dwellings in the area—a settlement size far beyond the official claim that Quang Ngai was "virtually uninhabited." Indeed, the AAAS team determined that the region actually supported a population of more than 5,000 persons, or about 180 persons per square kilometer. Moreover, comparisons between current air photos and the 1965 map suggested that the area had not experienced a rapid expansion of cultivation. They also learned—from other military sources—that the Montagnards had grown rice on terraced fields for a long time. The team's conclusion: "Our observations lead us to believe that precautions to avoid destroying the crops of indigenous civilian populations have been a failure and that nearly all the food destroyed would actually have been consumed by such populations" (Boffey, 1971: 45). Moreover, other reports corroborated that the "use of starvation as a weapon [had] not been very effective militarily inasmuch as soldiers can generally forage for themselves at the expense of the civilian population." Neilands (1970: 227) concludes:

> At Nuremberg the Allies defined as a very serious war crime the destruction of civilian food supplies as practiced by the German High Commissioner in Holland ... who was responsible for the opening of dikes and the flooding of about 0.5 million acres of agricultural land. The destruction of rice and other food staples

in Vietnam, while of dubious military value, is certain to increase the misery and suffering of the civilian population.

POPULATION AND THE (DESTRUCTION OF) THE ENVIRONMENT (PART II)

> In my estimation, we have just one moral obligation—and that moral obligation is for us to develop at the earliest possible moment that agent which will kill enemy personnel most quickly and most cheaply.
> —Lieutenant General (retired) Jimmy Doolittle[7]

> All day and night, the sounds of bombs, jet planes, gunships, and HU-1As circling above are deafening. The forest is gouged and scarred by bombs, the remaining trees are stained yellow by toxic chemicals. We're affected by the poison, too.
> —Dang Thuy Tram[8]

The use of chemical defoliants constitutes just one form of ecological warfare. Indeed, as the work of the geographer Yves Lacoste has demonstrated, there are many other ways of geographically regulating (or killing) populations than with chemical weapons. Lacoste (1973: 2), explains that "ecological warfare" is best understood from a geographical perspective. He writes: "To achieve a limited number of political and military objectives there has been destruction of vegetation, the transformation of the physical characteristics of the soil, the deliberate precipitation of new erosional processes, the rupture of hydrological systems in order to change the level of the water table (so as to dry up wells and rice paddies), and also a radical change in the distribution of population." The purpose is to more effectively regulate populations to achieve political and military objectives. Lacoste (p. 2) concludes that "such forms of destruction are not simply the unintended consequences of the massive scale of lethal means available for technological and industrial warfare; they are the result of a deliberate and minutely-articulated strategy, the elements of which are scientifically coordinated in time and space."

American military strategists had contemplated the use of ecological warfare against Japanese rice crops during World War II. Crop-killing chemicals, including ammonium thiocynate, for example, had been developed and tested. Other schemes included the placement of small incendiary bombs on Mexican free-tailed bats. These "animal bombers" would be used to burn down buildings in Japanese cities as well as to strike fear in the population. Crane (2002: 242–243) explains that after overcoming a host of technological problems—ranging from creating a light enough munition with adequate incendiary power to freezing the bats to make them quiescent enough to be armed—the project demonstrated its potential when some escaped fire-bats burned down Carlsbad Auxiliary Army Airfield. Further testing indicated that a plane full of "batbombs" could indeed start more fires than a comparable load of conventional incendiary devices. The project, however, was terminated in 1944 so that more monies could be transferred to the Manhattan Project and the development of the atomic bomb (Crane, 2002: 243).

During the Korean War and its immediate aftermath, military strategists continued to focus attention on the strategic potential of biological warfare against crops and large numbers of people (Crane, 2002: 244). By the mid-1950s, the U.S. Air Force had 5,000 tons of anticrop chemicals. Delivery systems included bombs, spray tanks, and 24,000 biological antipersonnel and 63,000 chemical nerve gas clusters waiting for fill (p. 248). It was in Vietnam, however, through the massive use of herbicides, defoliants, and strategic bombing of agricultural areas, that the biosphere was systematically assailed for military purposes (Barnaby, 1976: 40).

Between March 1967 and July 1972 the U.S. Army in Vietnam attempted to modify Vietnam's weather through rainmaking. Hundreds of operations were conducted in attempts to intensify the normal monsoon rainfall over the Ho Chi Minh Trail; clouds were seeded with silver and lead iodide from aircraft as nearly 50,000 canisters were dropped during more than 2,500 sorties (Barnaby, 1976: 41). These operations failed to produce any significant effects on Vietnam's weather. Also used were "Rome ploughs"—33-ton armored tractors, each equipped with a blade to shear and push over trees of almost any size. These vehicles were used to destroy forests and crops, and to raze villages; a company of 30 tractors could remove heavy jungle at a rate of 99 acres per day and light jungle at a rate of 395 acres per day. An estimated 803,100 acres of Vietnam's forests were cleared through this manner; in addition, thousands of acres of rubber plantations, fruit orchards, and agricultural fields, including irrigation systems, were also destroyed (p. 43). Westing (1975: 222) found that "the extensive land clearing shown to be feasible with Rome ploughs leads to locally serious ecological debilitation. The cleared areas undergo severe site degradation and become occupied with long-lasting biotic communities of low plant and animal species diversity, reduced biomass, and diminished productivity."

More devastating was the deliberate targeting of dikes in Vietnam's northern delta.

In the summer of 1972 Lacoste conducted fieldwork in the Red River delta region of northern Vietnam. His investigations were made in conjunction with the International Commission of Inquiry into War Crimes. His purpose was to ascertain how the modification and destruction of the "geographic milieu" was being used to "obliterate those very geographical conditions which are indispensable for the lives of several million people" (Lacoste, 1973: 2). The Red River delta comprises an area of approximately 3,500 square miles. During the war some 10 million people lived and farmed in the region; in some areas, population densities exceeded 800 inhabitants per half square mile.

Geographically, the delta is divided into two parts (Lacoste, 1973: 8 passim). In the west lies the upper delta. Here, alluvium-choked rivers emerge from the mountain valleys of northwestern Vietnam. Over centuries, the rivers in the western region progressively built up a large number of alluvial cushions. Sediment is carried eastward into the lower delta and flows above natural levees that are less high. According to Lacoste (p. 8), these differences of configuration between the upper and the lower delta have important consequences for the topographical localization of villages: in the upper western part the villages have been built above easily flooded areas on top of the alluvial cushions; in the eastern part of the lower delta most of the villages are located below the level of the rivers, in areas easily flooded should a break in the dikes occur.

Analyzing bombing patterns, Lacoste (1973: 8) found that "a large majority of the bombed dikes are situated in the eastern part of the delta, where most of these easily-flooded villages are to be found." Specifically, during the period April 16 to July 31, 1972, the hydraulic installations in North Vietnam were the objective of over 150 air attacks; hits were recorded in 96 different places. Of these, 58 were situated in the Red River delta and the majority (54 out of 58) were located in the eastern part of the delta (p. 6). This region was the most densely populated and the most important in terms of agricultural production. Furthermore, Lacoste (p. 8) argues that "the most frequently hit points on the dikes are the ones that, at high-water, are subjected to unusually strong pressure by water." Lacoste (pp. 8–9) elaborates that the dikes had been hit in the concave part of the bends—at points where they are subjected to the perpendicular pressure of especially powerful currents.

Lacoste (p. 12 passim) likewise examined the effects of the bombing campaigns. With respect to munitions, the most frequently used bombs weighed between 500 and 1,000 pounds; the resultant explosion of these munitions produced craters from 20 to 22 feet deep and about 35 feet in diameter. In addition, the shock caused by the explosions caused a series of fractures and cracks over a radius of 50 yards. Such devastation to the physical environment could result in massive flooding, potentially resulting in the immediate drowning deaths of hundreds or thousands of people, the destruction of rice crops, and the consequent death of perhaps millions more by starvation. In conclusion, Lacoste found no evidence of "military" targets in the delta region, beyond that of killing large numbers of people via drowning or hunger.[9]

Studies in other parts of Vietnam found similar results. Westing (1975) calculated that bomb craters in South Vietnam had a combined surface area of 365,700 acres and a combined volume of 706 trillion cubic feet. He concluded:

> Each of the 66,000 bombing sorties flown against South Vietnam by the B-52s alone (the major instrument of carpet bombing) left a crater field averaging 65 hectares in size. The combined area of such disruption just from this source amounted to one-quarter of the land area of the entire country. Thus, the direct damage from conventional high-explosives to the biota of South Vietnam, both immediate and delayed, combined with the indirect damage to it via habitat destruction, has resulted in what may well be the most serious (and least recognized) long-term ecological impact of the Second Indochina War. (p. 218)

Ecological warfare via the bombing of dikes in flood-prone regions conformed with the attrition strategy favored and forwarded by U.S. military strategists. Consequently, ecological warfare emerges as a crucial technique in the discipline of bodies and the regulation of populations. As such, it is possible to draw from this example important lessons that emerge at the interface of nature, violence, and population.

Nature, as Castree (2001: 5) explains, is both a concept and all those physical things to which the concept refers. It is also a contested term and concept, fraught with different meanings and different usages. Accordingly, many geographers have approached nature as a discourse—a social construct—that is also an instrument of social power. Demeritt (2001: 32) explains that "claims about the social construction of nature might be understood as claims about the social construction of our knowledge and concepts of nature." Much of this work has been encompassed by the phrase "the production of nature," a concept that directs attention to how people have shaped nature for profit. Nature is constructed as a resource to be conserved, preserved, or exploited. In the context of warfare, the struggle for nature has emphasized one of two relationships. On the one hand, researchers have documented that resource scarcity may give rise to conflict, while, on the other hand, it has been noted that resource abundance may also facilitate conflict (le Billon, 2001). Furthermore, as Nevins (2003: 688) finds, many of these studies have conceived of violence too narrowly, "limiting it to individual physical acts or events of physical brutality." Needed in these studies is a conceptualization of violence that includes "not only acts that involve physical brutality, but also institutionalized and indirect practices that contribute to physical injury and/or create, maintain, or exacerbate social injustice" (p. 688). Nevins concludes that

> This moves us beyond a focus on the intent of the perpetrators of violence, requiring that we accept the premise that individuals and social entities are responsible for the likely or predictable consequences of their actions.... To the extent that control of, access to, and distribution of environmental resources (and their associated benefits and detriments) are institutionalized in such a way as to harm human beings in that they contribute to the denial of basic human rights (such as that to adequate food, shelter, clothing, and medical care or the right to fair and just remuneration for work), they are examples of structural violence. (p. 688)

In Vietnam, we see the "destruction of nature" as a concerted effort to deny the Vietnamese people their livelihoods and homes. The destruction of nature, from the perspective of military strategists, was a legitimate technique of warfare, but one that had (and has) far-reaching consequences that extend beyond war itself. These spatial practices—including the denial of vegetated cover to the "enemy," the destruction of food crops, and the inducement of terror through biological and chemical agents—were designed solely to decimate populations through the annihilation of the environment. Little consideration was given to distinctions between "ally" or "enemy" because in the end the Vietnamese were simply seen as the Other. And all were morally excluded from the considerations of Rostow, Westmoreland, Nixon, and the other planners who managed the war.

THE CONTROL OF POPULATIONS

> At Mo Duc, military vehicles plowed through the hamlets. The villagers fled. Many cadres perished, crushed in their shelters by the enemy's vehicles....
> —DANG THUY TRAM[10]

In 1969 the U.S. military initiated Operation Pipestone Canyon. The location of the operation was 12 miles south of Da Nang, on a small island—Go Noi—located within the meandering branches of the Ky Lam River. About 5 miles long and 2 miles wide, Go Noi was the site of at least nine U.S. Marine operations in a 4-year period, dating to 1965. The area, however, had been heavily contested for many years during the Franco–Vietminh War.

By 1969 American officials were frustrated at the continued level of insurgent activities, and of not being able to pacify this small area of rice paddies and thatched houses. Under Operation Pipestone, U.S. Marine Corps engineers leveled the island with plows and bulldozers. The inhabitants were resettled in "strategic hamlets," isolated encampments surrounded by watchtowers, barbed wire, and armed guards. Christian Appy (1993: 160) quotes an after-action report that emphasized the "positive" aspects of the operation: The island was clear, mission accomplished. He also quotes the following assessment: "Go Noi island had been converted from a densely-populated, heavily wooded area to a barren wasteland; a plowed field."

Le Ly Hayslip, author of the 1993 best-selling memoir *When Heaven and Earth Changed Places* (and the subject of Oliver Stone's 1994 film,

Heaven and Earth), was born in Ky La Hamlet on Go Noi. She (along with Pham, 2006: 146) describes her understanding of strategic hamlets:

> Instead of trading life in the lands of the ancestors for security in a new village, the unfortunate people of the countryside usually found themselves lost and forgotten by their own government, women and children tucked away like herds of animals. Instead of being measures of social welfare, the Strategic Hamlets became places to impose and ensure governmental control. Driven from their homes, the residents of the new Strategic Hamlets ... found themselves abandoned, betrayed, jobless victims of governmental manipulation.

She (p. 151) concludes that "villagers and hamlet people were the ones who constantly came into contact with the realities of war; they were the ones who suffered the most, and who bore all of the burdens of war."

It has been described as the "other" war, the war to win "hearts and minds." In actuality, it did more harm to the people of (especially South) Vietnam than any good. It was the attempt to pacify people for political purposes. Even the term is Orwellian: to pacify, to calm, as a mother would an unruly child. But this technique of biopower was far from maternal. The pacification campaign was not simply a technique of spatial exclusion, it also served to morally exclude the Vietnamese.

The pacification effort—the war for hearts and minds—conformed with the Rostow doctrine of war. It was accepted that the North Vietnamese were supporting the NLF and that the survival of an independent South Vietnam was in jeopardy. A strategy was required therefore to stabilize areas deemed critical and to deny NVA soldiers and the NLF insurgents "safe havens" in which to operate. As Prados (1996: 242) explains, "Counterinsurgency theory suggested population resettlement." Consequently, advisors such as William Porter believed that it was incumbent on the United States to ensure that the Vietnamese population be isolated and secured (Cable, 1991: 127). The spatial strategies that emerged were practices of concentration and enclosure.

Discipline, Foucault (1979: 141) argues, proceeds from the distribution of bodies in space. He explains that when conceiving spaces of confinement, planners and strategists must consider carefully how this distribution is produced. In particular, the spatial arrangement of confinement will not only produce a space in which individual bodies may be isolated and mapped, but also spaces in which populations may be regulated into a productive collective. Foucault (p. 143) explains:

> Each individual has his [sic] own place; and each place its individual. Avoid distributions in groups; break up collective dispositions; analyse confused, massive or transient pluralities. Disciplinary space tends to be divided into as many sections as there are bodies or elements to be distributed. One must eliminate the effects of imprecise distributions, the uncontrolled disappearance of individuals, their diffuse circulation, their unusable and dangerous coagulation; it was a tactic of anti-desertion, anti-vagabondage, anti-concentration. Its aim was to establish presences and absences, to know where and how to locate individuals, to set up useful communications, to interrupt others, to be able at each moment to supervise the conduct of each individual, to assess it, to judge it, to calculate its qualities or merits. It was a procedure ... aimed at knowing, mastering and using. Discipline organizes an analytical space.

The spatial concentration of Vietnamese, from a Foucauldian perspective, resonates well with McNamara's and Rostow's analytical approach to the war.[11] In Vietnam, the confinement of Vietnamese civilians carried a twofold purpose. On the one hand, spaces of enclosure were to keep South Vietnamese peasants untainted from communist influence. U.S. military officials, in particular, harbored deep suspicions regarding the Vietnamese peoples' "true" loyalties and political commitments. It was argued by strategists that physically controlling the Vietnamese peasants, and keeping them confined to heavily policed encampments, would effectively neutralize the influence of the NLF. In other words, these concentration camps would prevent the "uncontrolled disappearance" of Vietnamese peasants and hinder "their diffuse circulation." Such encampments would further ensure a greater ability to "locate individuals" and to monitor their comings and goings. On the other hand, these spaces were also intended to deny NLF insurgents access to recruits, food supplies, and sanctuary from bombings. Consequently, these encampments would satisfy a key component of the demographic war of attrition: deny the enemy an ability to reproduce its numbers through recruitment. For Kolko (1994: 132), what was required was the physical control of the population, whose desires and needs were, for practical purposes, minimized; simply put, "It was demographic change and social transformation, not military action, that would set the critical context for the outcome of the war."

Beginning in the early 1960s American planners began experimenting with various forms of enclosure.[12] The Strategic Hamlet Program was one such project. As a counterinsurgency strategy, Vietnamese peasants were gathered together from their dispersed villages into heavily fortified hamlets. Designed to prevent interaction between the "good" peasants and the "bad" Vietcong, the hamlets were surrounded by moats, fences, and watchtowers; armed troops would stand guard. Ostensibly, the peasants would be able to take advantage of improved medical facilities, schools, and so on. The insurgents, conversely, would be denied sanctuary in the villages, as well as be denied sources of food and other supplies. In principle, from the perspective of McNamara and Rostow, the Strategic Hamlet Program would deny the NLF its ability to socially reproduce itself.

Apart from the perceived military gains, the Strategic Hamlet Program also conformed to Rostow's promotion of democracy and development in Vietnam. In effect, these programs may be seen as the Vietnamese counterpart to Johnson's "War on Poverty" in the United States. On the one hand, segregation and isolation of Vietnam's peasants would "bind" the people to the newly formed government and, through the reinstitution of village elections, contribute to the spread of democratic principles. On the other hand, the concentration of peasants in self-contained villages was thought (by Rostow, at least) to bring about a revolution in social attitudes and economic practices. With attendant programs of land reform, peasants were expected to set off on the stages of economic growth forecast by Rostow (Herring, 1996).

Rhetorically, these spaces were represented as models of land reform. As such, these were to provide viable alternatives to the grievances enunciated by the NLF. However, in practice, most U.S. officials did not believe that land-based grievances were important (Kolko, 1994: 131). Furthermore, men like Rostow refused to contemplate the idea that agrarian concerns (for example, issues of landlessness) could be a factor in the growing insurgency. According to Rostow's thesis, the insurgents—and the Vietnamese peasants in general—were simply "confused" by their rapid engagement with modernization. Any exhibited discontent had to be the result of northern communist propaganda (Kolko, 1994). Such reasoning further justified the confinement of Vietnam's peasant population.

In March 1962 a pilot project, termed "Operation Sunrise," was conducted in the Ben Cat district of Binh Duong province. This region was considered to be an NLF stronghold. The U.S. Information Service prepared a pamphlet entitled *Toward the Good Life* for distribution in the district. The population was subsequently removed and herded together; the majority of people were forced to leave their homes at gunpoint. The resettlement site, far from ensuring a "good life," consisted of a cleared area with a few concrete administrative buildings. Their "new" home was located—deliberately—so far from the nearest market town as to ensure hardship of movement. American funds, amounting to approximately US$300,000, earmarked for the new site were withheld until the resettled families indicated that they would never leave the hamlet (Young, 1991: 82).

Over the next few months, throughout the southern delta region, once-sprawling villages dispersed along canals and natural waterways were reconcentrated toward a centralized site. Houses were bull-dozed and farmers were herded at gunpoint into supposedly more defensible areas. Corruption, moreover, was rampant. The relocated villagers, for example, were required to pay the South Vietnamese government for the building materials (which had been donated by the American government) that would be used for the construction of new houses. Villagers were even required to pay for the barbed wire that encircled their new hamlet (Young, 1991: 83).

Under the Strategic Hamlet Program, the United States invested substantial resources for the "development" and "protection" of rural Vietnam. By 1965–1966 further attempts were made to coordinate the Strategic Hamlet Program. In 1966, for example, the Office of Civil Operations (OCO), under the direction of Deputy Ambassador William Porter, was established. In May 1967 the Civil Operations, Revolutionary Development Support (CORDS) program, led by Robert Komer, was inaugurated. CORDS was a wide-reaching program designed to monitor, administer, and control the Vietnamese population. Administratively and geographically, CORDS was a matrix organization; the integration and initiation of CORDS programs took place simultaneously in the four military regions, 44 provinces, and 234 districts of South Vietnam (McCollum, 1983: 113). Through this approach, Komer believed, it would be possible to most effectively coordinate ongoing and planned pacification practices. For Komer, progress in pacification had to be measured, otherwise there would be no way of knowing if it was effective (McCollum, p. 114).

Once the Vietnamese civilians were confined to their isolated concentration camps (that is, strategic hamlets), American officials believed that they were in a better position to observe, manage, evaluate, and regulate the South Vietnamese population. Within these quasi-prison camps, the Vietnamese people became objects—units of analysis—utilized to measure America's progress in the war. Beginning in 1964 a basic system for monitoring hamlets was developed jointly by American and South Vietnamese officials. In 1966, however, McNamara wanted a new system to better measure the progress of pacification. Through an arrangement with American authorities in Saigon, the OSA became the official repository in Washington for a highly detailed computerized data system, known as the Hamlet Evaluation System, or HES (Enthoven and Smith, 1971: 302). Developed by Komer, the HES was touted as a "sophisticated measurement of the political control asserted by both the South Vietnamese government and the Revolutionary forces" (Appy, 1993: 158).

Under the HES, hamlets were classified and compared—not in geographic terms, but rather through a political ranking. In Vietnam, soldiers routinely spoke of their difficulties in determining "friend" from "enemy." Consequently, U.S. advisors spent an enormous amount of time and resources seeking to quantify the political affiliations of the Vietnamese people. The HES was a statistical survey composed of 18 criteria—nine each on security matters and on matters of economic and political development. These criteria would supposedly be rated by U.S. advisors on a regular basis. Subsequently, these criteria would be used to classify hamlets into one of five categories (A through E) of governmental control. Those hamlets ranked A and B were considered "secure," meaning that the South Vietnamese government was thought to have political control over the people of those hamlets. Category C was "relatively secure," and categories D and E were "contested." Evaluation was hampered, however, by the fact that most of the American data gatherers spoke little or no Vietnamese, and the compiling of such monthly data on an average of 37 hamlets for each of them was only one of their many tasks; it was not uncommon for officers to fill out the forms without ever visiting the hamlets (Kolko, 1994: 241).

Within hamlets, individual bodies were likewise observed, classified, and controlled. Similar to the asylums, prisons, schools, and factories of which Foucault writes, strategic hamlets permitted a discipline through surveillance. These practices evolved from the advice of the noted counterinsurgency expert Robert Thompson and his experiences in Malaya. Beginning in 1962, for example, the National Police of the Republic of Vietnam initiated the Family Census Program. Strategically, a census is a basic source of intelligence in that it may reveal, for instance, who is related to whom. This is often considered an important piece of information in counterinsurgency warfare because insurgent recruiting at the village level is generally based initially on family ties. Consequently, in southern Vietnam, lists of names, coupled with photographs, were compiled and filed in police dossiers. Also included was each person's political affiliation, fingerprints, income, savings, and other information deemed relevant to the war effort. By 1965 there were 7,453 registered families (Valentine, 1990).

Just as pressure for high body counts led to gross inflation of the relevant statistics, so too did the hamlet evaluations prove farcical. Appy (1993: 159) explains that progress was defined by large numbers, hence the tendency among evaluators to inflate the numbers of "secure" areas. Consequently, populations deemed secure would include the millions of Vietnamese peasants who had been driven off their land, or people massed in the proliferating refugee camps and shantytowns. From a propaganda perspective, however, successive administrations consistently used the HES to publicly defend the efficacy of their war policies. Appy (p. 159) writes that the "statistics simply offered the illusion of progress and control. They were a surrogate for genuine understanding" in that any effort to manage the war, "to break it down into quantifiable units, seem[ed] to provide a sense of clarity and order about a war that was truly baffling and confusing." He concludes that rather "than admit their lack of real control or understanding, Americans looked for new measurements or 'improved' statistics. If the numbers did not fit, they could always be fudged. It was easier to change numbers than to change reality."

Many of these programs fell far short of expectations, doomed in part because of fundamental flaws inherent in America's dual strategy of "attrition" (that is, killing people) and "pacification" (that is, "winning hearts and minds" through confinement). Rostow and others never appeared to see the contradictions that the indiscriminate killing of people through cluster bombs and napalm was not conductive to pacification. Kolko (1994: 239) summarizes this tension: the American government "never explicitly chose between pacification in place and population displacement or between terror and material blandishments.... Ideologically incapable of defining a theory that condoned its consistent practice, it preferred justifying its enormous terror from the skies and its uprooting of a rural nation with liberal jargon"—in other words, "with the social science rhetoric of 'modernization.'" Furthermore, in theory, the Strategic Hamlet Program was intended to avoid massive relocations of peasants from their sacred ancestral lands. Such a move would no doubt serve to undermine the developing goal of winning the hearts and minds of the Vietnamese in the ideological contestation for the country. However, in the delta regions of South Vietnam, the establishment of hamlets could not be carried out without widespread displacement. The subsequent uprooting of thousands of villagers added to the already growing discontent of the people of South Vietnam. More disturbing, though, was the human cost. Land reforms were not implemented, and many peasants were left landless and jobless. And despite the American allocation of funds for the provision of health, education, and welfare services, South Vietnamese inefficiency and corruption kept most of the resources from reaching their intended destinations (Herring, 1996: 99).

EMBODIED INSTRUMENTS OF WARFARE

Discipline, in the words of Foucault (1979: 138), produces subjected and practiced bodies. More concretely, disciplinary techniques are used for specific purposes by specific institutions for specific objectives. In the context of producing docile, subjected bodies, Foucault discusses the emergence of "observatories," or locations where the techniques of disciplinary power are applied. Such observatories include military camps, prisons, schools, factories, hospitals, and the strategic hamlets designed by American officials in Vietnam. The exercise of discipline within these spaces thus presupposes a mechanism that coerces by means of observation. The entire system is designed to monitor, to track, and to chart those confined. Within the strategic hamlets, one's political affiliation was paramount.

For Foucault (1979; see also Philo, 2001), the enclosure of bodies and populations into confined areas transforms these spaces into "functional sites." According to Foucault (p. 143), "It [is] a question of distributing individuals in space in which one might isolate them and map them; but also of articulating this distribution on a production machinery that had its own requirements." Philo (2001: 483) explains that "this means that many of the spaces should be filled with work, with organised productive activity." Within the space of strategic hamlets, a principle type of "work" was that of winning a war: bodies were to be productive in the sense of facilitating America's military mission in Vietnam. Consequently, the confinement of bodies into strategic hamlets entailed not only a political function—to (re)produce Vietnamese peasants into loyal and obedient subjects—but also a military function: subjugated bodies became embodied instruments of warfare.

Confined to strategic hamlets, the people of South Vietnam were subject to routinized evaluation and monitoring. These entrapped bodies, however, also became instruments of America's war effort. People were recruited—or coerced—to spy, inform, and sometimes murder other Vietnamese. They became instruments to pacify a people—their own people—who were waging an anticolonial war. This practice is most evident in one of the war's most controversial programs, the Phoenix Program.

In operation between 1968 and 1972, the Phoenix Program was designed to complement the ongoing pacification campaign. One element of the program was to acquire relevant information on enemy activities, including the identification of NLF cadres. A second aspect was to gain the support and cooperation of the South Vietnamese people and to reduce military and political activities deemed detrimental to the war effort. A final component was to eliminate suspected NLF infiltrators and insurgents. Facilitated through the confinement of Vietnamese peasants, U.S. military advisors and CIA agents created a network of spies and informants. The intended target of the operation was a construct labeled "VCI," or Viet Cong infrastructure. The VCI was reportedly a "shadow government" that coordinated and directed NLF activities and provided food, intelligence, and recruits for the insurgency. The Phoenix Program sought to target and "neutralize" members of the VCI. Once suspected VCI members were identified, they were captured, interrogated, and/or executed.

Approved in June 1967 and made operational in 1968, the Phoenix Program was part of a joint civilian–military structure. Six regional offices were established and a CIA liaison office was opened in each of South Vietnam's 44 provinces. Operationally, progress of the overall program was assessed quantitatively, with a monthly quota of "VCI" assigned to the 247 district offices working under the program (Kolko, 1994: 388). A number of related demographic programs were also continued and/or expanded during the Phoenix Program, including the Hamlet Information Program (HIP).

The Phoenix Program was managed by Robert Komer and William Colby. Komer, as discussed earlier, was chief of the CORDS program. Prior to his involvement in Vietnam he worked for the CIA (1947–1960) as a Middle East expert. In 1960 he was appointed to the National Security Council and in 1965 served as deputy special assistant and, later, special assistant, to President Johnson. Colby was a former member of both the OSS and the CIA. In Vietnam, he was involved in the Strategic Hamlet Program, CORDS, and Air America. He also served as head of the CIA's Far East Division. Working under Komer and Colby were approximately 450 U.S. foreign service and army officers. Crucial to the workings of the program were the estimated 40,000 provincial reconnaissance unit (PRU) teams. Working in groups of 35–40, these were teams of Vietnamese "friendlies" who had been trained, funded, and directed by the CIA. PRU teams would collect information through any possible means, including bribery and torture, and placed suspects into one of three categories. People who were designated "A" were considered to be communist members and other enemy leaders; "B" people were cadres with considerable responsibilities; and "C" people were merely rank-and-file members. In general, those persons labeled "C" were ignored unless they took up arms. Colby believed that killing "C"-level foot soldiers contributed little if anything to the overall war effort. More important was the targeting and "neutralizing" of higher level members of the VCI (Langguth, 2000: 537).

Throughout the 4-year existence of the program, American officials claimed to have arrested 86,000 people (Kolko, 1994: 388). Government testimony before the U.S. Senate confirmed as many as 3,000 assassinations. Outside sources indicate, however, that the program was responsible for perhaps 20,000 assassinations.

Debates regarding the legality—and morality—of the Phoenix Program continue. For many critics, Phoenix was a corrupt, abusive, and brutal program. For example, subsequent studies revealed that the misidentification of South Vietnamese people was widespread. Such "mistakes" may have been deliberate, as when villagers settled old grudges by "leaking" names to the PRU operatives. Colby, in fact, attempted to respond to this acknowledged problem through tighter management. He established a rule that all suspects' files had to include three separate identifications before they could be listed as "enemies" (Langguth, 2000: 537). Others, including Colby, continue to maintain that the practice was justified. Indeed, after the war Colby explained that "they were *Communists*, those people. Just no damn good" (quoted in Langguth, 2000: 538).

CONCLUSIONS

> ... Politicians, policymakers, and supporters and opponents of the Vietnam War are still arguing about who was right or wrong, who won or lost the war in Vietnam ... [but] the only ones who truly lost out are the Vietnamese people.
> —Le Ly Hayslip and Dien Pham (2006: 155)

Colin Flint (2005: 4–5) concludes that "geography and war are the products of human activity; war creates geographies of borders, states, empires, and so on, and in turn these geographic entities are the terrain over which peace is maintained or new wars are justified." Wars, however, are also about people; more specifically, wars are about the regulation of populations through the control and elimination of bodies. Consequently, in this chapter I have attempted to raise the problem of war from the standpoint of an embodied population geography.

Population geography may facilitate a study of warfare through a focus on spatial strategies and techniques that are employed to control, regulate, and ultimately eliminate bodies and populations. Through a focus on space, power, and knowledge, population geography may also highlight the discursive practices used to legitimate and justify particular practices that result in the destruction of people and the environment. Attention to the demographics of warfare, furthermore, may provide insight into the horrors and ugliness that are often (and deliberately) hidden from view in public discussions of "just" wars. We see in Vietnam a panoply of spatial strategies—aerial bombardment and cluster bombs, chemical defoliants and ecowarfare, confinement and enclosure—that were used to subjugate the Vietnamese population. We see also the downward spiral of policy pronouncements, the increased willingness to subject "other" bodies to more and more violence. We see, in Clodfelter's (1988) words, the "insane logic" that condoned the repeated attempts to annihilate people, their livelihoods, and their homes.

For men such as Kennedy and Rostow, McNamara and Nixon, Westmoreland and Komer, the annihilation of people through "attrition," or the regulation of people through environmental destruction, were seen as "just" practices in the face of communist aggression. Here, and elsewhere (Tyner, 2007), I argue that America's involvement was not just, that there was not acceptable justification for the direct and structural violence that was meted on the people and environment of Vietnam. For others, however, this remains a debatable issue. But this is exactly my point. It is imperative for a retheorized population geography to engage directly with question of "justness" within the context of war. If Foucault (2003: 257) is correct, if war indeed is "not simply a matter of destroying a political adversary, but of destroying the enemy race," it is incumbent upon population scholars—as teachers, as researchers, as citizens—to challenge those governmental claims that seek to legitimate and justify the "death function" that constitutes biopower.

3

DEATH AND THE ERASURE OF SPACE

On April 17, 1975, Youkimny Chan was a 14-year-old boy living in Phnom Penh.[1] Growing up, he remembered the beaches of the Mekong River as wide and sandy, the river as sparkling blue. Nearby, fruit trees provided mangos, coconuts, and bananas for snacking. The air always seemed to smell of hibiscus and roses.

On that spring day, however, tanks rolled through the streets of Phnom Penh. Khmer Rouge soldiers with guns and loudspeakers ordered the residents to leave their houses and to evacuate the city. The soldiers told Youkimny and his family that they would only be gone for 3 days, and that the city was in danger of being bombed by American planes. Youkimny's family had no reason to disbelieve the truth-claims of their fellow Khmer—American planes had indeed been bombing Cambodia for over 5 years. In one 15-month span, under President Richard Nixon's illegal campaign designated Operation Menu, the U.S. Air Force flew over 3,600 B-52 raids over Cambodian territory, dropping more than 100,000 tons of bombs. So, when the Khmer Rouge warned of an imminent American attack on the city, Youkimny's family packed what belongings they could and began walking. The streets, hot and dusty, were filled with thousands upon thousands of people. All houses and hospitals were emptied; no one was permitted to remain.

Throughout the congested and chaotic streets, Khmer Rouge soldiers, many of whom were children themselves, searched the refugees for identification—or valuables. Those "noncombatants" who refused, or those who were identified as belonging to the former government, were shot without question. Pregnant women gave birth on the streets; elderly persons died from exhaustion. Bodies were left where they fell or were thrown into ponds. Youkimny saw a group of soldiers questioning two men with their hands tied behind their backs. The captives' heads were then cut off.

Youkimny and his family continued walking for 2½ months until they arrived in the province of Battambang. The villages there had been burned down and the refugees were told to rebuild them. They were then forced to farm rice.

There was no medicine and hardly any food. Youkimny watched as his 10-year-old nephew died of diarrhea. Then his 7-year-old nephew died. The children's mother, Youkimny's sister, went crazy with grief and died. Later, his grandfather—who had worked for the previous government—was taken away, his hands tied behind his back. Youkimny heard a gunshot deep in the jungle and knew that his grandfather was dead. Three months later, Youkimny's brother and brother-in-law were taken away. This time, young Youkimny secretly followed. He watched as his brothers were forced to dig a large hole while the soldiers held guns to their heads. He watched as the soldiers took large bamboo shoots and beat his brothers until they were dead. He watched as their bodies were kicked into the hole.

Over the next few months, Youkimny watched as another of his aunts died, then his grandmother, then his older sister. Next his mother died and his youngest brother. Last was his sister, Sinuoen. She, like many of Youkimny's other relatives, died of starvation. Youkimny remembers her last words: "Kimny, I don't know if I can live any longer. Can I have a spoon of rice?" To such a small request from a sickly girl, Youkimny had to respond, "I have no rice to give you. Drink this water." His sister sipped the water, then she died.

For 3 years, 8 months, and 20 days, as Cambodia—then known as Democratic Kampuchea—cannibalized itself, Youkimny and millions of other people suffered the horrors of exhaustion, starvation, and random executions. During the 1,364 days of Khmer Rouge rule, approximately 1,500 people died per day. Dunlop (2005: 190) argues that, by percentage of population, the Cambodian holocaust remains the worst to have occurred anywhere in the world, eclipsing the percentage of people killed in Nazi-occupied Europe and the Rwandan genocide put together. He forwards the idea that the Khmer Rouge remain the most effective mass murderers in modern history.

The leaders of Democratic Kampuchea—Pol Pot, Khieu Samphan, Ieng Sary, and other high-ranking officials of the Communist Party of Kampuchea—attempted to *make* their country into a modern, communal utopia. When the Khmer Rouge seized power, they did so with the intention of obliterating its hierarchical political culture in order to reconstruct Cambodian society as the world's most egalitarian, and therefore most revolutionary, social order (Jackson, 1989: 7). Moreover, as Carney (1989: 15) explains, "What the leaders did with their people after victory demands attention, all the more because the treatment of the population after April 1975 had a firm base in wartime population control policy." It is this disciplining of bodies and control of populations that draws me to the injustices and violence of Cambodia.

Population geographers have of course considered various facets of social engineering. Population geographers likewise have engaged, albeit minimally, with the geographies of death that surround mass violence and genocide. But here, set against the rice paddies of Cambodia, we witness Michel Foucault's biopolitics at a most horrific extreme. And, in the process, we might gain a greater understanding of how population policies and a government's assumed right over life and death are used to forward a particular geographical imagination.

SOWING THE KILLING FIELDS

"It is an extraordinary situation," Craig Etcheson (2005: 2–3) writes. Cambodia endured years of mass violence that are, in some respects, unparalleled. As much as one-third of the country's population died in just under 4 years. And yet many Cambodians do not believe it happened. And many Westerners, particularly those in the United States, remain woefully ignorant as to the horrors that were unleashed on the people of Cambodia. Etcheson (p. 3) asks, "How can it be that so much destruction occurred so recently, yet so few are aware of this history?"

The answer, on the one hand, is painfully simple. Cambodia is not perceived as being important. While the French and the Americans were waging war against the Vietnamese, for example, Cambodia was (in William Shawcross's words) a "bothersome sideshow." And today, a culture of impunity continues to haunt any attempt to bring justice to Cambodia. No senior leader of the Khmer Rouge has ever stood trial in a court of law. Indeed, the surviving leadership of the Khmer Rouge—until 2008—continued to live unmolested, treated with respect by the government, and free to go about their business (Etcheson, 2005: 2). Nuon Chea—"Brother Number Two"—lived in Pailin, a small village near the Thai border, listening to music and tending his garden. Ieng Sary, the vice premier for foreign affairs under the Khmer Rouge, divided his time between a luxury villa in Phnom Penh and a home in Pailin.[2]

On the other hand, the answer is decidedly more complex. The mass violence that gripped Cambodia—and not only during the nightmarish years of the Khmer Rouge—has a much longer history and a wider geography. The death and violence that were reaped in the Killing Fields of Cambodia had to be sown.

The historical geography of Cambodia did not begin with French colonialism. And yet it is here that I begin my story because it was under the French that a curious truth-claim of the Khmer people was constructed, one that would continue to circulate in the years to come and would justify the eugenical practices of two separate governments.

Cambodia's existence, by the mid-19th century, as a sovereign kingdom was in jeopardy. The glory years of Cambodia's past—materially evident in the form of Angkor Thom and Ankor Wat—were dim recollections. Between the ninth and the 14th centuries, a series of monarchs reigned over the greatest kingdom in Southeast Asia: Angkor. But now Cambodia's more powerful neighbors—Siam to the west and Vietnam to the east—threatened to absorb all of the territories of the former kingdom. Faced with the possibility of Cambodia ceasing to exist, King Norodom (r. 1860–1904) entered into a deal with the devil. The Khmer king gave timber concessions and mineral exploitation rights to the French in exchange for military protection. Caught in a geopolitical vise, Norodom believed that only through a visible French colonial presence could his country be saved. He was wrong.

Over the next decades French colonial authorities gradually assumed control of Cambodia and radically altered the social structure of the former kingdom. The French encouraged the inmigration of Vietnamese to staff Cambodia's civil service. Vietnamese workers were also widely employed throughout the rubber plantations that flourished in the eastern regions of Cambodia. To this were added many Vietnamese farmers and fishermen. Chinese merchants, likewise, were responsible largely for running the urban economies.

France did little to modernize its protectorate. Aside from building a few roads, created mostly to service the large plantations, French colonial authorities neglected Cambodia. Educational facilities were minimal, industry was stunted, and the country for the most part remained an agrarian outpost of French Indochina.

During World War II Cambodia, similar to Vietnam, was occupied by Japanese forces while still ruled by Vichy France. During these years a youthful Norodom Sihanouk was installed as a puppet monarch. From the perspective of the French colonial authorities, Sihanouk was ideal. Just 18 years of age, Sihanouk was, in the minds of his colonial masters, a pliable and inexperienced teenager who could easily be manipulated. This time, the French were wrong. On March 9, 1945, while under Japanese control and supervision, Sihanouk hastily declared Cambodia's independence. By August, however, Japan was defeated and the French returned to Indochina.

Many Cambodians, having experienced a brief moment of independence, sought to resist the reimposition of French colonial control. One such individual was Son Ngoc Thanh, an anti-French nationalist who served as foreign minister and prime minister during the Japanese occupation. In 1945 Thanh attempted to seize power from Sihanouk and to declare independence from France. He was arrested, however, and exiled to France. Over the next few years Thanh continued to foment revolution, forming his own guerrilla group, the Khmer Serei ("Free Khmer"). He believed that only armed struggle against the French, coupled with the end of the monarchy, would liberate Cambodia. Not an ideologue, Thanh looked first to Vietnam and later to the United States for support.

Other movements, albeit in a limited manner, were also underway. In 1945, for example, the Vietnamese-dominated Indochinese Communist Party (ICP) was formally abandoned by Vietnam. Acutely aware of being perceived as dominating the movement, Vietnamese officials believed that a more geographically representative alliance would best serve the anticolonial revolution against France. Consequently, the Lao and Khmer communists would each have their own organizations.

Thus, on April 17, 1950, the first National Congress of Khmer Resistance was held. The intent was to form a communist front, led by a revolutionary who went by the assumed name of Son Ngoc Minh—a fusion of Son Ngoc Thanh and Ho Chi Minh. Although it was attended by over 200 delegates, only 40 were Cambodian. The following year, the Khmer People's Revolutionary Party (KPRP) was founded.

The KPRP, though, had minimal appeal to indigenous Khmers who viewed communism with suspicion as a means of furthering Vietnamese dominance. Indeed, the KPRP was in fact under Hanoi's control; the Vietnamese determined the course of action and even wrote the statutes of the KPRP. Espousing a pragmatic understanding of the revolution's political geography, Vietnamese communists maintained that the revolutionary movements in neighboring Laos and Cambodia must be subordinate to the larger conflict in Vietnam.

The French, for their part too, were mostly concerned with events in Vietnam. Cambodia was, from the French perspective, a diversion, a "bothersome sideshow." By 1949 France had agreed to grant partial independence to Cambodia in a political move designed to reduce anticolonial sentiment. Within this context, however, Sihanouk saw an opportunity to reposition himself in anticipation of an independent Cambodia. Ever the pragmatist, Sihanouk angled for complete sovereignty. In 1953, he launched a "Royal Crusade" for independence. The prince declared martial law, abolished the national assembly, and then embarked on a well-publicized world tour to convince the French to transfer their powers to him to prevent a communist takeover. He argued that he alone could establish a neutral and independent Cambodia. Furthermore, he promised to forbid the communists use of Cambodian territory in their fight against the French. Sihanouk then returned to Cambodia and placed himself in a self-imposed "exile" in the northwestern province of Battambang. On November 9, 1953, Paris acquiesced to Sihanouk's request. In 1954, under the terms of the Geneva Convention, Cambodia was granted independence (as was Laos).

In 1954 few in Cambodia saw the need to continue any form of revolution. The French were departing and Cambodia was now recognized internationally as an independent state. The objectives of the revolution were apparently met. As a result, most members of the KPRP returned to village life. Not all revolutionaries, however, were content. For some, only half the battle was accomplished: the antimonarchical component was left unfinished. Meanwhile, Sihanouk worked to retain the status quo.

Sihanouk dominated Cambodian politics from 1954 to his downfall in 1970. In 1955 he abdicated, in favor of his father, in order to enter politics more directly. Sihanouk established his own political party, the Sangkum Reaster Niyum (People's Socialist Community). Throughout the 1950s and 1960s he attempted to maintain a nonaligned foreign policy. Given the past history of Cambodia, including its dominance by both Thailand and Vietnam, Sihanouk was less than eager to enter into any alliance that included these neighboring states. Consequently, Sihanouk was opposed to the idea of an American-based alliance that included both Thailand and the fledgling state of South Vietnam.

To neutralize anti-imperialist rhetoric, and to secure support from communist powers (North Vietnam and the PRC), Sihanouk—although not a communist—embarked on a leftist reorientation of the Cambodian economy. Geopolitically, Sihanouk assumed that the United States would ultimately lose in Vietnam and that China would become the dominant external influence in Southeast Asia. Sihanouk, though, was a pragmatist and a realist. Despite his overtures to China, he also continued to seek aid from the United States, so much so, in fact, that by the early 1960s aid from Washington constituted 30 percent of Cambodia's defense budget and 14 percent of its total budget. Between 1955 and 1963 economic and military aid from the United States totaled approximately US$400 million (Seekins, 1990: 32–34).

Domestically Sihanouk worked to secure his authority over Cambodia. Sensing the greatest threat from the small, but ever-present, communist movement, Sihanouk pursued a nondeclared—and largely covert—campaign against members of the Communist Party. Through assassination and intimidation, bribery and cajolery, Sihanouk moved both to coopt the appeal of the Left and to eradicate individual members of the Left (Kiernan, 1996).

By the late 1950s, as a result of government repression, the communist movement in Cambodia was largely nonexistent. Consequently, the communist leaders in Vietnam, in an effort to protect the embattled KRPR, decided to split the Khmer movement into two components. Such a move would potentially better enable the Vietnamese to dictate the activities of the Cambodians to facilitate their own struggles in Vietnam. Son Ngoc Minh, still identified as the highest ranking member of the KRPR, was encouraged to accompany approximately 1,000 Cambodian communists into exile in North Vietnam. There, they would receive training in military strategy and communist ideology. A second group of Khmer communists would remain in Cambodian. Those who remained would continue to participate in underground political work, including recruitment and training of new cadres.

Within Cambodia, the remaining Khmer communist movement was again divided, this time spatially. A former Khmer Issarak (i.e., a former resistance fighter) and founding member of the KPRP, Sieu Heng was placed in control of the Cambodian-based communist movement. Geographically, he oversaw control of political activities in the countryside. Tou Samouth, the third-ranking official behind Son Ngoc Minh and Sieu Heng, was made responsible for party affairs in the capital and the major provincial towns.

The geographic realignment of the communist movement in Cambodia set in place a drastic reconfiguration, one that would facilitate the emergence of a group of Paris-educated Cambodians that included a soft-spoken yet charismatic man known as Pol Pot. Born as Saloth Sar in March 1925, Pol Pot spent his formative years first in Kampong Thom and, later, in Phnom Penh. Pol Pot's family was far from being impoverished. His parents owned 50 acres of rice paddy and six buffalo. Furthermore, Pol Pot had royal connections. An older sister, for example, was a royal concubine and later was appointed head of the royal bedchamber with overall responsibility for all the palace women; a brother served as a palace officer (Chandler, 2000a; Short, 2004).

Pol Pot, as Kiernan (1996: 9–11) describes, never worked in a rice field or knew much about village life. Pol Pot spent a year in the royal monastery followed by six years in an elite Catholic school. At 14 he attended high school in Kompong Cham and later returned to Phnom Penh to study carpentry. In 1948 he received a scholarship to study radio electricity in Paris. In was in Paris that Saloth Sar adopted his nom de plume, Pol Pot, which means "the original Cambodian" (Kiernan, 1996). It was during his Paris years that Pol Pot became interested in Marxism and became involved in the Cambodian section of the French Communist Party. It was in Paris also that he met Khieu Ponnary, a woman 8 years his senior. She would become the first Khmer woman to earn a baccalaureate. She would also become Pol Pot's first wife.

Pol Pot befriended a number of other like-minded Cambodians in Paris, many of whom would remain his closest allies for the next four decades. One such man was Ieng Sary. Sary would ultimately emerge as the minister of foreign affairs of Democratic Kampuchea (DK). Sary would also marry Khieu Ponnary's sister, Khieu Thirith. Like her sister, Khieu Thirith was highly educated. In Cambodia she had graduated from the prestigious Lycee Sisowath and in Paris she majored in Shakespearean studies at the Sorbonne. In the process, she became the first Cambodian to achieve a degree in English literature. During the reign of the Khmer Rouge, Thirith would become a senior member in the administration, serving as minister of social affairs and head of DK's Red Cross Society. Other members of the Paris-educated elite included Khieu Samphan, Hou Youn, and Son Sen. Significantly, Khieu Samphan received a doctorate in economics from the University of Paris and would later become the Khmer Rouge head of state.

Upon their return to Cambodia, Pol Pot, Khieu Samphan, the Khieu sisters, and other Paris-educated Khmers worked to further the socialist revolution. From 1954 onward the Cambodian communists forwarded a three-pronged strategy. First, a legitimate political party, known as the Pracheachon, or People's Group, was established. Second, many Khmer Rouge, including Pol Pot, obtained influential occupations, such as teachers, writers, and journalists. Through these positions the Khmer Rouge were able to recruit new members and to disseminate party information. Third, and most broadly, members worked in secret to build the movement. Their objectives were to modernize Cambodia through the promotion of a socialist agenda. By necessity, they were both antimonarchical and anti-American.

A setback for the Khmer communists occurred in the late 1950s, however, one that would significantly impact future events. Sieu Heng defected to Sihanouk. He apparently saw no need to continue the revolution. With his defection, he provided the government with the names of Khmer communists living and working in the countryside. Sihanouk's principle military commander, Lon Nol, was sent to destroy these communist cells. By 1959 the Khmer Rouge had lost nearly 90 percent of its rural cadres. Some were murdered, some quit the movement out of fear of retribution, some simply disappeared (Becker, 1998: 81).

A geographic consequence of Sieu Heng's defection was that the rural stronghold of the Khmer communists collapsed. Only in the cities, and especially Phnom Penh, did the Khmer Rouge continue to function. And it was in the cities that Pol Pot and the other Paris-educated Khmer were in control.

In 1960 a series of secret meetings among the Khmer Rouge were held in railcars in Phnom Penh. Twenty-one members were present. It was decided to change the KRPR to the Workers Party of Kampuchea (WPK; in 1971 it was renamed again as the Communist Party of Kampuchea, or CPK). Son Ngoc Minh, still in Hanoi, was unaware of these events. In Phnom Penh, however, Tou Samouth, a long-time nationalist and communist, was elected as party secretary. Nuon Chea was pegged as second ranking, and Saloth Sar, the only member of the Paris Marxist Circle, was third. Nuon Chea, known as "Brother Number Two" was Pol Pot's right-hand man. Unlike Sary, Samphan, and Pol Pot, Nuon Chea did not attend university in Paris. Rather, he received his education in Thailand. It was through his Thai connections that he joined the Communist Party of Thailand (1950), later to join the ICP.

This period marked the beginning of the Paris-educated group's entry into the highest echelons of the Cambodian communist movement. This also marked the most palpable break from Vietnamese party dominance. As the WPK, party members articulated their own analysis of Cambodia's political and economic situation. They clarified the need for their own revolution, one that was not subordinate to the Vietnamese revolution. They also maintained that Cambodia under Sihanouk was neither independent nor free (Becker, 1998: 93). Only through a complete revolution could a modernized and sovereign Cambodia come into existence.

The timing of the Khmer communists was not happenstance. Between January and May of the previous year the Vietnamese Workers Party acquiesced to the demands of communists in the Republic of Vietnam to move from a political to an armed struggle against the United States–backed Ngo Dinh Diem regime. Within months the National Liberation Front (NLF) was established, thereby setting the context for a widening of the conflict. Indeed, leaders in Hanoi firmly believed that victory in Vietnam required an Indochina-wide strategy (Becker, 1998: 89).

As war in Vietnam edged closer to Cambodia, Sihanouk's policy of neutrality began to fail. Throughout the 1960s the prince continued to court favor both with the PRC and the DRV. He also appointed leftist officials to his cabinet—Khieu Samphan as secretary of state and Hou Youn as secretary of state for planning—and endorsed leading leftist intellectuals for his own Sangkum Party ticket. Concurrently, though, he also suppressed the Pracheachon and continued his violent repression of Khmer communists throughout the country. In a further attempt to distance his country from the influence of the United States, Sihanouk announced in November 1963 the termination of Washington's aid program to Cambodia. Hoping to neutralize the anti-imperialist rhetoric of his critics, and to secure support from the communists, Sihanouk embarked on a series of leftist economic reforms. Sihanouk, for example, nationalized private banks. Foreign trading companies were either closed or absorbed into a state-administered National Company for Export and Import. Foreign investment was restricted and prices were fixed in an effort to ward of competition from imported goods (Seekins, 1990: 20). As Chandler (2000a) suggests, Sihanouk most likely expected France and China to pick up where the Americans left off in terms of aid provision.

Politically, such moves were insufficient. Sihanouk failed to obtain any support from the growing leftist factions in Cambodia. Moreover, Sihanouk's decision to nationalize Cambodia's banks and its import–export trade angered the business elite, including the Sino-Khmer commercial elite and the pro-Western elite. Sihanouk's distancing of himself from the United States also frustrated Cambodia's military. Throughout the 1960s Cambodian politics had become increasingly militarized, typified by the ascension of Sihanouk's defense chief, General Lon Nol, to the post of prime minister.

By now the Vietnam conflict threatened to engulf Cambodia. As the United States intensified its military actions in Vietnam, both the military forces of North Vietnam and the NLF of South Vietnam used Cambodian territory as a sanctuary from the armed forces of the Republic of Vietnam and the United States. As Vietnamese communist forces sought refuge in the eastern highlands of Cambodia, American and South Vietnamese forces followed them.

The effects of the war were manifested in other, indirect aspects. The escalation of the war, for example, translated into increased troop levels, an occurrence that had deleterious effects on the Cambodian people and economy. Recruitment into the NLF in southern Vietnam, for example, quadrupled in one year, rising from 45,000 new recruits in

1964 to 160,000 in 1965. The offshoot was that large amounts of Cambodian-grown rice were smuggled into Vietnam to feed the growing armies. Economically, Cambodia depended on taxes from rice exports for its revenue. And whereas Cambodia enjoyed record rice harvests in the early 1960s, the rapid increase in rice smuggling plunged the country toward bankruptcy (Kiernan, 1996: 17).

In 1970 Sihanouk was ousted in a right-wing military coup. While traveling to France, Sihanouk had entrusted his government to Lon Nol and his pro-Western deputy prime minister, Prince Sisowath Sirik Matak. According to Chandler, Matak—Sihanouk's cousin—was the most prominent of the plotters. Matak was impatient with Sihanouk's mismanagement of the economy and was dismayed by the presence of Vietnamese bases on Cambodian soil (Chandler, 2000b: 208). While Sihanouk was away, Lon Nol and Matak launched attacks on Vietnamese communist positions, organized anti-Vietnamese demonstrations, and reestablished ties with various noncommunist groups, including the South Vietnam-based Khmer Serei. Sihanouk, hearing of these actions, condemned the moves of Lon Nol and Matak. In response, Matak pressured Lon Nol to lead a coup against Sihanouk.[3] On March 18, 1970, the National Assembly voted 89–3 to depose the ruler (Gottesman, 2003: 22).

The coup against Sihanouk plunged Cambodia into a disastrous civil war that lasted from 1970 to 1975. During these 5 years, as I discuss below, Cambodia experienced a genocidal campaign that singled out persons of Vietnamese ancestry for expulsion or eradication. This "other" killing field provided the context for the emergence of Democratic Kampuchea and the murderous reign of the Khmer Rouge.

THE OTHER KILLING FIELDS

Prasot was a small village near the Vietnamese border. On April 10, 1970, soldiers of Lon Nol's army forcibly removed the men, women, and children from the village and detained them in the yard of a farming cooperative. Approximately 100 civilians, all of Vietnamese heritage, were slaughtered at Prasot. Kamm (1988: 77) explains that when Western reporters came upon the scene of slaughter, the unapologetic government explained, in a blatant lie, that the victims had been caught in a crossfire during a Vietcong attack. In actuality, the Vietnamese were caught in a racially motivated pogrom initiated by the newly placed Lon Nol government. These deaths marked the beginning of "the other killing fields," a period of systematic and racialized mass violence that gripped Cambodia prior to the rise of Pol Pot and his own genocidal regime.

Prior to the massacre at Prasot, and indeed prior to the coup, anti-Vietnamese hysteria gripped Phnom Penh and its environs. Government radio broadcasts warned of the Vietnamese as being Cambodia's ancient enemies; newspaper headlines shouted: "Viet Cong, Sworn Enemies; Vietnamese, Hereditary Enemies of the Cambodians" (Kamm, 1988: 77). Leaflets were distributed, warning of Vietnamese communist infiltration and Vietnamese subversion.

Within weeks of the coup, detention camps and holding centers were established. Vietnamese residents—many of whom had lived in Cambodia for generations—were rounded up and detained as prisoners. Most of them were charged with being sympathizers with the Vietnamese communists who used Cambodia as sanctuary from the war in Vietnam. The Lon Nol government admitted to arresting some 30,000 Vietnamese (Becker, 1998: 125). The killings also continued. Two weeks after the attack on Prasot a Catholic Vietnamese settlement on the isthmus of Chrui Changwar was targeted. Government soldiers appeared at night and rounded up some 800 Vietnamese laborers. The captives' hands were tied behind their backs and they were shoved onto waiting boats. The soldiers then executed every Vietnamese captive and threw the bodies into the Bassac River (Becker, 1998: 125). Days later, former Southeast Asian correspondent for the *New York Times* Henry Kamm (1998) was present at the scene. He writes, "I took the ferry five days after the ghastly flow began and saw a group of five bodies tied together by their feet with rattan cord, as well as four bodies, their hands tied, floating singly toward Vietnam, about thirty miles downstream."

The massacre at Chrui Changwar was repeated in the town of Takeo, located south of the capital near the Vietnamese border. Here, approximately 150 Vietnamese men were rounded up and sequestered in a school. Each evening, the captives' wives and children brought food. One night, however, while the families were eating, soldiers fired point-blank into the mass of people. Estimates place the number of dead at 100. Trucks came to haul away the corpses (Kamm, 1998).

Elaborate pageants, parades, and festivals were held, ostensibly to promote Khmer nationalism. The day after the Prasot massacre, for example, the Lon Nol regime staged a patriotic mass rally in the Olympic Stadium in Phnom Penh. Kamm (1998: 78) describes the scene: For four hours, marching contingents from schools, ministries, and state enterprises paraded to a steady beat of martial music. Most carried clubs. Participants said that they wanted to beat the Vietnamese; that most of the Vietnamese living in Cambodia favored the Vietcong; and that the Vietnamese were enemies of Cambodia. Kamm (p. 78) relates that "in its strident chauvinism and xenophobia, the rally stirred in me unpleasant reminiscences from my childhood among the Nazis."

"There is a history of imaginary geographies," David Sibley (1995: 49) writes, "which cast minorities, 'imperfect' people, and a list of others who are seen to pose a threat to the dominant group in society as polluting bodies or folk devils who are then located 'elsewhere.'" This "elsewhere," Sibley contends, "might be nowhere" as when genocide occurs, or "it might be some spatial periphery, like the edge of the world." Consequently, such representations of marginal groups as defiling and threatening have been used to justify the perpetuation of unjust acts, including spatial exclusion (that is, deportation) and "ethnic cleansing."

In Cambodia, Khmer nationalists have traditionally portrayed the Vietnamese (and, to a lesser extent, the ethnic Chinese) as the quintessentially evil "Other" (Hinton, 2005: 215). Historically, though, as Alexander Hinton notes, part of this image was coopted from the French. Following Norodom's ill-fated agreement with, and concession to, France in 1862, the French effectively constructed Cambodia's people and their past. As Chandler (1997: 36) explains, the French were struck by the contrasts they perceived between the grandeur of the Angkorean ruins, on the one hand, and, on the other, the "decline" they saw in 19th-century Cambodia. He contends that the French invented Cambodia as a charming, powerless protectorate and subsequently took control of Cambodia's historical narrative.

This French-constructed knowledge, which Chandler (1997: 35) terms "Cambodge," "blended the grandeur of Cambodia's past, symbolized by the Angkor ruins, with an assessment of the Cambodian people as insouciant and needful of protection." Chandler (p. 37) explains:

France constructed a seductive, unserviceable heritage for their protégés, who were told that they were simultaneously needful of protection and the worthy descendants of the kings of Angkor. Inducing "memories" of mighty forebears in descendants thought incapable of governing themselves kept the population docile but occasionally brought on, especially among political leaders after independence, a severe case of *folie de grandeur*. These men assumed that with independence Cambodia had reverted to a pre-colonial level of grandeur, potential and accomplishment. Prince Norodom Sihanouk allowed himself to be compared to the Angkorean monarchs; his successor, Lon Nol saw himself as presiding over "the Cambodian race," and ... Pol Pot proudly declared that "If our people can build Angkor, they can do anything."

The French-constructed knowledge of Cambodia's historical geography would dominate the thinking of Sihanouk and Lon Nol; it would also overshadow the ideology of the Khmer Rouge (Chandler, 1997: 38). They were, in the words of Chandler (p. 38), "entranced by the 'otherness' of their own past, eager to compensate for colonially induced powerlessness, and entranced by what they perceived as Cambodia's incomparability."

Such geographic knowledge, however, was used in conjunction with a longer history of antipathy toward the Vietnamese. As Hinton (2005: 215) explains, French scholars provided the Khmer with an enduring ethnohistorical past, culminating in the Angkorean Empire. However, the long centuries of Khmer decline were fraught with dangers as the former kingdom was "threatened by evil others who schemed to 'swallow' Cambodian land and destroy the country and its people." Such a constructive narrative invariably positioned the Vietnamese as the evil Others. For Hinton (p. 215), such imagery constitutes an "ontologically resonant basis for Khmer nationalist political identity, providing a sense of self and community ('we' the pure Khmer) and a set of relational characteristics of belong (an essential moral purity contrasting with the various negative qualities of the evil 'other')."

There were ample stock representations of the Vietnamese from which the Lon Nol regime could draw. According to Hinton (2005: 215), numerous French historical reconstructions, Khmer royal chronicles, and local oral traditions all spoke of the "true" nature of the Vietnamese. Stories, passed down for generations, told of both the Thai and the

Vietnamese as aggressive, but the latter were especially singled out as being dangerous. Legends circulated as to the cruelty of the Vietnamese, of their evil nature. The Vietnamese, it was said, burned their victims and inflicted incredible suffering on their captives. The Vietnamese scorned their Cambodian neighbors and sought to destroy Cambodia and enslave its people. And all Vietnamese were viewed as composing a distinct and separate race: the race of the traditional enemy (Becker, 1998: 124).

Cambodia was in fact an ethnically and occupationally divided land. During the 1970s there were an estimated 400,000 persons of Vietnamese ancestry living in Cambodia. Many of these people had roots extending back many generations and, in general, most were anticommunist (Becker, 1998). There did exist, though, a certain animosity between the Khmer and the Vietnamese. There were cultural and linguistic differences, and there was a history of discrimination between the two groups. Vietnamese, as well as Sino-Khmer, tended to dominate the economic sphere of urban Cambodia. In the cities, the Vietnamese were employed as artisans, small traders, clerks, and domestic servants for Western residents. Poorer Cambodians were often unable to enter these occupations. In the countryside, the Vietnamese worked as fishermen along the rivers and the Tonle Sap (Gottesman, 2003: 19).

Throughout the late 19th and 20th centuries, divisions between the Khmer and ethnic Vietnamese became increasingly rigid. Unequal practices initiated by the French tended to favor the Vietnamese, who were viewed by the Western colonial authorities as more industrious and competent. The Khmer, it was claimed, were lazy and insolent. Later, during the regime of Sihanouk, these practices were reversed, favoring the Khmer. An extreme ethnonationalist government propaganda campaign, disseminated through speeches, the media, rallies, military indoctrination, and official publications, suggested that the Vietnamese—even those who had been living in Cambodia for decades and were strongly anticommunist—were a threat to the racial purity and survival of the Khmer (Hinton, 2005: 217). While still in power, for example, Sihanouk had issued a list of 18 occupations that were barred to the Vietnamese, although these were rarely enforced (Kamm, 1988: 76). It was not until the ascension of Lon Nol, however, that genocidal practices fully emerged.

Lon Nol took an exaggerated pride in calling himself a "true" and "pure" Khmer. He encouraged his soldiers to call him "Black Papa," in reference to his darker complexion that served as visually proof of his pure origins (Becker, 1998: 119). Throughout his career Lon Nol positioned himself as a champion of anticommunism. As he rose through the political ranks, and as he assumed a greater control of the Cambodian government, Lon Nol "seemed to relish the idea of confronting the North Vietnamese, whom he blamed for all the indignities Cambodia had suffered at the hands of Vietnam over the centuries" (Becker, 1998: 119).

An extreme nationalist, Lon Nol served tirelessly in both Cambodian political and military affairs. In 1946, as part of Cambodia's first national elections, Lon Nol founded his own political party, the Khmer Renovation Party; in 1955 he merged his party with Sihanouk's Sangkum Party. During the First Indochina War, at the request of Sihanouk, Lon Nol fought against the Issaraks and the rebel Vietminh. He was later appointed chief of staff of the newly independent Cambodian army in 1955. Becker (1998: 119) describes Lon Nol as "politically loyal, not militarily competent." He was "a man with peasant sensibilities and not much apparent talent, a man who had climbed to power through the military as Sihanouk's loyal hatchet man." He was also "a religious reactionary, a firm devotee of the occult and a practicing mystic who carried around the battered talismans given him in his youth by his village wiseman" (p. 120).

After the coup of 1970 Lon Nol was determined to realize his dream of purifying the Khmer race, culture, and religion of all the foreign pollutants that he believed had, in Becker's (1998: 120) terms, "sapped the country's energy and eaten away its identity and territory." Indeed, long fixated with purifying the Khmer race, culture, religion, and land, Lon Nol had published his manifesto, a narrative of Khmer history, in a slim volume entitled *Neo Khmer*. Drawing on French representations of Cambodia's past, he wrote:

> At the peak of its splendour, our country earned the surname of Chenla the Rich and the people lived an easy, comfortable life. This sweet life was forgotten by the menace of war, and the Khmer people, after having known a period of glory and peace, were invaded by the Siamese in the fourteenth century.... In the seventeenth and eighteenth centuries, a double attack by the Annamites [Vietnamese] and Siamese sowed disorder in the

country and our people, after having known glory and power, entered into a period of difficulty.... [T]hen all of Asia fell under the "domination of the white." (quoted in Becker, 1998: 127)

Lon Nol continued that the goal of the Vietnamese was to "systematically destroy our socioeconomic structure and our civilization: they want not simply to make our people subservient to them but to change our way of life, to modify our way of thinking and abolish our religious beliefs" (quoted in Becker, 1998: 127).

The pogroms against the Vietnamese under the Lon Nol regime must be viewed from the perspective of genocide. Vietnamese people, legally residing in Cambodia, were detained, arrested, tortured, and executed. Those not confined or killed were forced to flee; many went to neighboring Vietnam, where they would live for years in exile. And within Cambodia, a culture of impunity developed. Kamm (1988: 82) explains that "as the certainty of widespread atrocities grew, so [too] did the silence of the regime and the ostentatious indifference of private Cambodians." In part, this culture of impunity materialized because the messages were there for all to see. As Hinton (2005) explains, the killings were simultaneously a symbolic performance. The brutal practice of tossing the bodies into the Mekong River, Hinton (p. 217) explains, where the corpses would float toward Vietnam, illustrates the bodily inscription of violence. Through these acts, Khmer soldiers "transformed the bodies of the 'disordering' ethnic Vietnamese into an impurity (grotesque, waterlogged corpses) that was 'cleansed' (by being killed, plunged into water, and expunged from Cambodia) and 'reordered' (by being sent back to the 'true' place where they belonged, Vietnam)." The killings and tossing of the bodies into the river was thus a practice of spatial purification, a technique designed to cleanse the population geography of Cambodia. Such a graphic and embodied message would be repeated 28 years later in Rwanda.

Discursively and materially, the Lon Nol regime unleashed a genocidal campaign against those people considered to be impure Khmers. And at this level, there is not much to distinguish between the rightist, pro-Western Lon Nol regime and the Marxist–Leninist Khmer Rouge; both embarked on genocidal xenophobic campaigns against perceived ethnic Others. Both sought to achieve their own geographical imaginations of a pure society.

The people of Cambodia would pass from one nightmare to another.

THE BIRTH OF DEMOCRATIC KAMPUCHEA

On April 17, 1975, columns of Khmer Rouge soldiers marched into Phnom Penh. Their arrival marked the beginning of a 4-year period of unimaginable horrors, a genocidal regime that lasted until 1979. With the formation of Democratic Kampuchea (DK), the state of Cambodia disappeared from the map. The year 1975 was to be "Year Zero" and it would usher in a new phase of Cambodian history.[4] Pol Pot's Communist Party of Kampuchea (CPK) used the devastation wrought by American military actions as recruitment propaganda and as an excuse for its brutal radical policies and its purges of moderate communists and supporters of Sihanouk (Kiernan, 1996: 19).

The CPK sought to transform Cambodia into a modern, communal utopia. In doing so, Pol Pot and his cadres attempted to replace what they saw as impediments to national autonomy and social justice with revolutionary energy and incentives (Chandler, 2000b: 209). As Ian Brown (2000: 25) writes, Pol Pot and his comrades had been planning their "extreme version of a socialist revolution since their student days in France in the 1950s and, thereafter, during years of isolation in the jungles of eastern Cambodia. Their ideology was a radical blend of Maoism, with its emphasis on collectivization and national self-sufficiency, and rabid chauvinism, directed principally against Vietnam."

In their attempt to create—not *re*-create—a utopian society, the leadership of the Khmer Rouge embarked on a massive program of social and spatial engineering (Tyner, 2008). The ideological origins of such a transformation did not materialize overnight. Both in theory and in practice, party leaders drew on the radical extremities of Mao Zedong's 1956–1958 "Great Leap Forward" in an attempt to bring about a complete and rapid transformation of the Cambodian economy. Agricultural production was to take priority through the intensified production of rice. Eventually, after having achieved economic self-sufficiency, hard currency earned from rice exports would be used to finance industrialization.

The impetus for the revolutionary practices of the Khmer Rouge is also found in the writings and, indeed, doctoral dissertations of many of the top-ranking Khmer Rouge leadership. Khieu Samphan's economic dissertation, for example, provides a thorough (albeit slightly erroneous) exposition of Cambodia's political economy. Entitled *Cambodia's Economy and Industrial Development*, Khieu Samphan's dissertation—although not a template—would prove highly influential in subsequent policies of Democratic Kampuchea. In this document Khieu Samphan forwarded a series of interrelated theses. He stated that Cambodia's economy was backward, locked in a feudal and precapitalist mode of production. This condition, he maintained, resulted from Cambodia's unequal and dependent integration into the French colonial economy and the continuance of unfair trade relations. Liberation for Cambodia's economy could only occur through autonomous development, namely, a withdrawal from the international market. Lastly, it was imperative for Cambodia to confront the existent structural inequity between what he perceived to be a productive countryside and an unproductive city.

The Khmer Rouge leadership believed that most, if not all, of Cambodia's problems were derived from its subordinate position in an international economic system that was dominated by, among others, the United States, China, and France. Consequently, having violently wrested control of the country, the leaders of Democratic Kampuchea sought to achieve both total independence and self-reliance for their fledgling government. However, the basis of their revolution was to bring about an immediate and total economic transformation, one that required a new set of Khmer social values (Jackson, 1989: 39). Spatially, as Kevin McIntrye (1996: 730) explains, the evacuation of the cities and towns in the newly formed Democratic Kampuchea was "intrinsic to the Khmer Rouge's strategy of transforming Cambodia society."

The transformations of Cambodia envisioned by the Khmer Rouge were to be total, permanent, and pervasive. For the revolution to succeed, from the standpoint of the Khmer Rouge, the entire population of Cambodia was to be affected. Lefebvre (1991: 412) writes that "each society to which history gave rise within a framework of a particular mode of production, and which bore the stamp of that mode of production's inherent characteristics, shaped its own space." In 1975 Cambodia, as such, the landscape would have revealed vestiges of an "indigenous" and "precapitalist" Khmer society, a French colonial-mercantilist presence, and a newly applied veneer of American capitalism. The Khmer Rouge, however, were not content with retaining, and building on, the past inscriptions of previous modes of production and spatial practices. Rather, the Khmer Rouge explicitly attempted to "unwrite"—to erase—both history and geography to create (in their geographical imaginations) a pure utopian communal society. The Khmer Rouge sought not to turn back the pages of time to an earlier era, but instead to rush forward at a dizzying pace regardless of the consequences (Jackson, 1989: 59). The people of Cambodia would pay with their lives for the Khmer Rouge's misguided idea of social justice.

THE PLACE-DEATH OF CAMBODIAN CITIES

> From noon onwards, the masses in the streets multiplied as Communist troops uprooted more and more families.... There was a huge crowd of every age and condition, young, old and sick ... virtually everybody saw corpses rapidly bloating and rotting in the sun. Then the water supply ceased throughout the city.... No stores of drinking water, no stocks of food, no shelter had been prepared for the millions of outcasts. Consequently acute dysentery racked and sapped life from bodies ... already weakened by hunger and fatigue.... We must have passed the body of a child every 200 yards.[5]

The Khmer Rouge's evacuation of urban areas following their victory on April 17, 1975, constitutes one of the world's worst crimes against humanity. Countless people were forcibly uprooted and forced into the countryside; many died from exhaustion, lack of medical care, or murder. And for many scholars, the actions of the Khmer Rouge constitutes "the single most inexplicable event of the Cambodian revolution" (Jackson, 1989: 46).

An understanding of the Khmer Rouge's place-annihilation of Phnom Penh, however, provides crucial insights into the disciplining of bodies and the regulation of populations through a control of space. Attempts to understand this unjust and violent practice underscore the necessity of developing a reinvigorated population geography. As the story of Youkimny Chan vividly illustrates, having defeated the military forces of Lon Nol, the Khmer Rouge set upon the herculean task of depopulating Phnom Penh and other major cities throughout Cambodia. The capital city, in particular, had swollen in size as hundreds of thousands of refugees fled the countryside in the face of intensive American bombings campaigns and civil war. Indeed, the evacuation was encouraged by the Khmer Rouge, who forwarded the very plausible explanation that American planes were about to bomb the city.

In reality, the explanations for the evacuations are more complex and reflect a long-standing agenda of the Khmer Rouge leadership. As the scholarship of Karl Jackson, François Ponchaud, and Kevin McIntyre reveals, the Khmer Rouge targeted urban areas for a variety of reasons. First, there was the practical issue that the Khmer Rouge were in no position to feed and shelter the massive refugee population in Phnom Penh (not that they necessarily wanted to). More salient were security concerns, namely, the need to preserve the fledgling revolution. As Jackson (1989: 47) notes, for the Khmer Rouge cities were centers of foreign domination; cities were dominated, economically at least, by large Vietnamese-Khmer and Sino-Khmer bureaucratic and commercial populations. Moreover, cities were dominated by the institutions that had opposed the revolution, including the monarchy, the army, the foreign embassies, and the bourgeoisie. A forcible evacuation was deemed the most efficient means to disorganize any potential opposition. In this way, an amorphous heterogeneous population could be reorganized—following purges of the most counterrevolutionary elements—into more readily controlled and productive units. Likewise, the depopulation of urban areas would provide a surplus of productive labor and thereby facilitate the active construction of the Khmer Rouge's utopian dreams.

There is another aspect of the Khmer Rouge's depopulation policy, however, that needs to be explained. The Khmer Rouge envisioned their revolution to be immediate, total, and instantaneous. Pol Pot, Khieu Samphan, Ieng Sary, and other top-ranking leaders were not content to let the revolution take its course. Eschewing advice from Chinese officials, the Khmer Rouge forwarded their own "Great Leap Forward." In so doing, the Khmer Rouge deemed it necessary to completely erase, to wipe clean, to strip away any barriers to their revolution. The transformation of Cambodia was, from the perspective of the Khmer Rouge leadership, designed to literally crush all preexisting histories, geographies, and societies. Before a utopian communist society could be constructed, all the spaces of Cambodia required an unmaking.

Documentary evidence indicates that the decision to evacuate Phnom Penh and other major cities and towns occurred as early as February 1975. Indeed, the work of Jackson and McIntyre, in particular, argues that such a decision conformed readily with the political–economic practices advanced by Khieu Samphan in his 1959 doctoral dissertation. Specifically, the destruction of cities would, in a single stroke, deal an immediate blow to Cambodian involvement in the international economy that Khieu Samphan had identified as the single most obstructive barrier to an independent and self-reliant Democratic Kampuchea.

Accordingly, the forced evacuations of April 1975 were not without a skewed logic. As the Khmer Rouge increased their control in the early 1970s, they embarked upon smaller scaled depopulation operations. Beginning as early as 1971, Khmer Rouge forces began to systematically burn rural villages and hamlets under their control to force peasants into new communal agricultural systems (Quinn, 1989: 181). "Liberated" zones were reorganized into cooperatives and collectives, while the urban areas were razed and emptied of their people. In September 1973, for example, CPK troops seized half of Kompong Cham city and "took fifteen thousand townspeople into the countryside with them" (Kiernan, 1985: 371). In March 1974 a combined force of CPK northern and southwestern zone troops, led by Pauk and Ta Mok, overran the former capital of Oudong, north of Phnom Penh. Having captured the city, the Khmer Rouge led the populace of 20,000 persons into the countryside, killed all schoolteachers and government officials, and deliberately razed the town (Kiernan, 1985: 384).

Such physical destruction was intended to provide a blank slate, an opportunity to radically restructure Khmer society and to mark a definite and ostensibly permanent break with the past (Ponchaud, 1989: 161). As Haing Ngor (1987: 247) explains, "When [the Khmer Rouge] talked about sacrificing everything for Angka [the Organization, or the Party], they meant it. Whatever got in the way of Angka's projects had to be eliminated, including people." The depopulation of urban areas was therefore essential to the Khmer Rouge's strategy of "revolution by eradication" (Jackson, 1989: 56). As such, it illustrates well the thoroughly modernist foundations of the Khmer Rouge leadership. Democratic Kampuchea was not, contrary to the claims of some accounts, an attempt to return to a golden era of Cambodian history. A return to the past might have motivated the genocidal Lon Nol; the same cannot be said of the Khmer Rouge. Instead, the motivations of Pol Pot, Ieng Sary, Nuon Chea, and Khieu Samphan was not to *re-create* the glories of Angkor Wat, but instead to make an entirely new, modern, productive communal society. The destruction—and subsequent *construction*—of urban areas bears this out.

Cities, for the Khmer Rouge, encapsulated all that hindered a successful communist revolution. Drawing more from Mao than from Lenin, the Khmer Rouge leadership believed that modern capitalist industry was neither historically necessary nor socialism's prerequisite; industrial proletarians were not necessarily the progressive force for a socialist future (McIntyre, 1996: 737). Consequently, the Khmer Rouge championed the idea of a peasant-based struggle. Urban areas were no longer the modern, revolutionary influence that Marx had imagined but sites of foreign domination. Cities were equated with alien influences, and the countryside with the true nation (p. 737).

In his doctoral work, Khieu Samphan described cities as unproductive sites, populated by individuals who contributed nothing to society but who, in return, capitalized on the exploitation and oppression of the rural-based peasants. According to Khieu Samphan and those who agreed with his interpretations, only agriculture, crafts, and small industry were productive. Tertiary activities, including commerce and banking, were considered unproductive. Moreover, Khieu Samphan deplored those activities that serviced the bourgeois, including boutiques, household servants, pedicab drivers, diplomats, foreign business personnel, and venders. He singled out those who worked in cafes, bars, restaurants, and hotels for special criticism. In his dissertation, written 17 years prior to the Khmer Rouge victory, Khieu Samphan had claimed that approximately 94 percent of workers in Phnom Penh and 96 percent of workers in Kompong Cham city were engaged in unproductive activities (McIntyre, 1996: 74).

Hinton (2005: 50) suggests that "their conviction that they had discovered the key to ending oppression and revitalizing Cambodian society seems to have given Pol Pot and his associates a sense of omnipotence and grandeur." He continues: "Like Buddhists who had achieved enlightenment, they had attained secret knowledge that would transform Cambodia and enable its inhabitants to reach a higher state of being." By literally tearing the great bulk of the country's population from its roots and familiar patterns of work and life, the Khmer Rouge leadership intended irrevocably and irretrievably to move toward a new egalitarian agricultural society (Quinn, 1989: 181).

WE ARE FAMILY, YOU ARE NOT

For the peasantry of Cambodia, it was not known until 1977—and even thereafter it was a hazy knowledge—who was in charge of the country. Many peasants, for example, believed that Sihanouk actually had returned to power—a myth that the Khmer Rouge were all too ready to exploit. All that was known was that *Angkar* had become the most central person/institution in their lives. Angkar was actually the name of the Central Committee of the CPK, but few peasants knew that essential fact.

Angkar was credited with nearly mystic omnipotency; its word was law and any attempt to break it was always discovered (Becker, 1998: 141). For years, during the genocide, who or what Angkar was remained a mystery. The term provided clues, but these were slippery and fleeting. *Angkar*, for example, is frequently translated as "organization." Linguistically, however, *Angkar* is derived from the Pali word *anga*, meaning a part of the body, as well as from the Khmer word *angk*, denoting a structure or a limb of a body. The term is also used in reference to "mana-filled" objects or orderly institutions. All of these meanings come into play when discussing the centralized authority of the Khmer Rouge.

Angkar was idealized through the use of kinship idioms and was often referred to as *puk-mae*, the "dad-mom" of its children (Hinton, 2005: 130). Consequently, as the dad-mom of the people, Angkar was conceived as having "true" knowledge and authority. Idealized in songs and poems, Angkar was the great benefactor; it cared for and protected its children (Hinton, 2005: 130; see also Ponchaud, 1989: 165).

Throughout their reign the Khmer Rouge adopted a Maoist saying, one that encouraged systematic violence directed against entire families. It stated: "To dig up grass, one must also dig up the roots" (Hinton, 2005: 91). The phrase is chilling in its simplicity. Much as a peasant farmer might tend his fields, it is necessary to remove unwanted weeds as well as those structures that provide nourishment to the odious plants. The goal, as Quinn (1989: 181) identifies, was to fundamentally and drastically change the nature of Khmer society, beginning with the family.

"Familyism" represented a threat to both Angkar and Democratic Kampuchea because the traditionally close bonds between family members constituted an alternative source of loyalty. Under the Khmer Rouge, the people of Democratic Kampuchea were to have a single loyalty, an all-encompassing attachment only to Angkar. As such, the Khmer Rouge used various spatial practices to sever the social bonds between family members and therefore to erase space. Combined, these practices served to instill loyalty, to promote a bastardized vision of egalitarianism, and to facilitate economic and political policies.

Village life was adversely affected long before the Khmer Rouge came to power by the escalation of the war in Vietnam, the bombing of the Cambodian countryside, a crumbling economy, widespread corruption, and civil war. As Ebihara (1990: 22) writes, "the fabric of customary peasant life was already being seriously torn" prior to 1975. However, whereas the devastating effects of civil war were, in some respects, an unintentional consequence of larger military decisions, the dissolution of village life and traditional familial arrangements under the Khmer Rouge was deliberate. The leaders of Democratic Kampuchea sought to create a new social order; as such, their policies were aimed at radically reformulating Khmer society and culture into a new revolutionary order (p. 22).

Upon achieving victory in April 1975 the Khmer Rouge began the brutal process of evacuating cities and villages. This policy of forced deportation and relocation, to be sure, was enacted to bring about a centralization of control for the Khmer Rouge, as well as to provide the labor for the Khmer Rouge's economic programs. However, these forced movements and geographic redistributions of Cambodia's population also spelled the loss of support systems fundamental to the functioning and survival of the family unit (Mam, 2004: 130). More specifically, the Khmer Rouge practice of evacuation and collectivization was one of population geography: a discipline of bodies through a control of space. The population policies of the Khmer Rouge struck at the heart of traditional Khmer familial arrangements.

Administratively, the Khmer Rouge initiated widespread changes that would impact the lives of individual Cambodians and their families. The old system of provinces was replaced by new territorial zones, each designated by a compass direction (for example, Northwest Zone, Eastern Zone). Symbolically, these designations served both to erase previous geographic identities and to impose a new, orderly, and rationale system onto the Cambodian political landscape. Each zone was further divided into *damban* (regions, or sectors), followed by *srok* (districts), *khum* (subdistricts), and *phum* (villages). This political organization was imposed to permit a greater surveillance of the Cambodian people by the Khmer Rouge. Each territorial level was administered by a local committee, with the administrative hierarchy ultimately reaching to the Central Committee of the CPK, or Angkar.

Leaders of the Khmer Rouge sought, through these political geographic changes, to foster a transformation of daily life. Villages were reorganized into communes. For the Khmer Rouge, these collective farms "represented a tabula rasa upon which the new Khmer culture was to be imprinted. To create a new system, a plan was implemented to eradicate old practices, beliefs, and social patterns" (Quinn, 1989: 191).

Prior to the revolution, the extended family was the center of Cambodian economic and cultural life. Families worked together as an economic unit responsible for household production and consumption (Mam, 1990: 129). According to Ebihara (1990: 18), villagers were primarily subsistence cultivators. The mainstay crop was rice. In addition, other foods and household items were produced at home. Families commonly owned fruit trees and palms; livestock was raised and vegetables and herbs were cultivated in kitchen gardens. It was not uncommon for households to raise fish in rice paddies during the rainy season. Other goods, such as baskets and mats, were woven.

Traditional villages were not entirely self-sufficient. Indeed, many villages were closely tied to regional and national market economies. Villagers, for example, were linked to the cash economy (for example, to pay taxes or to pay off debts). Monies were also required to pay for weddings or funerals. Consequently, villagers would sell surplus produce or provide labor in exchange for wage payment. Villagers might also raise pigs or chickens for sale.

Under the Khmer Rouge the ownership of production and consumption became increasingly communal. Cooperatives were established to cultivate specified crops, including rice, vegetables, fruits, and nonfood crops such as cotton, rubber, and jute. The collection and distribution of produce and goods was centralized. The establishment of large-scale collectives, coupled with irrigation projects and the development of a system of (poorly planned and constructed) reservoirs and dams, were designed to foster greater farm yields and to permit multiple crops. Furthermore, and consistent with their attempt to "modernize" Cambodia through socialist practices, the Khmer Rouge initiated a spatial practice to "rationalize" the arrangement of rice paddies. Formerly, rice paddies were broken into parcels of varying shapes and sizes, resulting in a pastiche of land-use patterns. Under the Khmer Rouge, though, rice paddies were reorganized into regular, quadrangular plots—supposedly a symmetrical and efficient spatial arrangement of farming practices (Ebihara, 1990: 26). Ranging in size from several hundred persons to several thousand, these communal farms were the site of concentrated labor activities that were meant to achieve economic self-sufficiency for the Khmer Rouge.

Of their work in the communal farms, Quinn (1989: 182) quotes a young Khmer Rouge cadre:

> From now on if the people want to eat, they should go out and work in the rice paddies. They should learn that their lives depend on a grain of rice. Plowing the soil, planting and harvesting rice will teach them the real value of things. Cities are evil. There are money and trade in cities and both have a corrupting influence. People are good, but cities are evil. This is why we shall do away with cities.

Hinton (2005: 86) concludes that "long work hours, starvation rations, lack of freedom, miserable living conditions, and constant terror soon erased their humanity." The peasants were reduced to an animal-like status. Their distrust of cities and the structural conditions of the rural–urban disconnect allowed the Khmer Rouge to crystallize and mark the differences between the "new" and the "old" populations (Hinton, 2005: 78). In short, the Khmer Rouge forwarded a population policy that was deliberately and literally designed to erase—to clean up—all previous spaces of Cambodia (Tyner, 2008).

The evacuation and relocation of people from the cities to the rural collectives was just one component of the Khmer Rouge's population policy. Further transformations were required, namely, the elimination of all previous forms of social reproduction. While collectives were clearly essential for the proposed economic policies of the Khmer Rouge, such (re)concentrations of people also facilitated (in principle) the dissolution of the family. As Mam (2004: 133) explains, the "collectivization of work and living arrangements attacked the very structure and foundation of the traditional Cambodian family."

Households in pre-Democratic Kampuchea society exhibited a variety of forms. Many families lived in nuclear arrangements; others lived in "stem" arrangements, wherein one child remains at home upon marriage and brings his or her spouse into the household. Indeed, these arrangements could be either patrilocal—with the wife living with the family of her husband—or matrilocal—with the husband living with the family of his wife. Still other families were considered extended, in which relatives (for example, an orphaned nephew or niece, or a widowed sister) would be taken into households (Ebihara, 1990: 20). Furthermore, traditional Khmer familial structure was organized primarily by age rather than by gender. According to Ponchaud (1989: 162), in most pairings (for example, uncle/aunt, husband/wife) the two genders are expressed on equal terms. Traditional Khmer society likewise did not differentiate between maternal or paternal lineages. And while religious practices might be tied to sexuality, and consequently place women at a rank lower than men, in daily life—and notably in work—women were held as equal to men. Conversely, no important decision could be made without first consulting the elders, be it the grandparents, parents, or other extended kin (for example, uncles and aunts) (Ponchaud, 1989: 163). Age was a defining element, and can be seen in particular social functions and institutions (for example, the raising of children and marriage arrangements).

Within Democratic Kampuchea, however, all aspects of quotidian life were to be regimented and geographically controlled to better serve the revolution. The spatial separation of daily life was augmented with respect to social relations. The Khmer people, for example, were divided into work "forces" or "teams" based on age and sex. Adults, those aged between 14 and 50, were forced into mobile work brigades termed *kong chalat*. Males belonged to *kong boroh* and females to *kong neary*. The heaviest work was performed by these two groups: They plowed fields; planted, transplanted, and harvested rice; and dug and carried dirt for irrigation projects (Mam, 2004: 134). Those who were younger and unmarried usually traveled great distances from their villages to work in forests cutting timber or working on construction projects (p. 135).

Older members of Democratic Kampuchea—those 50 years old and above—were grouped into work teams known as *senah chun*. Again, these were separated by sex, with males belonging to *senah chun boroh* and females belonging to *senah chun neary*. Those in the *senah chun* normally performed lighter work (for example, sewing, gardening, collecting wood, caring for children) and usually remained in or close to the village. Some did, however, labor in rice fields (Mam, 2004: 134). The children of Democratic Kampuchea, which included all boys and girls under the age of 14, were organized into work groups called *kong komar*, with boys and girls separated into *kong komara* and *kong khomarei*, respectively. These members had the lightest work, often watching after cows and buffalo, gathering firewood, or gathering cow dung for fertilizer (p. 135).

These age/sex divisions of the populace reinforced the severing of traditional familial bonds and redirected loyalties to Angkar. Since Angkar was the "dad—mom" of all the people, all children belonged to Angkar and not to their birth parents. Such transformed social relations were reaffirmed through particular spatial practices. Beginning around 1977, for example, with the formation of higher level cooperatives, children rarely lived with their parents. Those under 6 years of age were entrusted to the care of grandmothers who cultivated their revolutionary spirit through the narration of heroic tales while their mothers were at work. Those children between the ages of 6 and 12 lived apart from their parents, sleeping in separate quarters; alternatively, they were organized into groups of 10 and received schooling chiefly geared toward manual work. Indoctrination sessions informed all children to no longer act deferentially to parents or elders: all people were now equal. They were taught, moreover, that parents had no merit, that parents were enemies of the regime, and thus enemies of children. Angkar alone was the rightful parent (Mam, 2004: 151; see also Hinton, 2005: 130; Ponchaud, 1989: 165). The Khmer Rouge's policy of separating children from their parents thus worked to socialize the next generation of revolutionaries. This was part of the planned moral education that was to be promoted during the Khmer Rouge regime (Clayton, 2005: 508). This policy, however, also facilitated the reach of Angkar into the everyday lives of the masses of people.

Collectivization and the attendant collective dining further strained, if not severed, traditional familial bonds. As work and dining were increasingly collectivized between 1976 and 1977, people associated more with their work teams than with their families. Ebihara (1990: 60) explains that the "imposition of communal dining halls was not simply a means whereby the state controlled distribution; it further demonstrated that the work team or cooperative had superseded the family as the basic social unit in Democratic Kampuchea." Mam (2004: 143) further argues that

> collective dining was enforced ... because the regime feared that allowing families to produce their own food would encourage family interests and distract loyalty from *Angka*. As with other policies implemented by the regime, the purpose of collectivizing food and property was to eliminate individual dependency on the family and [to] force individuals to project this dependency towards the organization.

Through the erasure of traditional social relations and family bonds, the Khmer Rouge set in place new relations, and therefore new geographic conceptions of Democratic Kampuchea. One particularly well-documented example is the Khmer Rouge's attempt to construct a new society through control of social reproductive practices, namely, marriages. Traditionally, marriages were arranged in the interest of the family, as well as potential spouses; decisions involved the consultation and permission of parents and extended family (Mam, 2004: 146). An elaborate and complex set of decisions and social relations were involved in the arrangement of marriages in traditional Khmer society. Brides, for example, were expected to originate from slightly higher social backgrounds than their prospective grooms. At the same time, however, grooms were expected to be older (though in the same age group, roughly up to 7 years older). These marriages were thought through carefully, often taking into consideration the wishes of the potential brides and grooms. Parents would try to assess the compatibility of potential spouses; they would also consult elderly religious persons to make evaluations based on the birth timing of the bride and groom. Significantly, parents would discourage any attempt at marrying a daughter against her will (see Heuveline and Poch, 2006: 101–102).

Within Democratic Kampuchea, marriage was maintained as an institution, but now it was to serve the revolution and the state. Local officials, loyal to the party, replaced parents in the negotiation and regulation of marriages. Individuals were (in general, though not always) denied the right to choose their own mate; parents and families were also forbidden involvement in the decision-making process (Mam, 2004: 146). Marriages, instead, were forced upon the people. In practice, marriages were determined by the social groupings constructed within Democratic Kampuchea. People were only "permitted" to marry within their own category: young soldiers, male or female, for example, could marry only from within their own ranks. And until 1978, one could not marry someone living outside one's own village or cooperative (Ponchaud, 1989).

The wedding event was not to represent the union of a couple or the beginnings of a family; rather, the marriage spectacle actually drew attention away from the significance of the individual and the family and toward obligations to the revolution (Mam, 2004: 147). Symbolically, weddings in Democratic Kampuchea were not solitary events but instead communal tasks to be performed. Survivors speak of mass weddings, with upward of 50 couples at a time. Couples would line up in rows, as rank-and-file soldiers might, with females on one side and males on the other. During the ceremony, couples would hold hands and pledge their loyalty to Angkar. Wedding vows were made to Angkar, and even the vow to "be faithful to each other" became synonymous with being faithful to Angkar (Ponchaud, 1989: 166–167). Spatially, this conformed with the Khmer Rouge's understanding of the purpose of marriage. As Mam (p. 148) explains, marriages were usually forced upon individuals for reproductive purposes only. It was a method of weakening family ties and increasing state control over sexuality and reproduction. Spouses were not encouraged to establish relationships; indeed, the spatial practices of collectivization and population relocation decisions often worked to keep newly married spouses separate. And indeed, after a wife became pregnant, most couples were soon separated.

Through the regulation of marriage, the Khmer Rouge government was able to exercise control over the sexuality of its citizens. Ebihara (1990: 30) describes the Khmer Rouge as puritanical in outlook. Men and women were, as previously noted, strictly segregated in the various spheres of daily life (for example, dining halls, work brigades). Illicit affairs were punished. Dress codes, aside from signifying egalitarianism, also served to ensure a "proper" decorum. Thus the control of sexuality was associated with a reaction to the perceived ills and vices of the previous society. However, the regulation of marriage and sexuality by the Khmer Rouge performed another crucial function. Through the control of family formation, the Khmer Rouge was able to assume authority over the reproduction of future generations. This was considered an important component when Khmer Rouge leaders contemplated future additions to the labor force and the revolutionary ranks (p. 30).

The many spatial practices initiated by the Khmer Rouge, while designed to fracture and reorient familial and village life, resulted in the deaths of thousands of persons through forced and prolonged work, illness, malnutrition, and exposure. The Khmer people were denied medical treatment, subjected to poor rations, and exposed to inhumane sanitary conditions. They were likewise subjected to random punishments, torture, and detention (Quinn, 1989). Of all practices directed toward the dissolution of the family, however, the most complete was the direct killing of husbands or wives, sons or daughters, aunts or uncles. As Mam (2004: 131) explains, the deaths of family members (by whatever cause) devastated the surviving family. However, the targeting of *entire* families merits special attention. The Khmer Rouge, aware of the extent to which people were tied to family obligations, did not hesitate to eliminate entire families (Mam, 2004; Ponchaud, 1989).

Hinton (2005: 68) explains that the Khmer Rouge promoted a Cambodian concept of disproportionate revenge. He explains that revenge is largely premised on a logic of debt and reciprocal exchange. Through an ideal of disproportionate revenge, one may "defeat" the offender and elevate one's own honor. However, there also exists the idea that a person must "completely defeat the enemy" (*phchanhy phchal*) to deter further retaliation. Hinton (p. 69) explains that "those who bear a grudge know that after they have exacted revenge, their adversary will in turn desire to repay the bad deed. To prevent the cycle from continuing, it may be in the avenger's interest to make a preemptive strike that will mute this desire by fear or death." The most extreme form of this type of revenge, according to Hinton (p. 70), consists of killing one's enemies and their entire families.

Following a concept of disproportionate revenge, the Khmer Rouge sought to destroy—to annihilate—entire families and thereby start anew. When one member of a family was accused, and therefore judged guilty, of a crime, the entire family was often targeted. Survivor accounts and Khmer Rouge documents detail how entire families were taken to extermination centers and executed en masse. Thus the Khmer Rouge cadres attempted to take disproportionate revenge so as to "completely destroy" their enemies and future enemies (Hinton, 2005: 90; Mam, 2004). Such a practice, however, has a long history in Cambodia, whereby victorious Cambodian kings would, after winning a war, kill opposing individuals and their entire family lines (Hinton, 2005: 71). The destruction of familial lines therefore entailed more than simply revenge. The killing of individuals and their entire families entailed also a political practice of spatial purification. As Hinton (p. 91) concludes, because the Khmer Rouge were so powerful, they were able to engage in the most extreme form of *phchanh phchal*—killing off the enemy's line. It is to this aspect of mass violence I now turn.

SUBJUGATING THE POLITICAL BODY

Also killed 160 children today for a total of 178 enemies killed.[6]

Under the Khmer Rouge regime, both people and their way of life were subject to erasure. In order to create the "new socialist man" to inhabit his new society, Pol Pot was impelled to strip away the cultural, religious, and social infrastructures upon which traditional Khmer society was based. These were to be replaced with a new socialist order based on total acquiescence to Angkar and the subjugation of the individual self to the collective good (Quinn, 1989: 191). Policies and practices were aimed at creating this new political body as the Khmer Rouge deliberately set out to unmake and subsequently remake the bodies and the population of Democratic Kampuchea.

Surface appearances were most easy to alter. As the Khmer Rouge attempted to promote a singular sameness of people, one based on an idealized geographical vision of the peasantry, all people were made to dress and groom alike. Men and women were ordered to wear traditional black peasant garb; colorful clothing—a sign of urbanism or Westernization—was banned. Simply wearing prohibited clothes could result in instant death. Hairstyles, likewise, were regimented. Short hair was imposed on all: long hair was seen as synonymous with perversion and idleness (Ponchaud, 1989: 157).

Furthermore, through socialization practices and moral education, the Khmer Rouge attempted to implement a complete and total subjugation of the body and the mind. All aspects of individualism were to be destroyed. Khmer Rouge people were to lead simple rural lives based on equality and self-sacrifice. Everything was to be done for the masses and for the nation (Dunlop, 2005: 156). People's actions were no longer based on individual profit or self-fulfillment but rather on the promotion of a selfless dedication to the collective well-being of Democratic Kampuchea. Efforts were made to remove all incentives for individual accomplishment; this was done to teach each person that any deviation from the general party line—any selfish or individual action—would result in severe punishment and probable death (Quinn, 1989: 193).

What Pol Pot and his colleagues sought to achieve was the obliteration of individualism from the collective Cambodian psyche. By destroying every vestige of individualist thought, the Khmer Rouge envisioned a new society consisting of persons totally dedicated to, and knowing only, a collectivist regime (Quinn, 1989: 193). Ideologically, the key was to make a utopian society—more quickly and more completely—than any previous attempt, including both the Russian and the Chinese Revolutions. The intention was not to remake the old society, but to make it anew. This required an explicit attempt to wipe clean all that existed before the revolution. They sought to destroy any previous geographies and to start from a "pure" base. Instantaneously, *every member* of Khmer society was to be reduced to the same economic and social level; contradictions between rich and poor, educated and illiterate, rural and urban were to be wiped out (Quinn, 1989: 192).

In Democratic Kampuchea individual bodies were conceived as having a fixed essence; bodies in fact were seen as immutable and resistant to change. Consequently, under the Khmer Rouge, bodies were organized and somewhat arbitrarily assigned into various social groups.[7] It was through the differential treatment of these groupings that vestiges of individualism were to be removed.

During its brief reign, the Khmer Rouge constructed and thus identified many different populations that were subject to possible exclusion or eradication. Some groups were ethnically defined. Hence, reflecting a continuity with the genocidal practices of the Lon Nol government, the Khmer Rouge targeted all people who were perceived as racially distinct, including the Viet-Khmer, the Sino-Khmer, and the Muslim Cham. Other marginalized groups were based on previous occupation (for example, soldiers and officials of the previous government, merchants, capitalists, wealthy farmers and landlords, intellectuals, monks, students, dancers, poets, and musicians). Within Democratic Kampuchea, all people indeed were subject to possible exclusion or eradication based on fluid conceptions of "us" and "them."

Most prevalent, however, was the Khmer Rouge's division between "new" and "old" people. "New people" (also referred to as "the April 17 group" or "war slaves") consisted of urbanites and the rural refugees who had fled to the cities to escape the civil war. They were differentiated from the "old people" or "base people" who had lived in the Khmer Rouge–controlled zones during the war (Hinton, 2002: 81). These were people identified as belonging to the "basic classes" of the poor and lower-middle peasantry. Both new people and old people found their lives radically transformed in Democratic Kampuchea (Hinton, 2005: 9), but the new people were singled out for even more dehumanizing practices. New people, for example, received less food, were treated more harshly, had fewer rights, and were killed more readily than old people (Hinton, 2005: 86). Haing Ngor (1987: 247) describes life under the Khmer Rouge:

> To us war slaves, the old way of life was gone and everything about it half forgotten, as if it had never really existed in the first place. Buddhist monks, making their tranquil morning rounds, didn't exist anymore. Three-generation families, where the grandparents look after the little children, didn't exist anymore. Shopping for food in the markets and staying to gossip. Inviting friends over to eat and drink and talk in the evening. It was all gone, and without that pattern we had nothing to hold on to.

Such social divisions also created and reinforced the existence of a culture of impunity. Hinton (2005: 86) explains that "since 'new people' were less than fully human, there were fewer moral inhibitions in harming them. A 'new person' who did something wrong could be 'discarded'—a euphemism for execution—without many qualms." For those Khmer Rouge cadres who were responsible for the day-to-day executions, their "victims" were reduced to a state of being less than that of animals; they were considered to be less than human. A person's status in Democratic Kampuchea was further differentiated by other factors, including one's "political attitudes" and class background. Political attitude, for example, referred to a tripartite classification of membership in cooperatives. Persons with full rights, known as *penh sith*, were entitled to join the party and army and, within the cooperatives, could hold any political position and receive full food rations. Candidates, or *triem*, could hold some low-ranking political positions and were next in line for food distribution. Lastly were the depositees, or *bannhau*. These persons were generally "last on the distribution lists, first on execution lists, and had no political rights" (Ebihara, 1990: 25). Under the Khmer Rouge, it was possible to change one's political attitude—depending on one's actions—but class background and the old/new people designations were essentially fixed.

Within the genocidal framework of the Khmer Rouge, the killing of bodies had a clear and distinct purpose: a systematic eradication of persons who embodied or perpetuated the idea of individualism. Whether these people died via starvation, lack of medical care, or execution was inconsequential. Haing Ngor (1987: 247), for example, explains that to the Khmer Rouge, the new people "weren't quite people. We were lower forms of life, because we were enemies. Killing us was like swatting flies, a way to get rid of undesirables."

As Haing Ngor's observation reveals, the Khmer Rouge viewed certain populations as expendable. The purge of the Cambodian population was the translation into action of a particular representation of space. As detailed by Hinton (2002: 79), the Khmer Rouge made references to how they were in the process of "cleaning up" Cambodian society. This brutal vision of the dialectics of self and space, and the attendant spatial practice of purification, is illustrated in the various slogans disseminated over the radio and at public meetings: "The regime must be destroyed"; "The enemy must be utterly crushed"; "What is infected must be cut out"; "What is rotten must be removed" (Quinn, 1989: 186). Hinton (p. 81), in fact, relates a particularly salient example of how the

Khmer Rouge viewed their attempts to *make* the population geography of Democratic Kampuchea. According to Hinton, one Khmer Rouge official likened the process to that of separating spoiled from unspoiled fruit. When one approaches a basket of fruit, one could, for instance, pick out the bad pieces, leaving the other pieces untouched. Conversely, one could overturn the entire basket and only put back the good pieces. Hinton (p. 81) notes that this metaphor directly references the "othering process" in which certain groups are excluded (that is, were not put back into the Democratic Kampuchea "basket") from a newly "overturned" social order and are labeled as dirty and impure (that is, spoiled fruit that should be discarded). Bodies that have been spoiled cannot be repaired: they must be physically eliminated from the greater population. This explanation also speaks to the *complete* upheaval envisioned for Democratic Kampuchea. Even those "pure" pieces (that is, ethnically pure Khmer, untainted by Westernization) were not immune from the Khmer Rouge's practice of societal transformation. Even those who were to be *included* in Democratic Kampuchea were still subject to inspection, control, and possible violence.

Conceptually, we often understand the wholesale eradication of people and of social relations as ethnic cleansing. Indeed, the Khmer Rouge sought to construct a new and pure society not through transforming past geographies, but by erasing—cleansing—those spaces. The mass violence unleashed by the Khmer Rouge was not, in this sense, irrational or insane. And herein lies the greatest tragedy: the violence was quite *deliberately justified and legitimated by its designers*. This contains dangerous implications for the promotion of social justice, in that the injustices meted out to the people of Cambodia were justified from the point of view of the Khmer Rouge. Moreover, the logic of mass violence within Democratic Kampuchea also reveals the political basis of genocide.

The principle expression of sovereignty resides, to a large degree, in the power and the capacity to dictate who may live and who must die (Mbembe, 2003: 11). Following Foucault (2003: 240), in the classical theory of sovereignty, the right of life and death was one of sovereignty's basic attributes. In other words, to say that "the sovereign has a right of life and death means that he [sic] can, basically, either have people put to death or let them live, or in any case that life and death are not natural or immediate phenomena which are primal or radical, and which fall outside the field of power." Foucault also suggests that the sovereign cannot grant life in the same way that he or she can inflict death (although control over reproduction comes close). The right of life and death, therefore, "is always exercised in an unbalanced way: the balance is always tipped in favor of death." Ultimately, the "very essence of the right of life and death is actually the right to kill: it is at the moment when the sovereign can kill that he [sic] exercises his right over life" (Foucault, 2003: 240).

Based on his reading of European history,[8] Foucault makes the argument that this conception of sovereignty shifted with the emergence of nondisciplinary practices and the transition from a concern with the anatomopolitics of the body to that of biopolitics (see Chapter One). Within France, in particular, Foucault (2003: 248) argues that power was decreasingly viewed as the right to take life and increasingly the right to intervene to make live, or to improve life by eliminating the random elements of accidents and so forth. Power, consequently, was exercised not over death but over mortality. Once this transition has occurred, Foucault (p. 254) asks, "How is it possible for a political power to kill, to call for deaths, to demand deaths, to give the order to kill, and to expose not only its enemies but its own citizens to the risk of death? Given that this power's objective is essentially to make live, how can it let die?"

The answer, of course, lies in state racism.[9] It is at this point that racism (or any other classification scheme) intervenes to separate bodies into groups: populations that are categorized as "us" or "them," "good" or "bad," "ally" or "enemy." Foucault (2003: 254) states bluntly: "It is primarily a way of introducing a break into the domain of life that is under power's control: the break between what must live and what must die." It is a way of separating out types of bodies, of constructing different populations that are evaluated in such a way as to justify death over life. Foucault (pp. 254–255) elaborates:

> The appearance within the biological continuum of the human race of races, the distinction among races, the hierarchy of races, the fact that certain races are described as good and that others, in contrast, are described as inferior: all this is a way of fragmenting the field of the biological that power controls. It is a way of separating out the groups that exist within a population. It is, in short,

a way of establishing a biological type caesura within a population that appears to be a biological domain.

The regroupings of bodies into populations and subpopulations is an inherently spatial process. It is an activity of dividing and separating people for political and economic purposes. However, there is an additional component to these sociospatial separations, one that is immediately connected to questions of sovereignty and justice. Foucault (2003: 255) continues: "The fact that the other dies does not mean simply that I live in the sense that his death guarantees my safety; the death of the other, the death of the bad race, of the inferior race (or the degenerate, or the abnormal) is something that will make life in general healthier: healthier and purer." Such reasoning in fact conforms with traditional Khmer concepts of sovereignty and violence. In Cambodian folktales, for example, the act of murder is not normally conceived as an evil or as a uniquely reprehensible act. Rather, murder may assume a revelatory function, either in the sense that it serves as a prelude to a rebirth or in that it triggers an act of salvation (Ponchaud, 1989: 161). Consequently, the killings of (perceived) corrupt and irredeemable elements was understood by the Khmer Rouge as a prelude to the birth of a moral and properly ordered society.

We thus arrive at a practice of spatial purification in the name of building a nation-state. The construction of a pure society, such as that envisioned by the Khmer Rouge, required the eradication and elimination of essentialized primordial Others. These bodies, conceived as forever separate, could not be reformed or reeducated. Political rehabilitation was not an option. There emerged a perceived necessity to simply exterminate the unwanted Other.

Bodies within Democratic Kampuchea were to be either economically and/or politically useful. Bodies, in other words, were to exist solely for the state. For the Khmer Rouge, policies and practices were implemented to make society pure through the elimination of the impure. Their regime was totalizing. Violence was neither limited to nor directed at "racial" groupings, as in other genocides, but rather was an integral component within a complete transformation of society to which all inhabitants were subjected. Democratic Kampuchea was conceived as an authoritarian, normalized society. And, as Foucault (2003: 256) explains, "When you have a normalizing society, you have a power which [facilitates] an indispensable precondition that allows someone to be killed, that allows others to be killed."

The Khmer Rouge saying, "If you live there is no gain; if you die there is no loss," approaches this conception of life and death. The phrase speaks to the liminal position of bodies within Democratic Kampuchea. Bodies—*all bodies*—were inconsequential on their own. It was only within the context of the revolution, and by extension the state (for the state and the revolution were viewed as one), that bodies mattered. Bodies were to be economically useful (for example, by performing labor on collectives) and/or politically docile. If not, bodies were considered inconsequential. This is why Pol Pot, on his deathbed in 1998, continued to show no remorse for the deaths he unleashed in the 1970s. From his point of view, he did not kill anyone; he simply removed so much detritus that threatened the sovereignty of Democratic Kampuchea. The mass violence of the Khmer Rouge, as such, marks the epitome of state-sanctioned dehumanization.

CONCLUSIONS

The Khmer Rouge project was, in effect, a projection. It was a colossal attempt to promote both spatially and temporally a particular vision of a modern and communal utopian society. Such a projection, however, could not be cluttered with the material or symbolic debris of earlier geographies. For the Khmer Rouge ideologues, the landscape of Cambodia needed to be erased prior to the construction of a new Democratic Kampuchea.

The spatial practices of purification sanctioned by Pol Pot and other high-ranking officials of the Khmer Rouge were designed to achieve a number of objectives: economic self-sufficiency, centralization of control, the dissolution of family structures. However, a primary objective—and one that most directly influenced the life or death of the people of Cambodia—was political. Simply put, the systematic violence—including both structural and direct forms of violence—of Democratic Kampuchea was justified as a desire not to *return* to a past geography, nor to build upon existing geographies. Rather, the Khmer Rouge advanced a genocidal practice that was deliberately, and literally, designed to erase—to clean up—all previous spaces of Cambodia.

According to Foucault (2003), the state must present itself as the guarantor of the integrity and purity of society; it must defend itself against groups perceived as impure. Chandler (1991: 41) explains that Khmer Rouge leaders subscribed to the Maoist doctrine of permanent revolution; as such, it was necessary for party members to continuously create counterrevolutionary enemies for purges to assure the safety of the party and to maintain the revolution's purity. Other groups, and hence other enemies, were thought to be everywhere. As Pol Pot explained in a speech delivered on December 20, 1976,

> ... there is a sickness inside the Party.... We cannot locate it precisely. The illness must emerge to be examined. Because the heat of the people's revolution and the heat of the democratic revolution were insufficient at the level of the people's struggle and at the level of class struggle among all layers of the national democratic revolution, we search for the microbes within the Party without success. They are buried. As our social revolution advances, however, seeping more strongly into every corner of the Party, the army and among the people we can locate the ugly microbes. They will be pushed out by the true nature of social revolution. (Chandler, Kiernan, and Boua, 1988: 183)

Although the Khmer Rouge claimed to be constructing an egalitarian society, they were in actuality constructing (and subsequently destroying) multiple and disparate population geographies.

4

SPACES OF PLANNED VIOLENCE

"They took the women to the bush and told us that they were going to kill us. They started to beat us. Some women were beaten to death. Then they took those of us who were still alive and forced us to walk to Nyamabuye [the neighboring commune]. There were about 200 women from two communes. They chose among the women. They raped many of us. They were saying 'We want a Tutsi wife.' When we reached Musumba sector they said that they were going to leave us inyenzis [cockroaches]. They kept asking us 'How do you want to die?' They kept threatening that they were going to rape all of us and that they were going to beat us to death.... [Later] they took our clothes and made all of us sit down in a big area. At night they came around with torches to look for the beautiful women. They shone the torches in our faces and they kept saying 'You come, you come.' The first time they chose six women. They were all raped by up to five militia. They kept changing the women through the night. When they chose me, I begged them, 'please kill me.' I was raped by three men.... The next day after I was raped, all the women were forced by [the militia] to walk on the road naked like a group of cattle. At all the roadblocks that we passed, the other [militia] were shouting to them 'Kill them, you have to kill them. They will make Tutsi babies.' Those [militia] who were keeping us for rape would answer that they would kill us later. By this time, we all smelt because we had not washed. We had no clothes. We were covered with blood. Blood was everywhere. When I urinated blood was coming out."[1]

The above narrative is that of Marie, a young Tutsi woman who survived the genocidal pogrom that ravaged her country. Samantha Power (2002: 334) describes the Rwandan genocide as "the fastest, most efficient killing spree of the twentieth century." Indeed, in just 100 days, over 800,000 Tutsi were slaughtered. Another 10,000 to 30,000 Hutu sympathizers were likewise murdered. In total, approximately 11 percent of Rwanda's population was annihilated in 3 months.

Marie's story seemingly substantiates many of the initial media reports of the Rwandan genocide, of a "society gone amok" (Lemarchand 1999: 17), of the culmination of centuries of conflict between two 'natural' enemies. However, as Ronayne (2001: 153) explains, "Contrary to the perceptions of many outside observers, the genocide in Rwanda was not simply the result of ancient hatreds between two ethnic groups." Lemarchand (p. 17) concurs, noting that the "Rwanda genocide is neither reducible to a tribal meltdown rooted in atavistic hatreds nor to a spontaneous outburst of blind fury." Gérard Prunier (1995) is even more blunt in his assessment. According to Prunier (pp. xi–xii), "What we have witnessed in Rwanda is a historical product, not a biological fatality or a 'spontaneous' bestial outburst. Tutsi and Hutu have not been created by God as cats and dogs, predestined from all eternity to disembowel each other because the tall thin men came from Egypt and the short stocky ones were born on the shores of Lake Kivu."

The genocide, as explained by Peter Ronayne (2001: 157), also did not result from a "failed state," but rather was the result of a "racist Hutu power leadership of an activist and centralized state apparatus [that] put into motion a premeditated, well-conceived, and deliberate plan to exterminate the Tutsis." Indeed, Berkeley (2002: 107) maintains that "Rwanda represented the opposite: a state that was all too successful in mobilizing its people along rigidly hierarchical lines from the top down, from the head of state and his ruling clique of coconspirators down to the last village mayor."

The Rwandan genocide was in fact a planned—and thoroughly modern—corporeal annihilation; it resulted from an explicit policy to rid the country of a marginalized population. An entire social group, with no ontological basis, was to be excluded from the country. Decades of moral exclusion and structural violence combined to marginalize this group. In the years leading up to the 1994 genocide, dehumanizing representations dominated the media and these practices set in place a culture of impunity. The Tutsi victims were constructed as the root of all problems; only through the elimination of this diseased, impure, and immoral group could the legitimate heirs to the state flourish. The violence that was unleashed on Rwanda entailed its own "structuring logic," as individual Rwandans lashed out against a perceived internal other who threatened, in their imaginary, both their personal integrity and the cosmic order of the state (Taylor, 2002: 139).

The experiences of Marie encapsulate many disturbing but crucial elements of a refigured population geography: the discipline of bodies, the regulation of populations, the control (and production) of space. In this chapter I consider at length the constructedness of the Rwandan genocide, of how particular bodies and groups were constructed as alien and nonhuman, of how these bodies and populations were morally excluded from a utopian fantasy of racial purity. In short, I discuss how the violence in Rwanda was anything but natural.

COLONIAL CONSTRUCTIONS

Present-day Rwanda is a small, compact state located south of the equator in central Africa. Ecologically and culturally, however, the region is exceptionally complex. The people who have settled this region compose part of the cultures and societies of a vast region astride the Congo–Nile watershed separating the two great African cultural zones of the Congo River Basin and the Great Lakes region. The societies that came to be included in present-day Rwanda drew in important ways from both cultural zones as well as from local ecological realities (Newbury, 2001: 259). For example, Newbury (p. 263) describes at least nine "microregions" of Rwanda, each of which brought separate characteristics to the region and maintained separate ties to outside areas.

Present-day Rwanda came under European control as part of the "scramble for Africa" of the late 19th century. In the years following its unification in 1872, Germany began to duplicate the steps of other European powers in the colonial partitioning of Africa. In November 1884 the German chancellor, Otto von Bismarck, convened the Berlin Conference. Bismarck, newly converted to colonialism, sought to bring order to the confusion of European interests developing in Africa and perhaps thereby gain the upper hand over his rivals (Griffiths, 1995: 38). Rules were established whereby the European powers, plus the United States, regulated the territorial division of the African continent. It was through this process that Germany acquired its colonial possessions in what was then known as German East Africa.

German colonial rule was brief and relatively inconsequential. Far more influential was the imposition of Belgian rule, beginning in 1916 and formalized in 1919. In that year, following Germany's defeat in World War I, the western provinces of German East Africa, Ruanda-Urundi (now present-day Rwanda and Burundi) were given to Belgium under a League of Nations mandate. Having added to their African colonial holdings, Belgium pledged to ensure freedom of speech and religion for its newly acquired colonies. That Belgium failed to deliver on its promises should come as no surprise, given its history of brutal colonial rule in the Congo. Belgian colonial administrators disrupted the old state apparatus; money was introduced; Western education was organized for the sons of the (primarily Tutsi) chiefs; and forced labor was instigated, mainly to build roads to benefit Belgian colonial exploitation (Melvern, 2004).

More damaging to Rwanda, however, was the imposition of European notions of race. Precolonial Rwanda was organized socially, economically, and politically as a structured monarchy. It was a semifeudal society, replete with aristocrats and vassals, peasants and slaves. The administrative structure was organized on four levels: province, district, hill, and neighborhood. Each level was linked in social relationships of mutual dependence. Ethnically, the region exhibited tremendous diversity and fluidity. Newbury (2001: 266) explains that many identities were associated with physical features on the landscape: "Each had its own story to tell, and their separate historical and cultural characteristics continue to affect politics and identity even today." Newbury (p. 266) continues: "The process of forging a common identity occurred in an uneven fashion; 'national' cultural identity coexisted, sometimes rather uneasily, with the legacy of regional awareness, an awareness that often remained relevant even within highly centralized state structures."

The early European explorers noted that many occupations and social relations in Rwanda appeared to be racially based. Three groups were identified: the Hutu, the Tutsi, and the Twa. Administratively, higher level chiefly functions, including those at the hill, district, and provincial level, were generally performed by Tutsi. The monarchy, likewise, was Tutsi-dominated. At the lowest, neighborhood level,

Hutu generally administered affairs. Although the population was linguistically and culturally homogenous—they spoke the same Bantu language, lived side-by-side, and intermarried—the Europeans inappropriately identified these divisions as "tribal" or "racial" (Prunier, 1995: 5). Newbury (2001: 272) writes that "the tendency has been to extrapolate to an entire cultural category the characteristics of an unrepresentative sample—if the ruling lineage was Tutsi, then all Tutsi were presumed to have been powerful; if some Hutu were landless, then all were said to have lived on the edge of poverty. Such generalizations deny logic and belie the empirical record."

Neither historians nor anthropologists can agree on the origins of these divisions that have been so crucial to Rwanda's terrible history (Melvern, 2004: 3). Contemporary anthropologists acknowledge that these divisions did not represent strictly defined groups, nor did such divisions constitute an unbending class system. Rather, precolonial Rwandan society was exceptionally malleable; Hutu could become Tutsi and Tutsi could become Hutu (Ronayne, 2001). Newbury (2001: 266) bluntly states that broad classificatory labels, such as "Hutu," "Tutsi," or "Twa" carry little explanatory meaning in a historical sense.

In the Kinyarwanda language the word *Hutu* meant "subject" or "servant" and the word *Tutsi* meant "rich in cattle." To a considerable extent, most people identified as Hutu were peasants who cultivated the soil while those defined as Tutsi were cattle herders. However, perceived differences were not solely based on wealth or class. Not only were there Hutu and Tutsi in the same class, but not all Tutsi were wealthy (Melvern, 2004: 4).

Newbury (2001: 271) explains that ethnicity was important to social processes, but in ways very different from the popular image. He elaborates:

> Ethnic identities were not primordial, they were contextually created; they altered over time, and they evolved differently in different places and contexts. Thus ethnic groups cannot be seen as internally homogeneous, externally distinct, and constantly in confrontation with other groups. Like many other social categories, ethnicity was not an institution but an identity, and hence ethnic categories were contextually defined. In some cases, ethnic identity and class identity overlapped. (p. 271)

In his account of Rwanda's precolonial population geography, Newbury (2001: 271–272) notes, for example, that there existed a group of people called *Ingabo*. This term applied to the descendants of warriors; these individuals held their own land and paid taxes to the army chief. They were treated as neither Tutsi nor Hutu. For the European colonists and missionaries, however, given the "almost obsessive preoccupation with 'race' in the late nineteenth-century anthropological thinking, this peculiarity soon led to much theorizing, romanticizing and at times plain fantasizing" (Prunier, 1995: 5).

These social groups did, however minimally, exhibit an "average" dominant somatic type, but certainly not all individual members conformed to it (Prunier, 1995). Newbury (2001: 272) explains that there existed (and exists) wide physical variations within each ethnic category, and significant physical overlap between the groups. Nevertheless, the Europeans placed considerable weight on the physical features of these three groups. The Twa were described as "small" and "chunky" with "monkey-life flat faces" and "huge noses"; the Hutu, likewise, were characterized as "generally short and thick-set" with "big heads" and "jovial expressions."

The Tutsi, conversely, were the prized "race" of the European colonialists. Physically, the Tutsi were described as "very thin" with "fine features." They had "high brows" and "thin lips" and were perceived to be lighter in complexion. Tutsi women, especially, were thought by the Europeans to be very beautiful. The Tutsi, in fact, were considered to be so beautiful that they must have originated outside of Africa. Consequently, the racially obsessed 19th-century Europeans forwarded a number of hazardous hypotheses on the Tutsi's possible origins (Prunier, 1995: 6). Called "African Arayans" or "Black Caucasians," the Tutsi were believed to be descendants from a foreign population that migrated into Africa. One theory held that the Tutsi originated from India; other theories postulated that the Tutsi came from Egypt, Asia Minor, Melanesia, the Garden of Eden, or the lost continent of Atlantis (Prunier, 1995; Ronayne, 2001).

Throughout the early 20th century, Belgian colonial authorities continued and expanded the racial mythology of Tutsi superiority. Colonial accounts became a "scientific canon" and these theories conditioned the views and attitudes of the Europeans. Through the years, these racial theories would also significantly impact the Rwandese as well, both Hutu and Tutsi (Melvern, 2004; Prunier, 1995; Ronayne, 2001). The construction and rigid social classifications of Rwanda's population became internalized and were manifested in specific colonial practices.

As colonial administrators, the Belgians continued Germany's practice of indirect rule. Between 1926 and 1931, for example, Belgian authorities implemented a series of reforms that set in place a Tutsi chiefly complex and a system of indirect administration (Prunier, 1995: 25). This resulted in a near complete domination of all political functions by those classified as Tutsi. Furthermore, in positions of greater authority, Tutsi were able to modify traditional land and contractual rights and were gradually able to acquire sizeable holdings of lands previously administered by Hutu.

Perhaps most damaging, however, was the regulation of Rwanda's population. There is a growing literature, as Kraly and McQuilton (2005: 225) discuss, on the role of population systems in the abuse of human rights. They detail how demographic accounting and registration systems were used to support the forced removal of Aborigines in Australia and how other discriminatory practices were buttressed by population registrations and classifications of lineage. Further, as detailed earlier, various population registers were used in the so-called pacification strategies employed by the United States in its war in Vietnam. In Rwanda, however, we see how the imposition and continuation of a population registration system aided directly in the genocidal slaughter of hundreds of thousands of people.

In 1933 the Belgian administration began a process that would codify social divisions within Rwandan society. A census was introduced in Rwanda, with teams of Belgian bureaucrats arbitrarily classifying people as either Hutu, Tutsi, or Twa. Every Rwandan was counted, measured, and classified. The Belgians actually measured their colonial subjects, recording, for example, their height, length of nose, and shape of eyes. For many subjects, it was not possible for the Belgians to determine race with "accuracy"; accordingly, many people was classified haphazardly. Some people, for instance, were given a Tutsi identity simply because they had more money or more cows (Melvern, 2004: 6). Subsequently, all people were assigned identity cards, with their ethnic groupings clearly marked. This amplified the importance of what was once a fluid division and increased its rigidity (Ronayne, 2001: 154).

Over the years, a previously permeable society hardened into a nation sharply divided along strictly interpreted racial classifications. Two dominant but unequal social groups—Hutus and Tutsis—were produced. And resultant from racially based (and biased) colonial practices, these social groupings were accompanied with significant discrepancies in economic and social power (Ronayne, 2001: 154). Spatially, these groups were conceived as having separate origins. The Tutsis, it was claimed, were foreigners; the Hutus, conversely, were indigenous to the nascent Rwandan state. In time, these geographical imaginations would be used to legitimate both direct and structural violence.

INDEPENDENCE

There is no trace in Rwanda's precolonial history, writes Prunier (1995: 39), of systematic violence between Tutsi and Hutu. Certainly wars existed, both "domestic" and "foreign." These conflicts, however, were either fought with Hutu and Tutsi fighting side-by-side as a collective against perceived foreign kingdoms, or within, with chiefly lineages wresting seats of local power. The remarkable history of violence throughout Rwanda following independence must accordingly be situated as a legacy of colonial-induced material inequalities between constructed social groups.

After World War II, Belgium continued to administer the mandated territory of Ruanda-Urundi as a United Nations trusteeship. In 1957–1958 a number of political parties were established, responding in part to diminishing Belgian authority. Among the first were the Mouvement Social Muhutu (Hutu Social Movement, or MSM), founded in 1957 by former schoolteacher Grégoire Kayibanda, and the Association pour la Promotion Sociale de la Masse (Association for the Social Promotion of the Masses), created in 1957 by the Hutu businessperson Joseph Gitera. Two years later the MSM redefined itself as the Mouvement Démocratique Rwandais/Parti du Mouvement et de l'Emancipation Hutu (Rwandese Democratic Movement/Party of the Movement and of Hutu Emancipation, or MDR-PARMEHUTU). Opposing these and other Hutu parties was the Tutsi-created Union Nationale Rwandaise (Rwandese National Union, or UNAR), founded in 1959. Aside from being pro-Tutsi, the UNAR was exceptionally monarchist and hostile to Belgian rule (Prunier, 1995: 47–48).

As the region was caught up in the decolonization movements sweeping Africa, Rwandan politics continued to be racially defined, not only by the Hutu and by the Tutsi, but also by outside participants (for example, the United Nations). Moreover, cold war politics began to intervene. During the late 1950s UNAR began to receive financial support and military backing from the Soviet Union. This furthered the increasingly hostile division between the Tutsi and the Belgians, and, in fact, contributed to the latter's support of Hutu-led parties. Belgium, however, was also responding to other forms of international criticism, namely, its support of Tutsi minority rule. For this reason, as well, Belgian authorities began the arduous task of replacing Tutsi chiefs and subchiefs with Hutu leaders (Prunier, 1995: 48).

Violence erupted in 1959. Following a Tutsi attack on Dominique Mbonyumutwa, a Hutu subchief and PARMEHUTU activist, Hutu activists began attacking Tutsi chiefs, their families, and known UNAR members. UNAR supporters responded in kind. The violence spread rapidly throughout the region. Thousands of people were killed and thousands more fled to neighboring countries (see Melvern, 2004: 6–7; Prunier, 1995: 48–49). As Melvern (p. 7) concludes, the killing of Tutsi in 1959 was the first of several alleged genocides.

After United Nations intervention, the Belgian trusteeship was ended in 1962 and Rwanda was established as an independent state. But independence did not bring an end to ethnic-based political power. Instead, the Hutu revolution, begun in 1959, merely inverted the previous hierarchical relationship between Hutu and Tutsi. This inversion was promoted enthusiastically by Kayibanda, Rwanda's first president. According to Melvern (2004: 8), Kayibanda is considered the founding father of Hutu nationalism. He ruled through a local network of Hutu on every hill. He continued and augmented the idea that Tutsi were "foreigners" who had invaded and occupied Rwanda. As outsiders, the Tutsi were not considered "true" citizens. The Hutu, by contrast, were constructed as "native peasants" who were historically enslaved by an influx of aristocratic invaders (Melvern, 2004; Prunier, 1995). Prunier (p. 80) concludes that the Hutu, from the 1960s onward, saw themselves as "the only legitimate inhabitants of the country." The Hutu "were the silent demographic majority, which meant that a Hutu-controlled government was now not only automatically legitimate but also ontologically democratic."

In light of increasing Hutu dominance and violence, many thousands of Tutsi fled to neighboring Uganda. An estimated quarter of a million Tutsi lived in poorly equipped and infrequently supplied refugee camps (Melvern, 2004: 8). In November and December 1963, however, in an effort to return home, approximately 1,500 Tutsi refugees attempted to invade Rwanda with the goal of removing Kayibanda from power. The attempt failed, however, and the Kayibanda regime began a concerted and planned campaign to kill Tutsi. Political opponents were targeted and, according to Prunier (1995: 56), all surviving Tutsi politicians who were still living in Rwanda in 1963 were executed. Murder, however, was not limited solely to politicians; in the ensuing slaughter, an estimated 10,000 to 14,000 Tutsi were killed (Melvern, 2004: 8–9).

Over the next 10 years, as racially charged violence continued to grip Rwanda, other political machinations were in the works. On July 5, 1973, 10 army officers, calling themselves the Committee for National Peace and Unity, ousted Kayibanda in a military coup d'état. It was claimed that the coup was necessary in order to bring stability to the country and to end the violent repression against the Tutsi. Reality, though, was vastly different from the rhetoric: the new government continued the genocidal policies of its predecessor. The newly installed president, former minister of the national guard and police, Juvenal Habyarimana, was a believer in Hutu superiority. He transformed Rwanda into a brutal totalitarian state. In 1974 Habyarimana formed his own political party, the Mouvement Révolutionnaire National pour le Développement (MRND) and banned all other parties. All citizens of Rwanda were required to be members (Melvern, 2004: 11).

To facilitate ethnic discrimination and persecution, Habyarimana continued the use of identification cards. This also enabled the government to monitor and regulate the movement and settlement patterns of its citizens. Population movement was tightly controlled. Travel within the country was permitted, but severely restrained. If one desired to move, he or she was required to obtain authorization; such clearance was generally not granted (Melvern, 2004; Prunier, 1995). Other facets of daily life were likewise regimented. For decades, peasants had been told exactly when and what to farm, and could be fined if they did not comply with such instructions (Hintjens, 1999: 270). Prunier (1995: 77) concludes that the administrative control in Rwanda was probably the tightest in the world among noncommunist countries.

Discrimination against the Tutsi was widespread. Politically, Tutsi were marginalized and largely barred from office. There were no Tutsi *bourgmestres* (mayors) and only two Tutsi were members of parliament (out of 70 members). Those officially listed as Tutsi were subjected to strict quotas in secondary and higher education and in public employment (Hintjens, 1999: 247). Ironically, some Western agencies viewed these policies as positive, as an indication of Habyarimana's attempt to "integrate" Tutsis into Rwandan society, based on democratic majority (Melvern, 2004: 12). In actuality, those identified as Hutu controlled all facets of Rwandese society.

With an area of just 26,338 square kilometers, Rwanda is a densely populated state. Moreover, it has registered substantial growth throughout the 20th century. For example, its population rose from approximately 1,595,000 in the 1930s to nearly 7 million in the 1980s. Its arable density, consequently, increased from approximately 85 persons per square meter in 1934 to over 380 persons per square meter in the 1980s (Prunier, 1995: 4). Given these trends, President Habyarimana promoted a policy that food production should increase faster than population growth. This was to be achieved through the establishment of agricultural self-sufficiency and the attainment of "food security." Rwanda, according to Habyarimana, was to become a self-sufficient, agrarian-based state. Consequently, through the promotion of food security, Rwanda's peoples would be best in a position to achieve both economic growth and development.

Similar to the attempts promoted by the Khmer Rouge, the Habyarimana regime initiated several draconian policies to achieve its dream of an agrarian utopia. Building on earlier colonial practices, all Rwandans were forced to participate, both individually and collectively, in the government's mass mobilization strategy. In order to increase agricultural productivity, Rwandans were required to perform manual labor for the state. One such practice was the *umuganda* policy. *Umuganda* is a Kinyarwanda word that refers to the wood used to construct a house. Under the Habyarimana regime, however, it referred to a harsh policy of forced labor. On February 2, 1974, the president issued an order that every Rwandan would perform a set amount of unpaid collective work

1 day per week—though in practice this one day stretched into many more days. All Rwandans were to "voluntarily" contribute their labor to various weekly collective works. This provided a tremendous reservoir of unpaid labor available to the state for construction of schools, roads, sanitation facilities, and health centers (Verwimp, 2004: 19). Promoted as the reestablishment of a traditional institution that preceded colonialism, the policy was portrayed as a reaction against the monetarization of the Rwandan economy.

The umuganda policy was coupled with other restrictions on the lives of the Rwandans. Habyarimana, for example, placed restrictions on movement through a policy of "ruralization." Verwimp (2004: 11) explains that peasants were forced to stay in the rural areas. Again, similar to the Khmer Rouge, Habyarimana considered cities places of immorality, theft, and prostitution. Consequently, many residents of urban areas were sent to "reeducation" camps. Those living in rural areas were frequently denied permission to move to the cities. Such restrictions on population mobility were explained as efforts to promote morality, to instill a peasant-based labor ethic, and to foster obedience to authority (Verwimp, p. 11). Ultimately, these policies would provide surplus labor for the promotion of agricultural.

In the 1970s Rwanda had one of the highest birthrates in the world. Habyarimana spoke often of Rwanda's demographic problem. In 1973, for example, he explained that "we are aware of the problems caused by the demographic growth of the Rwandan population and they should be getting our permanent and serious attention" (quoted in Verwimp, 2004: 15). However, as Verwimp documents, Habyarimana was inconsistent in his population concerns. In 1979, for instance, Habyarimana concluded that "the number of inhabitants of our country should not always be presented as excessive, nor always be presented as a constraint on development," and later, in 1980, he explained that "a Rwandan by nature wants to have a lot of children because he considers his children a source of protection, a source of production to secure his living" (quoted in Verwimp, pp. 15–16).

In practice the economic and population policies of Habyarimana worked against his goal of self-sufficiency. Habyarimana, for instance, most vigorously promoted the cultivation of coffee and tea for export. Vast tracts of land were set aside for the cultivation of these crops, to the detriment of thousands of landless (and increasingly starving) peasants. The setting aside of land for the cultivation of coffee was not conductive to the provision of food security for a densely populated state such as Rwanda. Furthermore, peasants were not allowed to cultivate the crops they wished, nor were they permitted to use the techniques of soil protection they wanted. Habyarimana, likewise, never promoted family planning as a solution to his selective claims of overpopulation.

Throughout much of the 1970s and 1980s Rwanda remained a small and impoverished country. Conditions worsened in the late 1980s as a drastic drop in coffee prices led to economic collapse. Despite claims to promoting agricultural self-sufficiency and food self-reliance, Habyarimana actively pursed the export of coffee and tea (Verwimp, 2004). These economic policies brought little improvement to labor-rich but capital-poor Rwanda during the 1970s and 1980s. With the downturn in the late 1980s, conditions worsened. In turn, health and education services suffered. The people of Rwanda, and not just the Tutsi, began to feel the brunt of Habyarimana's failed policies.

Outside of Rwanda, displaced Tutsi composed Africa's largest refugee problem. An estimated 900,000 Rwandan refugees were living in Uganda, Burundi, Zaire, and Tanzania. Many sought to return to their homeland, but Habyarimana, claiming overpopulation, steadfastly refused any right of return (Melvern, 2004: 14). Consequently, Tutsi refugees, as part of the Uganda-based Rwandan Patriotic Front (RPF), attempted to force a change.

The RPF leadership, including second-generation Tutsi refugees and moderate Hutus, believed that a return home for the displaced Tutsi could only be achieved through military pressure. Additional demands included an end to ethnic divisions, the elimination of compulsory identification cards, the promotion of a viable self-sustaining economy, and a democratization of the security force (Melvern, 2004: 14). On October 1, 1990, an RPF force of approximately 5,000 men invaded Rwanda.

It was assumed by members of the RPF that the Habyarimana regime was in a weakened state, and that an initial push into the country would bring about the collapse of the presidency. However, the RPF both underestimated the strength of the regime and failed to account for external assistance, namely, French military support of the Habyarimana regime (Lemarchand, 1999; Verwimp, 2004).

The invasion itself was unsuccessful. Disastrously for the RPF, the failed military operation solidified the position of the Hutu extremists. Not content with merely staving off the attempted overthrow of his government, Habyarimana set in motion a brutal pogrom aimed at Tutsi residents in Rwanda and their Hutu supporters. In the massacres that ensued, an estimated 10,000 people were arrested; many hundreds were detained, tortured, and executed.

Hutu extremists circulated reports that those Tutsi living in Rwanda were accomplices of the invading rebel group, and that the Tutsi were planning to exterminate the Hutu. In November 1992, for example, Leon Mugesera, a senior member of the president's party, addressed an MRND gathering. With clear reference to the colonial constructs of Tutsi as foreign invaders, Mugesera claimed that "the fatal mistake we made in 1959 was to let [the Tutsi] get out.... They belong in Ethiopia and we are going to find them a shortcut to get there by throwing them into the Nyabarongo River. I must insist on this point. We have to act. Wipe them all out!" (quoted in Power, 2002: 340).

PREPARATIONS FOR A GENOCIDE

During the early 1990s Hutu extremists actively cultivated a particular representation of space, one that prefigured a pure society. Tutsi had been produced, through colonial and postindependence practices, as a marginalized group, with primordial origins outside Rwandan territory. As outsiders, Tutsi were increasingly excluded from the body politic. But in time, even minimal participation was too extensive. As Hintjens (1999: 242) explains, "racialist ideologies mainly served as a mask or pseudo-justification for the more fundamental goal of regime survival under conditions of sharp socioeconomic crisis and growing political opposition." Hutu extremists embarked upon a massive campaign to rid their country of the unwanted Other.

The preparations for genocide were politically designed. Preeminent was the existence of the *akazu* ("little house" in Kinyarwanda), a core group of influential politicians consisting of President Habyarimana and his immediate entourage. This included his wife (Agathe), his three brothers-in-law (Protee Zigiranyirazo, Seraphin Rwabukuma, and Elie Sagatwa), and a group of trusted advisors. Next down in the chain of command were various rural-based organizers, numbering anywhere from 200–300 (Lemarchand, 1999: 21). Structurally, other political bodies were formed to perpetuate ethnic hatred. One important development was the formation of the Coalition pour la Défense de la République, or CDR, a party that emerged as an offshoot of the MRND. The proclaimed purpose of the CDR was to defend the republican institutions that emanated from 1959. For the CDR, however, this goal translated into a vitriolic anti-Tutsi agenda. The CDR rejected the idea that Rwandans were one people and called for a new, pure Hutu nation (Melvern, 2004: 51).

The dissemination of Hutu extremist hate propaganda, which included the spreading of ethnic hatred and inciting ethnocide and genocide, began in earnest in 1990 with newspaper and magazine articles aimed at persuading Hutu intellectuals and other literate members of the population that their lives were menaced from inside and outside Rwanda by Tutsi infiltrators aided by Hutu supporters of democracy (Chalk, 1999: 187). One crucial outlet was the journal *Kangura* ("Wake Up" in Kinyarwanda).[2] In print from 1990 to 1993, the journal was started by Hassan Ngeze and financed by members of the MRND, the military, and intelligence agencies. Twice a month, between 1,500 and 3,000 copies were printed and distributed throughout the country. For those Rwandans who could not read, stories from the paper would be read aloud at public meetings and at rallies (Melvern, 2004: 49).

Given its strong connections to the military and intelligence community of Rwanda, the journal was able to print remarkably accurate reports of various happenings throughout the country. These "objective" and well-informed stories, therefore, provided greater weight—and legitimacy—for other, more sensationalistic reports on the evils of the Tutsi. Such a juxtaposition of "fact" with propaganda made it all the more easier for Hutu to instill constructed fears of ethnic discord (Melvern, 2004: 49).

Through the pages of *Kangura* and other outlets, the Tutsi were morally excluded from the spaces of Rwandan society. The spatial extent of this moral exclusion was exceptionally pervasive. It was not enough to confine Tutsi to a few select encampments within Rwanda. Instead, the entire country needed to be purged. Tutsi elimination was to be complete. This goal carried a strong demographic component. Population fears would become pivotal to the genocide that engulfed

Rwanda. For the ordinary rank-and-file Hutu peasant there was a feeling that there were too many people on too little land. With a reduction in Tutsi numbers, however, there would be more land for the Hutu victors (Prunier, 1995: 4).

The journal devoted pages to the promotion of interethnic hatred. One key document, and one that has been widely analyzed, is titled "Ten Commandments of the Hutu." It appeared in the December 1990 issue. As a manifesto for genocide, Power (2002: 338) compares these "Ten Commandments" to Hitler's Nuremberg Laws and the Bosnian Serbs' 1992 edicts. Significantly, the first three of the 10 commandments proscribed sexual relations between the two "races": "Every Hutu should know that a Tutsi woman, wherever she is, works for the interest of her Tutsi ethnic group. As a result, we shall consider a traitor any Hutu who: marries a Tutsi woman; befriends a Tutsi woman; employs a Tutsi woman as a secretary or a concubine"; "Every Hutu should know that our Hutu daughters are more suitable and conscientious in their role as woman, wife and mother of the family. Are they not beautiful, good secretaries and more honest?"; and "Hutu women, be vigilant and try to bring your husbands, brothers and sons back to reason" (quoted in Nowrojee, 1996). Other representations of Tutsi women were widely circulated, including the belief that Tutsi women were sexually promiscuous but forbidden from Hutu men; that Tutsi women were spies and saboteurs; and that Tutsi women were "weapons" of the Tutsi.

Kangura and other media outlets likewise ran fictitious articles. Documents allegedly captured from Tutsi rebels were widely circulated; these reports detailed Tutsi plans for genocide or assassination attempts. One such article, titled "17 Rules of the Tutsi" appeared in a 1993 issue of *Kangura* (Hintjens, 1999). According to this document, Tutsi were called to "identify all Hutu" and that the "Tutsi should kill all Hutu children" (Hintjens, p. 265). Such fabrications were used to spread fear among the Hutu population and to legitimate the violence that was being planned.

More effective than newspapers or magazines as a means of promoting hatred was the radio. Indeed, in countries where most of the population is illiterate, and television sets are rare, radio is the premier means of reaching the public (Chalk, 1999). During the summer of 1993 the privately owned Radio-Télévision Libre de Mille Collines (RTLM) began transmitting over the air waves. An "independent" radio station,

RTLM was in fact founded with the assistance of a wealthy businessman, Felicien Kabuga, whose daughter was married to a son of President Habyarimana, and by other members of the akazu. RTLM, furthermore, was aided by the staff and facilities of Radio Rwanda—the official government-owned station—and powered by electric generators at the Presidential Palace (Chalk, 1999: 188). To ensure widespread dissemination, moreover, the government made available hundreds of cheap, portable radios in the shops and marketplaces throughout the country. In 1992 radio ownership in Rwanda was estimated at 25 per 100 persons; for all of sub-Saharan Africa, ownership was just 13.5 per 100 persons (Chalk, 1999: 188).

With its disc jockeys, pop music, phone-in shows, and widespread use of street language, RTLM catered to the youth of Rwanda's society (Melvern, 2004: 53). Unlike the journal *Kangura*, RTLM made no attempt to carry factual reports, but instead provided a steady diet of commentaries and interviews testifying to the malevolence of the Tutsi people (Chalk, 1999; Melvern, 2004). According to Lemarchand (1999: 19), programs regularly created "an image of the Tutsi as both alien and clever, not unlike the image of the Jew in Nazi propaganda." Consequently, Tutsi were both disqualified from being members of the national community and identified as a threat to the unsuspecting Hutu (Lemarchand, 1999). Hintjens (1999: 267) furthermore notes that "such propaganda also had the desired effect of shifting blame for every Rwandan problem onto the RPF and the Rwandan [Tutsi], presumed to be its allies." She continues (p. 267) that similar to other minorities transformed into scapegoats, the Tutsi came to be held responsible not only for economic recession and political unrest, but even for their own victimization.

Thousands of young Hutu men, many of whom were jobless, responded to the politically disseminated messages of hatred and fear that enveloped the country. From this mass of discontented youth, a number of militias were formed. Under the guidance of the MRND, for example, a youth group, called the *Interahamwe*, was created. Translated as "Those who work closely together and who are united," the Interahamwe was structured as a nationwide self-defense force. Members were given military training, including the use of various weapons and explosives; they were also trained to kill at high speed (Melvern, 2004: 26).

Reports also surfaced, in late 1992, that the government had formed death squads. Modeled after the infamous death squads in Latin America, these were structured as small groups of well-trained operatives who would carry out assassinations and other forms of violence. They were managed by a secretive organization known as Le Réseau Zéro (Zero Network, or Network Zero). The name is perhaps in reference to the number of Tutsi its members intended to leave alive in Rwanda. The Zero Network was formed by high-ranking officials, many of whom had personal and familial ties with the president.

Hutu government officials also worked to arm their newly created militias. Melvern (2004: 56–57) notes that between 1990 and 1993, Rwanda—one of the world's poorest countries—became Africa's third largest importer of weapons and agricultural "tools." Resulting from an agreement dating to October 1990, Rwanda was subject to a Structural Adjustment Program and its economy was in the hands of the World Bank and the International Monetary Fund. Approximately US$216 million were earmarked for Rwanda, and of this, nearly half (US$100 million) was spent on weapons and "tools." By 1992 over 85 tons of munitions and 581,000 machetes were imported into Rwanda. Also purchased were razor blades, nails, hoes, axes, screwdrivers, scythes, saws, spades, knives, pliers, pincers, scissors, hammers, and shears (Melvern, p. 56). Throughout 1992 and 1993 these implements were stockpiled throughout the country.

For some, the purchases of the Rwandan government raised eyebrows. Five missions, in fact, were conducted by the World Bank between June 1991 and October 1993. Representatives, however, failed to find anything suspicious. When questions were raised as to why so much money was spent on weapons in light of widespread famine and deteriorating health and welfare systems, the president's response was that Rwanda needed to defend itself from foreign aggression (Melvern, 2004: 57).

The hate messages, militias, and weapons soon converged. Supposedly in response to a Tutsi plot to assassinate prominent Hutu leaders, the akazu issued an order to local authorities to engage in a special collective work session to "clear the brush," a euphemism for killing Tutsi (Melvern, 2004: 27). The RPF, in the minds of the Habyarimana clique, had to be destroyed as a political force. This meant the rejection of any kind of political compromise with the RPF, including ad hoc alliances with its representatives during the transition to multiparty democracy (Lemarchand, 1999: 20).

From late 1990 to 1993 militia forces and Hutu militants attacked and killed hundreds, if not thousands, of Tutsi in separate incidents (Ronayne, 2001: 155). On March 4, 1992, for example, approximately 300 people were brutally murdered by roving bands of Interahamwe militia. Pregnant women were disemboweled; the penises of men were cut off. Others were bound by hand and foot and thrown into rivers. Families were burned alive in their homes (Melvern, 2004; Prunier, 1995).

In response to the ongoing violence, the United Nations belatedly intervened to end the civil war and to create a viable multiethnic democracy (Ronayne, 2001). Signed on August 4, 1993, the Arusha Accords proposed a comprehensive settlement between the RPF and Habyarimana's government. This was to be a power-sharing compromise, including a new system of governance based on parliamentary procedures. Such a move would significantly reduce the presidential powers; the president, in effect, would become a figurehead, with most decision-making power being transferred to a prime minister. Other components of the accords established that the government would be based on political pluralism. As part of the power-sharing arrangement, the RPF would receive five cabinet seats out of 21, placing them on par with the MRND. The armed forces, likewise, would be integrated: 40 percent of all troops and 50 percent of the officer corps would consist of RFP elements (Lemarchand, 1999; Melvern, 2004). To facilitate these changes, the Arusha Accords set in place a transitional government that would include representatives of the RPF. A newly established U.N. Assistance Mission for Rwanda (UNAMIR) was charged with overseeing the implementation of the accords, while military observers from the Organization of African Union (OAU) were to monitor the cease fire.

Not surprisingly, the Arusha Accords were seen by many hardline Hutus as a betrayal. The CDR in particular accused the president of capitulating to the Tutsi and to international pressure. Habyarimana, of course, was a hardline Hutu extremist. However, following his acquiescence to the accords, perceptions changed and he was seen as a traitor to his people. Consequently, to derail the peace process, hardline Hutu extremists embarked on an even wider campaign of brutal terror. As

Lemarchand (1999: 21) concludes, the wanton killing of Tutsi civilians became the quickest and most "rational" way of eliminating all basis for compromise with the RPF.

GENOCIDE UNLEASHED

On the evening of April 6, 1994, a plane carrying President Habyarimana and his Burundian counterpart, President Ntariyamira, was hit by two surface-to-air missiles as it approached Kigali International Airport. The plane exploded and crashed in the garden of the presidential palace. Also killed were most of those responsible for the country's security, including Elie Sagatwa, head of presidential security, and army chief Nsabimana (Melvern, 2004: 133, 137). Even before details of the crash were reported, roadblocks had been established throughout the capital. What followed was a coordinated plan of attack, a campaign of murder that was intended to cleanse the country of unwanted elements.[3]

A series of planned assassinations began moments after the crash. Members of the Presidential Guard, on the basis of preestablished lists apparently prepared by Protais Zigiranyirazo and in the presence of Habyarimana's widow, hunted down and killed Tutsi and Hutu opposition leaders and other political allies of the RPF (Melvern, 2004: 278; see also Lemarchand, 1999; Prunier, 1995). Other "priority targets," including journalists, civil rights activists, lawyers, and intellectuals were executed. These targets were seen as potentially threatening to the Hutu extremists' geographical imagination of a postgenocidal society (Ronayne, 2001).

The planned annihilation of Tutsi and their Hutu supporters was not limited to individual bodies. Instead, the genocide was a collective endeavor, one intended to eliminate an entire social group. Hutu extremists mobilized the army and the many militias to take the killings to the cities and the countryside. The slaughter was promoted and aided by radio broadcasts. After the genocide began, broadcasts served to perpetuate and in fact coordinate the killings. When reports of Habyarimana's death were announced, these were accompanied with cries to "avenge the death of the president." By

May, as the genocide proceeded, RTLM was blatantly calling for the country to be completely cleansed of Tutsi (Ronayne, 2001: 157). To accomplish the killings, RTLM disc jockeys would broadcast information about specific "targets." Reports would contain information on where to find certain people. Names, addresses, and descriptions were announced; requests for resupplies of weapons were relayed. As Li (2002: 118) explains, it "goaded ordinary people into joining the killings—the most famous of its entreaties being the uncharacteristically blatant 'The graves are only half full! Who will help us to fill them?'" One broadcast told listeners: "You have missed some of the enemies.... Some are still alive. You must go back and finish them off" (Ronayne, 2001: 158).The radio, Melvern (2004: 208) concludes, became "the voice of genocide."

The ensuing genocide broadened and rapidly spread throughout Rwanda. Members of the Interahamwe and other militias canvassed the countryside under orders from their political superiors. Armed with machetes, rifles, grenades, or make-shift weapons, Hutu militia tracked down and killed Tutsi and Hutu moderates (Ronayne, 2001). These killings, moreover, followed a certain geographic "logic." In the rural areas, for example, for generations Tutsi and Hutu lived side by side, in similar huts, with no noticeable difference of economic level. And given the demographic ratio, each Tutsi household was usually neighbored by several Hutu families. Concealment of identity during the genocide, therefore, was virtually impossible: ethnic classification was public knowledge. Consequently, the targeting of Tutsi and moderate Hutu for death was easily accomplished (Prunier, 1995: 249).

In the cities people did not know each other. Mass violence therefore required a different strategy, an organizational plan that would facilitate the targeting of unwanted people. As Ronayne (2001: 158) writes, "To track down their victims, the killers and their leaders made use of election rolls, census figures, and national identification cards." Such practices speak volumes about the underlying population geography of Rwanda's genocide. Similar to the Phoenix Program in Vietnam, or the extensive use of autobiographies by the Khmer Rouge, population registers and other forms of bodily information were used as an extreme form of biopolitics.

THE EMBODIMENT OF RWANDA'S GENOCIDE

Geographers have made significant contributions to our understandings of the "body" and corporeal geographies (Longhurst, 1995, 1997, 2000, 2001). Drawing on a panoply of feminist and poststructuralist theorists, such as Iris Marion Young, Elizabeth Grosz, and Susan Bordo, a number of geographers have explored "how dominant cultures designate certain groups (elderly, homosexual, obese, female, ethnic minorities, and so on) as 'other.' Subordinate groups are defined by their bodies and according to norms that diminish and degrade them (for example, as ugly, loathsome, impure, sick and deviant)" (Longhurst, 2000: 8). The ongoing research of Robyn Longhurst, Steve Pile, Heidi Nast, Larry Knopp, Michael Brown, and Linda McDowell, among others, has significantly altered our conception (and perception) of bodies. This work has, in the words of Bordo (1995: 165), illuminated the ways in which the body is a "medium of culture." Furthermore, as Bordo (p. 165) continues, the body is seen not simply as a text of culture, but instead as a "direct locus of social control." Theoretically, this work resonates with emergent scholarship that has considered the corporeality of genocide.

The genocide in Rwanda was a spatial practice, designed and implemented to purify the country of a perceived Other. As such, the bodies of Tutsi and Hutu sympathizers became political and symbolic resources, texts upon which the akazu's geographical imagination were inscribed. The violence meted out on these bodies thus formed part of a ritual: it was both practical (from the genocides' leaders' perspective) and spectacular. The torture of bodies, and not simply the killing, was not an extreme expression of lawless rage, but rather a technique of disciplined terror directed against *individual bodies and collective populations*.

Foucault (1979: 33–34) writes that torture forms part of a ritual, a practice that includes two components. First, torture must mark the victim: it is intended to physically (as in mutilation) or symbolically (through the spectacle of pain and the display of bodies) brand the victim with guilt. However, it is not the individual bodies—those living people with names, families, and histories—that is most important, but rather what their bodies signify *in the minds of the perpetrators*. The torture and killing of a Tutsi body, from the perspective of the killer, was an act of purification, intended to eliminate a threatening social group as a collective. As Taylor (2002: 139) explains, the violence in Rwanda "followed a cultural patterning, a structured and structuring logic, as individual Rwandans lashed out against a perceived internal other who threatened, in their imaginary, both their personal integrity and the cosmic order of the state." Second, and related, the public torture and killing must be spectacular. Physical torture thus becomes an integral part of the ritual process intended to inculcate society's norms and values (Taylor, p. 141).

How was this manifested in the Rwandan genocide? Taylor (2002: 139) maintains that the brutal and horrific slaughter of Tutsi as sacrificial victims was "a ritual intended to purge the nation of 'obstructing beings,' as the threat of obstruction was imagined through a Rwandan ontology that situates the body politic in analogical relation to the individual human body." I find in Taylor's argument a compelling (albeit disturbing) understanding of torture as a physical and symbolic practice that both disciplines bodies and regulates populations.

Drawing on studies of health practices and popular medicine, Taylor (2002: 146 passim) argues that a basic metaphor underlies Rwandan conceptualizations of the body. These conceptualizations are

> characterized by an opposition between orderly states of humoral and other flows to disorderly ones. Analogies are constructed that take this opposition as their base and then relate bodily processes to those of social and natural life. In the unfolding of human and natural events, flow/blockage symbolism mediates between physiological, sociological, and cosmological levels of causality.

Similar to other studies in geography, Taylor (2002) finds the prevalence of bodily fluids as especially salient. Taylor (1992: 9–10) explains that fluid "substances are of interest for their movement; fluids circulate in an orderly fashion or they may be excessive or insufficient. In the simplest form of expression, substances are perceived to operate according to a dialectic of 'flow' versus 'blockage.'" Consequently, popular healing techniques attempt to restore bodily flows (for example, of blood, semen, breast milk, menstrual blood) that have been obstructed. These healing techniques, moreover, concentrate on particular sites of the body, including digestive tracts and reproductive organs. These metaphors hold not only for the "body" within Rwanda, but also for the "body politic" that is Rwanda.

In precolonial Rwanda, rituals of state were conducted under the aegis of the sacred king (*mwami*). Through a study of ritual texts, Taylor (2002: 153; see also Taylor, 1992, Chap. 1) identifies a recurrent preoccupation with maintaining orderly fluid flows and, implicitly, that of imaana. There are many translations of this term, usually in the form of "God" or "supreme being." However, *imaana* is also likened to a generalized creative or transformative force. Taylor (p. 153) explains that "gaining access to the powers of *imaana* and keeping the fluids of production, consumption, and fertility in movement were arguably the most important ritual functions of the Rwandan king (mwami). The mwami was the ultimate human guarantor of the fertility of bees (for honey), cattle, women, and land."

Concepts of sovereignty and authority were (and are) intimately connected through the body of the mwami. The mwami was "the kingdom's most giving or 'flowing being'; his body was a conduit" (Taylor, 2002: 154) for all that circulated within his domain. However, the mwami was not a passive entity, nor was he entirely benign. The mwami was directly responsible for the protection of his kingdom. The king, consequently, was as much a "blocking being" as a "flowing one." As an active agent, the mwami was possessive of the power of life and death over his subjects. He could reward or punish as he saw fit.

Typically, in precolonial Rwandan society, threats appeared in the form of individual bodies, namely, those of sorcerers or other malevolent beings. Not infrequently, these "dangers" were female figures. One myth, for example, tells of an old woman who sheltered, in her uterus, Death (who was being pursued by a mwami). Literally, in this narrative, Death is associated with beings (old women, or *agakeecuru*) whose fluids do not or no longer flow (that is, the old woman did not menstruate). Other myths include girls who had reached childbearing age but lacked breasts—girls who were called *impenebere*—and girls who had reached childbearing age but had not yet menstruated—girls who were called *impa*. In both of these cases, the girls were seen as "blocking beings"; they constituted a threat to the normal and beneficial flows of the physical and spiritual worlds and were potential sources of misfortune to the kingdom. Consequently, both types of girls could be "legitimately" sacrificed, as one of the mwami's responsibilities was to eliminate beings who posed a threat to "flow" (Taylor, 2002: 155). Taylor (1992: 37) elaborates that "usually they were taken just beyond the limits of Rwanda and then killed; their blood as it flowed upon the earth was thought to vitiate the fertility of the foreign land, as well as bring it other forms of misfortune."

Although many concepts of "flow" and "blockage" fell into disuse throughout the decades of colonialism, there is a continuity of certain key elements. For example, one may see in the actions of President Habyarimana a continuation of the role of the mwami. All forms of population movement (flows) were strictly regulated by high-ranking officials; labor policies and agricultural quotas were rigidly set in place, designed (ostensibly) to increase the fertility of Rwanda's lands. However, previous interpretations of evil—the "blocking beings"—were radically altered. Whereas in precolonial Rwanda the image of the "blocking being" was confined to a limited number of individuals, such as the *impa* and the *impenebere*, during colonialism, as privileges were awarded by the colonial rulers on the basis of Hutu or Tutsi identity, entire groups of people (populations) could be thought of as obstructions to the polity as a whole (Taylor, 2002: 170). Throughout the Habyarimana regime, the Tutsi were increasingly constructed as foreign elements—"blocking beings"—who obstructed the beneficial flow of Rwandan society. Consequently, as dehumanized and impure Others, their elimination was necessary to allow the flow of imaana.

During the genocide, Taylor (2002: 158) argues that the killers and "torturers manifested a certain proclivity to employ violent methods with specific forms. These forms betrayed a preoccupation with the movement of persons and substances and with the canals, arteries, and conduits along which persons and substances flow: rivers, roadways, pathways, and even the conduits of the human body, such as the reproductive and digestive systems." In short, the genocide exhibited a spatiality that connected the body and the body politic with the physical geography of Rwanda. This is seen in three key areas: rivers, roadblocks, and bodies.

In Rwanda's history, rivers have held symbolic importance. In a kingship ritual known as the "Path of the Watering," for example, Taylor (1992: 40–49) details how the Nyabugogo and Nyabarongo Rivers served to revivify the magicoreligious potency of the dynasty by recycling and reintegrating the ancestral benevolence of deceased kings.[4] Such imagery was likewise prevalent in the genocide. Recall the earlier quote by Mugesera, and in particular his statement that Tutsi belonged in Ethiopia and that they were to be thrown into the northward-flowing Nyabarongo River. On the one hand, this imagery is similar to that of the violence inflicted on the Vietnamese by Lon Nol's soldiers in Cambodia: the Mekong River would carry the bloated corpses of the Khmer enemy back to its homeland. Likewise, the Nyabarongo River would carry Rwanda's ancestral enemies back to their homeland. Taylor (2002: 159) argues that the Nyabarongo, as the means by which Tutsi will be removed from Rwanda, serves an important ritualistic function, that of purifying the nation of its internal "foreign" minority. In short, he concludes that "Rwanda's rivers became part of the genocide by acting as the body politics' organs of elimination, in a sense 'excreting' its hated internal other" (p. 159).

A second component entails *Gusiba Inzira* (or "Blocking the Path"). A defining feature of the Rwandan genocide, presented in the 2005 film *Hotel Rwanda*, is that of the roadblock. Indeed, Rwanda's roadblocks are as horrifically iconic as are the showers and ovens of the Holocaust, or S-21 of the Cambodian genocide. During the Rwanda genocide, the most frequent loci of execution were roadblocks. Manned by Rwandan government forces, Interahamwe, militia, communal police, or simply gangs of criminals, these were sites of intense cruelty. Victims were slashed with machetes or bludgeoned with nail-studded clubs. Accounts from survivors and other eyewitnesses relate how some victims paid for a quick death by a bullet (Melvern, 2004; Prunier, 1995; Taylor, 2002).

Roadblocks were ubiquitous, particularly in the cities and towns. In part, these barriers served to prevent the escape of terrified Tutsi and Hutu. However, these also served to monitor and regulate the population of Rwanda. It was at these barriers that people were forced to confirm their ethnic identity, to disclose their identification cards, and to await judgment. For Taylor (2002: 161–163), though, these barriers also served a symbolic function; roadblocks became part of a ritualized performance that extended far beyond any "strategic" function. Roadblocks, for example, were pervasive, often located just a few hundred yards from one another. From a tactical sense, such a redundancy of roadblocks was counterproductive. The imposition of so many barriers diverted manpower, which was needed in the ongoing military operations against the Rwandan Patriot Front rebels. Symbolically, however, these physical barriers may be seen as "ritual and liminal spaces where 'obstructing beings' were to be obstructed in their turn and cast out of the nation" (Taylor, 2002: 161).

As sites of ritualized torture, roadblocks facilitated the normalization of killings and, in fact, generated a culture of impunity. For example, accounts indicate that many Hutu who were stopped at the roadblocks were required to kill captive Tutsi before proceeding. Taylor (2002: 161) notes that such practices may seem unnecessary and sadistic, but he emphasizes that these forced killings performed an important psychological function. By forcing Hutu to engage in such acts, and especially those Hutu who were perhaps morally opposed to the slaughter, a widespread culture of impunity was constructed. From the point of view of the genocide's perpetrators, Taylor (pp. 161–162) explains, the transference of killing removed

> the ambivalence of the sacrificial act and the stigma of the sacrificer/executioner by passing these on to everyone. The ritual obfuscated the boundary between *genocidiares* and those who were otherwise innocent Hutu. Not only were Tutsi and Hutu "traitors" being killed at the barriers; innocent Hutu were also being forced to become morally complicit in the genocide.

A culture of impunity thus spatially expanded at each roadblock, an expansion that permitted mass violence to continue unabated. Symbolically, therefore, the physical roadblocks became conduits for the unfettered flow of genocide.

A final component to consider is that of the body as conduit. This is seen, first, in the literal impediment of bodies through violence. Taylor (2002: 163) explains that "if the movement of people could be obstructed with barriers, it could also be hindered by directly attacking the body." After the genocide, thousands of corpses were discovered that had had their Achilles tendons severed or their legs and feet slashed. Taylor (p. 164) concedes that this technique of cruelty has a certain logic in that in the presence of a large number of potential victims, too many to kill at once, militia might immobilize fleeing victims by a quick machete blow to one or both of the Achilles tendons. The killers can then proceed at a more leisurely pace in their executions. However, surveyors of the carnage discovered that many victims, including the elderly, infants, or infirm, were in no position to flee, and yet still had their Achilles tendons slashed. Given such evidence, Taylor (p. 164) suggests that these violent acts carried a symbolic logic, one of "blocking the path." He explains that such an act inscribes on the victim's body the killers' intentionality. By physically and ritualistically "blocking the path" of threatening beings, the perpetrators of the genocide were able to claim and assert their power over the Other.

Second, many embodied techniques of torture were directed toward the digestive tracts and reproductive systems. One particularly gruesome practice, for example, was that of impalement. Throughout the genocide, Tutsi men were impaled from anus to mouth with wooden or bamboo poles, or metal spears, while Tutsi women were impaled from vagina to mouth (Taylor, 2002: 165). Archival sources indicate that in precolonial and even in colonial times, impalement was used as form of torture directed against cattle thieves. Executioners would insert a wooden stake into a thief's anus and drive it through his body cavity until it exited his neck or mouth. Once impaled, the pole with the victim would then be stuck into the earth and left standing for days. This form of torture provided a visual warning and possibly worked to deter other potential cattle thieves. However, the spectacle of torture also carried another message. Within Rwandan society, cattle are important material resources but they also are important as a means of commemorating the most significant social transitions and relations, such as marriage. Consequently, diverting socially appropriate flows of cattle vis-à-vis thievery is a way of "blocking the path" between individuals and groups. The theft of cattle threatened the conduits of social exchange (Taylor, 2002: 166). By analogy, the impalement of bodies, and hence the literal blockage of bodily functions with a pole or a spear emerged as a symbolically appropriate form of torture and punishment (pp. 168–169). During the Rwandan genocide, the Tutsi (similar to cattle thieves or other malevolent bodies) exerted their power, their threat, on the social group not so much by what they did as by the inherent qualities that they supposedly embodied. Tutsi were constructed as "blocking beings," the nemeses of Rwanda tradition that threatened socially appropriate relations. Taylor (p. 168) concludes that Tutsi "were obstructors of the cosmic unity of the nation as that unity was imagined by the Hutu extremist elite: a purified nation with a purified, reified 'Hutu culture' expunged of all elements of 'Tutsi culture' and rid of all who would resist the encompassing powers of the state." In this manner, the "torturers not only killed their victims; they transformed their bodies into powerful signs that resonated with a Rwandan habitus even as they improvised upon it and enlarged the original semantic domain of the associated meanings to depict an entire ethnic group as enemies of the Hutu state." As Taylor (p. 171) observes, "Killing one's adversaries while communicating powerful messages about them and oneself are not mutually exclusive."

One important message that permeated the Rwandan genocide hinged on the sexual politics of sovereignty. It is to this last component I now turn.

THE BIOPOLITICS OF GENOCIDAL RAPE

> Don't tell me that you won't have tasted a Tutsi woman.
> Take advantage of it, because they'll be killed tomorrow.
> —JEAN-PAUL AKAYESU[5]

Between April 1993 and June 1994 Jean-Paul Akayesu served as *bourgmestre* (mayor) of Taba commune in the Gitarmam prefecture of Rwanda. Married, with five children, Akayesu previously worked as a teacher and then as an inspector of schools. He entered politics in 1991 and was a founding member of the Mouvement Démocratique Républicain (MDR). In 1998, after a 17-month trial that resulted in four thousand pages of transcripts and 125 evidentiary documents, Akayesu was found guilty of aiding and abetting acts of sexual violence by allowing them to take place in his presence in or near the municipal building and by verbally encouraging the commission of those acts (Magnarella, 2002: 315, 320).

Much has been written on the trial of Akayesu (Brunet and Helal, 1998; Karagiannakis, 1999; Magnarella, 2002). His indictment and conviction marked a significant turning point in international justice, not least of which is that the justices of the International Criminal Tribunal for Rwanda (ICTR) established that acts of sexual violence constituted genocide, provided that these acts were committed with the specific intent to destroy, in whole or in part, a particular group. In the Akayesu judgment, the trial chamber "recognized that rape was an integral component in a pattern of behavior directed at Tutsi women and designed to ensure the maximum suffering before they were killed. Accordingly, this form of violence preceded death and could be characterised as one of its mediums" (Karagiannakis, 1999: 487). Furthermore, the trial chamber found that rape is a constituent act of genocide in that it causes serious bodily or mental harm to members of the group and should be included with other acts of mental or physical torture, inhumane or degrading treatment and persecution (Karagiannakis, 1994: 487).

From the standpoint of population geography, the establishment of sexual violence as a genocidal act warrants closer attention. Sex and sexual violence have emerged as "a means of access both to the life of the body and the life of the species" (Foucault, 1990: 146). Furthermore, it has become "the theme of political operations, economic interventions (through incitements to or curbs on procreation), and ideological campaigns for raising standards of morality and responsibility: it was put forward as the index of a society's strength, revealing of both its political energy and its biological vigor." Recent events provide grim testimony to the politics of sex and to sexual violence, all of which reinforce Foucault's (p. 146) broader argument that there exists "a whole series of different tactics that combine in varying proportions the objective of disciplining the body and that of regulating populations."

Historically, rape and other forms of sexual violence have long been (mis)characterized and dismissed by military and political leaders as a private crime or the result of the unfortunate behavior of a few renegade soldiers. Rape has been naturalized as "just part of war" or even of genocide (Nowrojee, 1996). Hynes (2004: 432), among others, notes that "data on wartime morbidity and mortality is collected by the military and includes primarily the direct effects of combat and combat-related exposures on combatants and less frequently on civilians." Moreover, "Rape and sexual exploitation in war, on the other hand, have been systematically disregarded (even when documented) as war atrocities and crimes until the recent revelations of the genocidal rape of Muslim women during the conflict in the former Yugoslavia and of Tutsi women in Rwanda." Hynes (p. 433) concludes that "because military data gatherers have ignored military sexual exploitation and violence against women, a substantial portion of the harm of war to women and girls has been overlooked and, thus, uncounted within the 'official' tally of war casualties."

More properly, rape should been viewed as a deliberate instrument of both direct and structural violence; it is a technique of terror that inflicts both physical and psychological trauma. Furthermore, it carries a crucial symbolic component. In many societies, women are not equal to the nation (or society), but symbolic of it (Domosh and Seager, 2001). In part, this symbolism derives from the so-called natural role of women: to bear children (Yuval-Davis, 1996: 17). As Booth (2006: 151) argues, across disciplines and in many different struggles feminist scholars and activists have demonstrated that nationalist ideologies as well as material processes of state formation depend fundamentally on elites' ability to control which citizens have how many babies and whether they have them or will be allowed to prevent themselves from having them. According to Eisenstein (2007: 28) bodily violation—including rape and genital mutilation—destroys established gendered stereotypes. In particular, a "violated female is no longer a woman that a man wishes to lay claim to. In war [or genocidal] rape, females are reduced to their patriarchal definition as a body vessel and also denied the status of privileged womanhood. In war rape the woman is totally occupied.... " Women's bodies become battlegrounds upon which discourses of moral inclusion and exclusion are contested. As a political/military strategy, rape is intended to degrade not just individual women, but to strip humanity from a larger group. It is an extreme form of direct violence that serves another purpose, namely, to further marginalize and dehumanize a population.

The effects of war- or genocide-related rape, furthermore, continue long after the violent act itself. Rape may trigger cultural gender-based norms, for example, that perpetuate discrimination against women. In some societies, women who are raped are ostracized, isolated, and marginalized. Survivors of rape, moreover, may suffer recurrent health problems, including sexually transmitted diseases and HIV/AIDs. Also, rape serves to affect future generations. Babies born of war- or genocide-related rape are often called "children of hate" or "children of bad memories." According to Rehn and Sirleaf (2002: 16),

> In Liberia and Sierra Leone thousands of babies were born to women and girls who had been abducted and forced to accompany combatants into the bush, where many gave birth without medical help. Up to 20,000 women are believed to have been raped during the fighting in Kosovo, and many of them bore children. In one month alone, January 2000, the International Red

Cross estimated that 100 babies conceived in rape were born in Kosovo, and that many other women gave birth to children born of rape but decided not to identity them as such.

In Rwanda, an estimated 2,000 to 5,000 of these births resulted from the genocide (Nowrojee, 1996).

Rape, within the context of war or genocide, is both a discipline of bodies and a regulation of populations. This form of biopolitics, subsequently, is used to perpetuate a morally exclusive geographical imagination of territorial integrity. Of the many crucial issues that demand the attention of population experts, one would be hard-pressed not to consider war- and genocidal-rape as one of the most important. And yet, as Hynes (2004: 437) finds, "until very recently, little has been known about the prevalence and scale of sexual abuse of women by men in war." Only within the past three decades has "a growing number of women journalists, lawyers, physicians, and human rights activists ... uncovered and exposed the war crimes against women, namely rape, abduction, sexual torture, and trafficking for prostitution" (p. 437).

In the late 1980s, Hynes (2004: 432) notes, the term "genocidal rape" was coined to describe the depth of men's inhumanity to women in war when Serbs—though in actuality all sides—intentionally detained and raped Muslim women in camps to destroy them and their people by sexually "contaminating" the women. In practice, however, rape as an instrument of war and terror has a longer history (Brownmiller, 1975; Milillo, 2006). Early accounts are found in ancient Greece and during the Crusades. More recent studies have documented widespread rape and sexual abuse during World Wars I and II, the Vietnam War, and Bangladesh's war of independence. More recently, in 2002 Elizabeth Rehn and Ellen Johnson Sirleaf released a report commissioned by the United Nations Development Fund for Women. Based on interviews with women in 14 countries throughout Europe, Asia, Africa, and the Middle East, Rehn and Sirleaf found that women were raped and tortured in front of their husbands and relatives; pregnant women were beaten to induce miscarriages, or had their wombs punctured with guns; rifles were forced into vaginas; and women were forced into rape camps and subjected to gang rapes. Renh and Sirleaf (2002: 11) describe how "women are physically and economically forced or left with little choice but to become sex workers or to exchange sex for food, shelter, safe passage or other needs; their bodies become part of a barter system, a form of exchange that buys the necessities of life." They conclude that government officials, aid workers, civilian authorities, and their own families have all been complicit in using women in this way.

In Rwanda, patterns of sexual violence clearly reveal that acts of rape and sexual mutilation—directed at women as well as at men—were not by-products of the killings. Neither were these acts opportunistic assaults. Instead, these horrific bodily acts were deliberate. As militia killed and pillaged, some members often singled out women to be held for their personal sexual service. At times, the perpetrators locked women in their own homes or in the captors' homes; such women were often called "women of the ceiling" because their captors hid them in the crawl spaces between the roof and the ceiling to prevent their being discovered and killed by others (Nowrojee, 1996).

Rape was carried out with the aim of eradicating the Tutsi. Many survivors, in fact, reported that the attackers enunciated their intent to destroy them and their people during the attacks (Baines, 2003; Nowrojee, 1996). Often rape was accompanied or followed by mutilation of the sexual organs, or of features held to be characteristic of the Tutsi ethnic groups. Such acts included pouring boiling water into the vagina, opening of the womb to cut out an unborn child before killing the mother; cutting off breasts, slashing the pelvic area, and mutilating vaginas (Nowrojee, 1996). Women, of course, were not the only targets for sexual mutilation and violence. Hutu perpetrators frequently emasculated Tutsi males, even those too young to reproduce, by slashing off their penises.

The practice of rape, and the sexual mutilation of both men and women, exhibits "a preoccupation with the reproductive system, and specifically with parts of the body that produce fertility fluids" (Taylor, 2002: 168). For Taylor, such violence combined both symbolic and pragmatic functions. On the one hand, these acts served to destroy the future capacity of both individual bodies and the collective population to reproduce. On the other hand, symbolically, the violent acts transformed their victims' bodies into the equivalent of "blocked beings." Consequently, those who were raped and mutilated embodied the superiority and sovereignty of Hutu over Tutsi. In Rwanda, this right over life and death was applied to future generations through the mutilation, rape, and murder of women; the evisceration of pregnant women; the slaughter of the unborn and the newborn; and the killing of children. We see, with the deliberate infliction of pain and suffering on pregnant women, a further symbolic ritual associated with Rwanda's genocide. As the work of Robyn Longhurst and Joyce Davidson details, pregnancy and pregnant bodies are viewed as disruptive and transgressive. Longhurst (2001: 55), for example, notes that "pregnant women undergo a bodily process that transgresses the boundary between inside and outside, self and other, one and two, subject and object." Within Rwanda, the wombs of women became contested sites between Hutu superiority and Tutsi inferiority.

These horrific acts targeted at reproduction of a society certainly, but genocidal rape and other forms of sexual violence directed against women in Rwanda (and some men) was also an exercise of power: a symbolic attempt on behalf of the perpetrators to construct their society anew. As Taylor (2002: 172) concludes, during the chaotic political time of transition, following the death of Habyarimana, these violent and inhumane acts "made symbolic sense during the 1994 violence to make the claim of power—when power was no longer clearly defined, no longer in the hands of a single hierarchical authority, when power was diffuse and in the streets—by eliminating all who would subvert the encompassing order of the Rwandan state." Consequently, this "entailed obstructing the obstructors, sacrificing the malevolent 'blocking beings' in the nation's midst, as these latter represented both the potential pathology to individuals and a threat to the collective order" (p. 172).

CONCLUSIONS

In 1978 Michel Foucault (1990: 137) suggested that "wars are no longer waged in the name of a sovereign who must be defended; they are waged on behalf of the existence of everyone; entire populations are mobilized for the purpose of wholesale slaughter in the name of life necessity: massacres have become vital." His thesis was based on his argument that, historically, a privilege accorded to a sovereign power was the right to decide life and death. In precolonial Rwanda, for example, this is seen in the mwami's right to "block the path" of those who threatened the flow of society. Such "obstructing beings" could take the form of prepubescent girls or cattle thieves. Furthermore, according to Foucault, if a sovereign was threatened by external enemies, he or she could wage war and thereby require his or her subjects to take part in the defense of their homeland. The ability to wage war, therefore, was an exercise of indirect power over life and death. A sovereign (generally) does not specifically order his or her subjects to their death, but must acknowledge that these decisions might result in a loss of life.

Foucault suggests that a transformation of these mechanisms of power occurred. He identifies (based on his reading of European history, but a trend, I believe, that is applicable elsewhere) a shift in the right of death. Now wars are fought for social bodies, collectivities, nation-states. Foucault (1990: 137) argues that "it is as managers of life and survival, of bodies and the race, that so many regimes have been able to wage so many wars, causing so many men [and women] to be killed." The genocide in Rwanda was a planned campaign to rid the country of a group perceived as threatening, as outsiders. The survival of a prosperous civilization, it was claimed by Hutu extremists, was at risk. At stake was the biological existence of a (constructed) population. Genocide emerged as a *legitimate* strategy to provide for the Hutu population through the annihilation of Tutsi bodies.

5
POPULATION AND PEACE EDUCATION

> Contemporary students of human geography surely cannot avoid the impression that the most exciting developments in the discipline focus on new understandings of why geography matters, prompted by theoretical concerns such as those found in the post-colonial or feminist literature. Even if their interest lies in subject matter—such as birth, death or migration—that population geography has traditionally claimed, the questions they ask and the approaches they adopt may encourage them to identify with other adjectival geographies.
> —Elspeth Graham and Paul Boyle (2001: 390)

> What seems to be emerging is a field that lacks a single core, a clear hierarchy, an agreed-upon set of methods, or theories, or ontology, but which nevertheless seeks knowledge that informs society about the intersections between population and geography.... [Population geography's] institutional label is still alive ... but it is increasingly appearing as an aesthetic, "made" by those interested in producing and acquiring knowledge (scholars, states, communities, activists), made by its past reputation and space–environment–place "sound," made by its representation in the media and civic society and made by its relation to the ongoing institutionalization of geography within academia.
> —Adrian Bailey (2005: 166)

The motivation for this book lies in the on again, off again debate that has permeated population geography for nearly two decades: from Allan Findlay and Elspeth Graham's (1991) initial challenge for population geography at the millennium, through White and Jackson's (1995) momentous call to retheorize the field. Mostly, though, I find myself responding to Findlay's (2003: 177–178) proposal that population geography should contribute to holding to account states and other organizations claiming to govern populations in an ethical and equitable fashion.

This book is also a product of a particular moment—a particular confluence of violent geographies. During the writing of this book, an illegal war continues to ravage what once was Iraq. The toll on the people of Iraq has been catastrophic. Between the United States-led invasion and occupation of Iraq on March 20, 2003, through July 2006, for example, there have been approximately 655,000 "excess" deaths in the country as a result of the war; of these deaths, over 90 percent are due to direct violence, the most common cause being gunfire (Burnham, Lafta, Doocy, and Roberts, 2006: 1421). This politicomilitary project itself followed years of economic sanctions (especially during 1994–1999) that adversely affected the peoples of Iraq. Writing in *The Lancet*, for example, Mohamed Ali and Iqbal Shah (2000: 1851) note that infant mortality rose from 47 per 1,000 live births during the period 1984–1989 to 108 per 1,000 in the period 1994–1999, and under-5 mortality from 56 to 131 per 1,000 live births (see also Aziz, 2003; Kapp, 2003).

People also continue to die in Darfur as the international community once again turns a blind eye toward genocide; perhaps upward of 400,000 people may have died in the region since 2003. Additional millions—perhaps 4 million—continue to suffer (and possibly die) from direct violence, starvation, and disease in internally displaced person (IDP) camps in Darfur and neighboring Chad.

Apart from war and genocide, millions of people on all continents barely survive, living in horrific conditions of abject poverty, governmental repression, and multinational exploitation. We need, as Fisher (2001: 25) argues, "to change social structures that disempower and marginalize certain groups of people and to radically question the meaning and application of basic democratic values."

In response to these two motivations, I have attempted to provide a radical alternative to population geography, one that places peace and social justice at the forefront of our endeavors. Within *War, Violence, and Population* I have argued for a greater engagement with social justice and the building of peace through education. I have sketched just one approach, one directed toward violent injustices as manifested in war and genocide. No claims are made for a universality of appeals to justice; I recognize that social justice is found in the particularity of the political. Instead, I have sought to promote discussion, to encourage appeals, to enlarge the forum, to redirect population geography toward a path of peace education.

Through three cases studies—the Vietnam War and the genocides in Cambodia and Rwanda—I have detailed how bodies are spatially disciplined and populations are regulated. Furthermore, I emphasized the production of knowledge-claims that legitimize and justify the perpetuation of violence. In all three cases, the perpetrators of violence enacted specific representations of space, geographical imaginations, that were used in connection with various spatial practices to subjugate and morally exclude people constructed as the Other. For what purpose were people morally excluded and, in many instances, murdered? David Keen (2006: 160) writes that "Many catastrophes—across a wide range of cultures and time-periods—have brought forth a call for explanations and for associated 'purifications'." In Vietnam, the United States unleashed a massive, technologically frightening arsenal to bomb the Vietnamese into submission. The goal, ostensibly, was to rid the region, and the world, of communism. In actuality, the militarized subjugation of Vietnam's people and landscape was designed to facilitate the accumulation of capital and to support a military–industrial complex that profited through the killing of people. In both Cambodia and Rwanda, a select few sought to annihilate people who were constructed as threats to a conceived utopia. For the Khmer Rouge, an assortment of social groups were produced—new people, traitors and spies, intellectuals, and foreigners—and subsequently excluded from society. For the Hutu extremists, it was the supposedly alien Tutsi, a group that was conceived as being a primordial Other, an illegal invader and occupier of a Hutu homeland.

Howard Zinn (2005: 54) contends that "we have learned from historical experience that people can change their opinions dramatically if they get new information." This is why the media and educational institutions are so contested. These are not only sites of information dissemination, but also of information production. In order to rid the world of war and genocide, we need "to expose the motives of our political leaders, point out their connections to corporate power, show how huge profits are being made out of death and suffering" (Zinn, p.

55). We need to demonstrate how acts of violence—war, genocide, and other forms—are part and parcel of wider networks of capital circulation and identity formation. We need, following Zinn (pp. 55–56), to teach history—and geography—to see how war and violence

> corrupts everyone involved in it, how the so-called good side soon behaves like the bad side.... [W]e have to show, in the most graphic way ... the effect of war on human beings. And how wars, even when they are over, leave a legacy of death in the form of land-mines.... We need to point to the reckless waste of the world's wealth in war and militarism, while a billion people in the world are without clean water, and a hundred million suffer from AIDS and other deadly illnesses.... A fraction of the money spent on war and preparations for war would save the lives of tens of millions of people.... We need to hold out a vision of a different world, in which national borders are erased and we are truly one human family, in which we treat children all over the world as our children, which means we could never engage in war.

As Calderwood (2003: 305) concludes, "When change does finally come about, it is often because public sentiment has moved, so that formerly radical ideas [such as peace] seem reasonable and just and former norms [such as war and violence] seem unjust and in need of revision."

Population geography needs to be reoriented. Adrian Bailey (2005: 193) is correct when he suggests that this reorientation "involves moving beyond method and a concern with technique, with a desire to articulate new visions of alternatives futures." Required is an explicit attempt to promote an alternative future that is predicated on social justice and the building of peace.

In most Western-based societies, peace has been presented as the opposite of war: this is a product of binary thinking that obfuscates as much as it illuminates. Indeed, even a cursory examination of the discursive history of peace illustrates a more complex concept. For example, the "promotion of peace" suggests an attitude that human beings should resolve conflicts without resorting to violence. Parents may teach their children, for example, that the best way to resolve disputes is through discussion and not physical force. Peace, furthermore, as the opposite of war, does not necessarily entail a "just" or "benign" society. As Harris and Morrison (2003: 12) explain, a state not at war may not be peaceful. Indeed, societies may exhibit high crime rates or high infant mortality rates. People may live under oppressive conditions sanctioned by a totalitarian government. Governmental regulations may restrict population movements, reproductive decisions, and choice of marriage partners—conditions that permit forms of structural violence. To many observers such a society would hardly constitute a "peaceful" existence, even if war was not underway.

Peace educators, in general, distinguish between "positive" and "negative" connotations of peace. In its negative form, peace implies the stopping of some existing or pending violence. Positive forms of peace, conversely, follow standards of social justice and involve concrete human actions—processes—concerned with building up a just and humane world (Vriens, 1997: 28). Social justice, therefore, is not to be confused with theories of justice. The latter, as Rickie Sanders (2006: 53) explains, seek to derive salience from a narrow range of fundamental principles that apply to all or most societies regardless of concrete social relations. In a perfect world, she writes, a theory of justice is possible. In our less-than-perfect world, however, such a theory is impossible. Social justice, conversely, *is* situated in concrete social and political practices and strives to be emancipatory. Sanders (p. 53) elaborates that social justice "is contingent on everyday meanings to which people attach importance and which to them appear unproblematic. This everydayness and ordinariness gives social justice a political and mobilizing power."

Social justice often entails a conception of what is fair and unfair, and of the social arrangements necessary to ensure that members of society are treated justly (Nagel, 1999: 133). This understanding, however, is often reduced to that of distributive justice: of the morally proper distribution of benefits and burdens among society's members. David Smith (2000: 24) explains that "a central issue in distributive justice is how to justify differential treatment, or how to identify the differences among people which are relevant to the particular attribute(s) to be distributed." However, a distributive understanding of social justice is often individualistic and thus has less relevance for social groups seeking to eradicate collective injustices (that is, structural violence); furthermore, given its emphasis on material goods, such an understanding tends to neglect the distribution of "nonmaterial goods" such as respect, opportunity, and integrity (Sanders, 2006: 53).

Consequently, as Iris Young (1990) counters, distributive justice is insufficient. Rather, one needs to include questions of oppression and domination. These, rather than a limited discussion based on distribution, must be the primary terms for conceptualizing *injustice*. As such, the structures responsible for inequality—including forms of direct and structural violence—may be more effectively dismantled, thus contributing to a broader understanding of social justice that includes not just issues of distribution, but also both self-development and self-determination. Pursuing this line of reasoning, Don Mitchell (2003: 30) contends that "attention to just distribution within its geographical contexts demands struggle toward the transformation of those geographical contexts." In other words, the structures and institutions responsible for oppressive and exploitative inequalities must be addressed. Obvious examples include various state apparatuses, including both military and intelligence agencies. Less obvious are the taken-for-granted, everyday systems that *discipline* and *regulate* our lives: identification cards, censuses, marriage licenses. In Vietnam, we have seen how statistical studies and field surveys were used to spatially constrain and control innocent people, or how empirical-based studies on the effectiveness of cluster bombs were used to strike terror in the lives of men, women, and children long after the initial air attacks were conducted. In both Cambodia and Rwanda, we have seen how the construction and classification of peoples into various groups meant life or death. Repeatedly, violent practices were enabled through the structural and institutional promotion of biological difference.

Mitchell (2003: 32) explains that "both oppression and domination are exercised through difference: it is difference that is oppressed and it is differentially situated actors who dominate. Autonomy—the freedom to be who one is—requires not just the recognition of difference but also its social promotion." This is where peace education enters into the process. As Caroline Nagel (1999: 140) writes, defining and achieving social justice is a contentious matter; justice emerges from debate and conflict. In other words, justice is a political concept, and the forums in which politics take place, for example, university classrooms, are of critical importance.

Recognition of the contingency and contentiousness of social justice and the promotion of peace, however, broaches an additional concern. If social justice is socially contextual, are not the meanings of "just" constantly contested? Such debates usually center on the (false) dichotomy between universality and particularity. Harvey (1996), for example, argues that to assert that a situation is unjust presupposes that there are some universally agreed-upon norms as to what we do or ought to mean by the concept of social justice. He is partly right. As Young (1998) explains, appeals to justice and claims of injustice are not a result; they are rather the starting point of a certain kind of debate. If we were to claim the existence of a (set of) predetermined, all-encompassing universal right(s), or even justice, then who would decide? Those stakeholders with the most resources? Could such an exercise possibly be objective? I think not.

There is no escaping the "fact" that *peace* and *social justice* are discourses; these are concepts—signifiers—with multiple and contested meanings. To invoke the language of justice and injustice is to make a claim; this is a political process. Here, I follow Jenny Edkin's (1999) distinction between "politics" and "political." For her, *politics* includes elections, political parties, the doings of governments, the state apparatus, treaties, international agreements, diplomacy, and so forth. However, what gets to be counted as "politics" is not predetermined; it is the result of contestation. What gets to be counted as "politics" is, in fact, part of the *political*. The "political" therefore encompasses the establishment of that very social order that sets out a particular historically and geographically specific account of what counts as politics; this also defines other areas of social life as "not politics." The political, furthermore, is not limited to the grand moments of openness or undecidability that arise in between established social systems, where the whole system of legitimacy previously in place has been effectively challenged and a new one not yet installed. The political also arises in the undecidability that is found in every moment of decision. The act of decision is a matter of a specific historical and geographical moment; it cannot be justified by an appeal to a general law (that is, universal human rights). The political, therefore, comprises in this sense an interminable process of decision making, of traversing the undecidable. So too with questions of social justice. It is a claim, a political process, a contested decision.

The lessons of Democratic Kampuchea are especially relevant. The Khmer Rouge justified their actions and condoned the death of millions of their own citizens. These deaths occurred via both direct violence (for example, murder and execution) and structural violence (for example, starvation, inadequate health facilities). And those spatial practices that permitted such violence—confinement, marital regulations, relocation, torture—were justified and legitimated in terms of promoting a just and egalitarian society. Ironically, the Khmer Rouge claimed to establish a universal understanding of right and wrong: all people were to be equal and the distribution of goods was to be just and equal. And here again lies the issue, and the fallacy, of claims for a universal human rights. Who decides? In Cambodia, the Khmer Rouge defined their understanding of a universal human right and approximately 2 million people died as a result. In Vietnam, the United States operated with a particular understanding of human rights, namely, the superiority of capitalism and democracy. Men like Richard Nixon, William Westmoreland, and Walt Rostow legitimated the killing of Vietnamese—both those labeled combatants and those labeled noncombatants—as a means of promoting world peace through the eradication of communism. How many Vietnamese died as a result of American actions promoting these supposedly universal values and rights? These are but two examples of the dangers that follow when an institution champions a *particular* vision of *universal* rights and justice.

How, then, is the political process of social justice appeals to be enacted? Young (1998) claims that in the course of debates about what the obligations of justice require, people will often formulate principles to support their claims. This does not mean, however, that we must agree on these principles *prior* to debate about policy. The claim of justice, in other words, does not presuppose an a priori agreement on the principles of justice. We aim to resolve our conflicts by discussion and negotiation, instead of through violent means, that is, through peaceful means. She continues that, indeed, through discussion and negotiation, other injustices might be identified that adversely affect "populations" or "social groups" that weren't previously considered. She does not, therefore, promote appeals to justice based on perceptions of similarity (which is not the same as solidarity) because that invites us to deny that we have obligations to those whom we perceive as different. She suggests, in turn, that we rest appeals to justice on the recognition that we are together, even though we may not see ourselves as part of the same community.

A focus on "difference" as a core concept underlying social justice is not without its problems (Tyner, 2006b: 161). While a focus on difference has drawn attention to the marginalization and powerlessness of specific social groups, there has also been a tendency to erode the sense of human sameness underpinning the ideal of moral equality crucial to a just society (Smith, 2000: 138). Accordingly, Smith maintains that a "geographical perspective on social justice has to work between universality and particularity." In short, we should work toward a sense of human sameness without abandoning insights gained from understanding the particularity of persons and places.

Will all people always be "included" in claims to social justice? It's doubtful. But the existence of socially constructed (and contested) claims to universal rights likewise will not provide a just life for everyone. By focusing on the process, however, the political contestation of social justice and injustices may be made apparent. Such is the task of peace education.

EDUCATING FOR PEACE

Education is by definition a future-oriented and optimistic activity (Vriens, 1997: 27). It is also a political forum. Consequently, peace education must be more than a lesson about a peace problem or a war situation. Lessons must be relevant to the subject matter at hand, and to enable one to understand the complexities of the situation under discussion (p. 28). Harris and Morrison (2003: 9) likewise suggest that peace education seeks to transform the present human condition by changing social structures and patterns of thought. Such a goal resonates with the promotion of a postcolonial approach to the study of populations.

In order to work toward the elimination (or at least a substantial reduction) of war and violence, Harris and Morrison (2003: 15) argue, people must understand, desire, and struggle to achieve peace. They suggest that

> if and when the desire for peace becomes strongly rooted in human consciousness, people will strive for it, demanding new

social structures that reduce risks of violence. Peace education provides not only a way to promote such a desire for peace within the human mind but also knowledge about peacemaking skills so that human beings learn alternative nonviolent ways of dealing with each other. (p. 15)

Within population geography, one possible route is through studies that interrogate the discipline of bodies and the regulation of populations through a control of space: investigations into the use of ethnic identification cards in the promotion of genocide (as in Rwanda), the use of censuses to facilitate assassination campaigns (as in the Phoenix Program during the Vietnam War), or the regulation of marriages to affect fertility (as in Democratic Kampuchea).

Following Fisher (2001: 44), therefore, a peace-building pedagogical approach is *teaching that engages students in political discussion of social injustice*. Such an approach necessarily entails a collective, collaborative, and ongoing process that pays special attention to people's experiences, feelings, ideas, and actions; seeks to understand and challenge oppressive and exploitative structures and institutions; supports and generates people's political agency by addressing "personal" concerns and taking them seriously; questions the meaning for differently situated people of oppression and liberation; and proceeds nonjudgmentally but cultivates the political judgement needed to act in response to violence and other forms of injustice. As Harris and Morrison (2003: 177) conclude, "Human beings have a choice about how to live on this planet. Education, by influencing students' attitudes, information, and ideas about peace [and social justice], can help create in human consciousness the moral strength that will be necessary to move toward a more peaceful future."

The abolition of violence—as manifested in war and genocide, for example—is an enormous undertaking, one that is challenged on many fronts (Zinn, 2005). One objection to the claims of peace education, for example, questions the connection between large-scale political decisions and the everyday reality of "common" people (Vriens, 1997: 26). Vriens (p. 26), for example, asks, "What has an ordinary person to do with, for example, the war in Zaire, or with the genocide in Rwanda, with the Israeli–Palestinian conflict, or with the ongoing abuse of human rights in countries like Indonesia, China, or elsewhere?" Indeed, as Patricia Calderwood (2003: 302), explains, "We live and work, for the most part, within a context of immediacy, a context so absorbing that it is easy to be blind to how we are situated within a web of connection to countless other lives, many of which we can barely imagine." In other words, we are often blind to the fact that we all inhabit a *global* population geography, that our actions and decisions do in fact intermesh with those of other people—most of whom we will never know. The clothes we buy, the foods we consume, the places we travel: all of these seemingly inconsequential and individual decisions have connections. Geography, and indeed population geography, is well situated to make visible these connections.

As educators, but also as inhabitants of the world, we have a responsibility *to act*. To not do something is also an action; it is an ultraconservative position that will maintain the status quo. To know that poverty exists (and to do nothing), to know that infants and children are dying from malnutrition and inadequate health care (and to do nothing), to know that people are being raped and killed through organized mass violence (and to do nothing) is to participate in and perpetuate a culture of impunity. As Opotow (1990: 2) explains, "Although harms that result from unconcern ... may not involve malevolent intent, [this] can nevertheless result in exploitation, disruption of crucial services, suffering, the destruction of communities, and death." It is widely recognized that the "international" community did nothing in the leadup to, and the early months of, the 1994 genocide in Rwanda. And yet the warning signs were there.

To promote peace and social justice, we must act to reduce and eradicate oppression, however distant we may feel from personal culpability for its enactment (Calderwood, 2003: 302). As educators, and particularly as educators of *geography*, it is our responsibility to bring to light these connections. This is why Findlay's concerns are so germane, and this is why a relational understanding of space is crucial. If, as Massey (2004: 5) contends,

> space is a product of practices, trajectories, interrelations, if we make space through interactions at all levels, from the (so-called) local to the (so-called) global, then those spatial identities such as places, regions, nations, and the local and the global, must be forged in this relational way too, as internally complex, essen-

tially unboundable in any absolute sense, and inevitably historically changing.

This rather poststructural approach to space therefore has important consequences for *personal engagement*, and consequently a challenge to a culture of impunity. To not make these connections between our lives and the lives of others is to participate in and to perpetuate a culture of impunity. Such a rationalized disengagement and detachment permits the status quo and allows instances of direct and structural violence to continue unchallenged. However, thinking through this spatially allows one the opportunity to "intervene in a charged political arena" and thereby to "combat localist or nationalist claims to place based on eternal essential, and in consequence exclusive, characteristics of belonging" (Massey, 2004: 6).

Peace education is also viewed as a promotion of utopian ideals, of forwarding unrealistic expectations. Detractors also denounce peace education as unattainable: they claim that peace will never be forthcoming. Harris and Morrison (2003: 29) acknowledge that "in a world which often looks bleak, full of genocide, environmental destruction, multiple holocausts, unemployment, terrorism, and continuing poverty, the achievements of peace is not something that is easily visualized." However, peace education does not try to make peace by means of education; peace education cannot make peace directly, but instead aims to make people able to judge in the service of political coresponsibility for peace (Vriens, 1997: 27). Peace education ultimately will work toward educating people to establish support for peaceful policies; it constitutes an attempt to transform society by creating a peaceful consciousness that condemns violent behavior. Professors can teach about the problems of war and peace, of militarism, and to pressure governments to adopt nonviolent policies (Harris and Morrison, 2003: 28).

Moreover, most proponents of peace education do not believe that through their activities all instances of violence, including war and genocide, will be prevented. As Harris and Morrison (2003: 13) explain, "since societies will always have hostilities, disagreements, and arguments, the pursuit of peace does not strive for an idealized state of human existence with no aggression or conflict; it strives, rather, for the means to resolve disagreements without resorting to warfare or physical force, and for justice where human beings are treated with dignity."

Peace education does teach about peace, because many citizens need more knowledge about the problems associated with militarism and violence. Peace education, consequently, is a long-term strategy to immediate threats. It "represents an indirect solution to the problems of violence. As a strategy, it depends on millions of students being educated, and for these students, in turn, to work also toward the eradication of violence" (Harris and Morrison, p. 28).

Critics of peace education question "whether peace education is too directive, maybe even whether it constitutes indoctrination" (Vriens, 1997: 26). Indeed, those who pursue a pedagogy based on peace face considerable pressure from (generally right-wing) critics. It is not uncommon, for example, for peace educators to be verbally attacked because they challenge hegemonic views of security and national defense. Such accusations have been especially pronounced in the United States with the rise of a neoconservative, neoliberal, and militarized society (the Ronald Reagan years, 1980–1988) and during the presidential administration of George W. Bush (2000–2008). Cries are raised that peace educators are not objective, that they engage in rhetoric or polemics, that their research and teaching is value-laden, and that they provide only "one side" of the issue. Foremost among these critics is David Horowitz, author of *The Professors: The 101 Most Dangerous Academics in America* (2006) and *Indoctrination U.: The Left's War against Academic Freedom* (2007a). For the past several years Horowitz (2007b) has waged a self-described "national campaign for academic freedom designed to promote the restoration of academic standards, including intellectual diversity, in institutions of higher learning." His understanding of academic diversity, however, is rather limited. He asserts that conservative ideas and ideals are ideologically suppressed by "faculty ideologues"; that students are required—hence, indoctrinated—to study radical and revolutionary concepts: feminism, Marxism, and the like. He dismisses the use of peace-related texts. Most recently, Horowitz has attacked the concept of "constructivism"—a concept that many population geographers, such as Allan Findlay and Elspeth Graham, have argued is central to a reoriented discipline. In short, Horowitz concludes that America's universities have become anti-American, anticapital, antimilitary, anticonservative, and antifamily. In a remarkable display of Orwellian logic, Horowitz would "protect" academic freedom through censorship.

The argument, however, that peace studies (or feminism, or critical race theory, or social theory more broadly) "is somehow value-laden, while traditional studies of history and other academic disciplines are not, may be seen itself as a polemical argument constructed to discredit a point of view that threatens those with power" (Harris and Morrison, 2003: 166). Vriens (1997: 28) concurs: "If people accuse peace education of being indoctrinating, they actually mean that peace education is one-sided and not neutral, or they do not agree with the information and choices which peace education offers."

Violence, as seen in its various forms—including domestic abuse, rape, and war—is frequently associated with a militarized society. Militarism, furthermore, emerges from the promotion of select values, opinions, and social organizations that support (and promote) war and violence as legitimate ways to manage human affairs (Harris and Morrison, 2003: 9). Wars are often represented—constructed!—as natural; violence becomes the normal state of affairs from which to interpret societies and the ways the world works. Such a constructed understanding of warfare, however, facilities the accumulation of capital via military force (as in Vietnam) and permits the continuance of a culture of impunity (as when the international community did nothing to stop Rwanda's genocide because war between the Hutu and the Tutsi was represented as natural). As Zinn (2005: 15) writes, "The most powerful weapon of governments in raising armies is the weapon of propaganda, of ideology. They must persuade young people, and their families that though they may die, though they may lose arms or legs, or become blind, that it is done for the common good, for a noble cause, for democracy, for liberty, for God, for the country."

Within such a context, education for peace becomes truly radical and revolutionary.

CONCLUDING THOUGHTS

As teachers and researchers, what are our responsibilities? And to whom are we responsible? As long as war and genocide—but also all forms of structural and direct violence—remain important problems of our world, we cannot deny our responsibility to help students understand these problems. If we are willing to accept this claim, then it will be possible for our students (and ourselves) to develop the skills and techniques to provide just and humane alternatives; to develop a sound basis for the competency to evaluate injustices; and to identify potentials and limitations in exercising their (and our) responsibility (Harris and Morrison, 2003; Vriens, 1997).

Over two decades ago Alan Jenkins (1985) argued for a geographic curriculum that promoted peace. He suggested that a "fundamental failure in many 'pure' geography courses [was] not so much their preoccupation with spatial patterns at the expense of process, but rather their failure to use their concerns for, and knowledge of, such patterns to confront the central economic, social and ecological issues of our times" (p. 204). However, Jenkins (p. 204) also believed that "geographers, through their knowledge of the content and methods of the discipline, have much to offer peace education either in specialist geography courses or in a different framework." A retheorized population geography should respond to this challenge.

The path to peace is a moral road. This world will not become more peaceful until citizens develop a moral revulsion to violent practices that promote the destruction of the natural habitat, the taking of human life, and the maintenance of social structures that perpetuate inequalities (Harris and Morrison, 2003: 177). Therein lies our responsibility.

NOTES

CHAPTER ONE

1. Curtis (2002) traces the emergence and deployment of the term "population" within Foucault's writings, a project joined later by both Legg and Philo. Broadly, Curtis charts the use of "population" as opposed to "populousness" and other related terms, such as the "social body" or the "collective body." Populousness, for example, has a complex history in Western thought, tracing back at least to the Greeks. In its earlier usages, "populousness" referred to the sense that some units of government (for example, kingdoms, empires, countries, and cities) contain greater or lesser numbers of entities (for example, hearths, soldiers, souls) that were distributed across different orders or classes (Curtis, 2002: 508). The term continued to be used throughout the 16th and 17th centuries and figured prominently in many of the earliest (European) censuses as well as in Thomas Malthus's writings. Furthermore, the concept as it was modified, implied a hierarchical differentiation of orders of the people (p. 508).
2. Both empiricism and positivism provided an ontological and epistemological framework for many of these sciences. The development of the scientific principles of Francis Bacon (1561–1626) and of scientific laws as evidenced by the work of Isaac Newton (1642–1727) influenced the development of population studies and highlighted the necessity for standardized and more complete population data. As Barnes and Hannah (2001: 379) elaborate: "Since the first comprehensive national censuses during the 18th and 19th centuries, and associated institutions for dealing with them, the inscription of figures, and later their joining to probability calculations within a bourgeoning set of both commercial and statist networks, produced worlds to be organised, controlled, manipulated, studied, and known."

CHAPTER TWO

1. Dang Thuy Tram was a medical doctor from Hanoi. She served during the war in the southern province of Quang Ngai between 1966 and 1970. While caring for the sick and wounded, Thuy compiled two diaries recording her wartime

experiences. She was killed by American troops on June 22, 1970. Among the few possessions found on her body was the second of her diaries. It was recovered by Fred Whitehurst, who was serving with a military intelligence unit at Duc Pho. For 35 years he kept the diary until, in 2005, Whitehurst was able to locate the surviving members of Thuy's family. Her diary was published in Hanoi in 2005 and released in the United States 2 years later. See Dang Thuy Tram (2007) *Last Night I Dreamed of Peace: The Diary of Dang Thuy Tram*, translated by Andrew X. Pham with an introduction by Frances Fitzgerald (New York: Harmony Books, 2007). See also Seth Mydans (2006) "Diary of North Vietnam Doctor Killed in U.S. Attack Makes War Real," *New York Times*, June 6, 2006. The quote is Dang's entry of May 20, 1969 (p. 121).
2. Dang (2007: 135).
3. Dang (2007: 137).
4. In 1968 the phrase "search and destroy" was changed in response to harsh criticism from the American public and politicians. The phrase made Westmoreland's strategy sound brutal and without a higher purpose than simply killing the enemy (Appy, 1993: 156). It was replaced with the more banal-sounding phrases "search and clear" or "sweeping operations." According to Young (1991: 163), Westmoreland wondered why some "friendly critic" didn't warn him how badly the phrase sounded.
5. Dang (2007: 142).
6. In Vietnam, three color-coded chemical agents were widely used. Agent Orange (a mixture of 2,4-D and 2,4,5-T) was used principally as a general defoliant, directed against forest cover and crops. Agent White (a mixture of 2,4-D and picloram) was also used against forests. According to Neilands (1970: 222), picloram is a product of Dow Chemical, and at the time was not authorized for application to any *American* crops. It was known at the time that the substance remains in the soil—and retains its phytotoxicity—for decades. Agent Blue (a solution of cacodylic acid) was used on rice and grasses. Cacodylic acid contains arsenic. In 1968 the AAAS asked that the use of this substance be discontinued in Vietnam (p. 222).
7. Quoted in Crane (2002: 245). Doolittle, of course, was the World War II hero who planned and led the April 18, 1942, bombing campaign of sixteen B-25 bombers against Japan. The mission was the first strike by the United States during the war against the Japanese homeland. The occasion of Doolittle's quoted remarks was an April 1952 interservice symposium whereupon he attempted to assuage the moral qualms of military leaders who were not supportive of the use of biological or chemical weapons.
8. Dang (2007: 125).
9. During the summer of 1972 there was not a massive loss of life resultant from flooding. Lacoste (1973: 3) argues that such devastation did not occur because it was not intended, but rather because the monsoonal rains of that year were particularly low—a phenomenon that occurs every 8–10 years. During August, when the floods are usually heaviest, water levels barely reached the level of the dikes throughout the delta. It was this meteorological occurrence, Lacoste maintains, that prevented a widespread loss of life.
10. Dang (2007: 159).
11. According to John Prados, Kennedy searched for other strategic ways to confine

the conflict in Vietnam. Prados (1996: 242) explains that "geography suggested the possibility of sealing off South Vietnamese borders, thus preventing the infiltration of weapons or men [sic] from the north or through Laos." This border control strategy was championed as early as May 1961 by Robert Komer, among others.

12. The American-based Strategic Hamlet Program built on earlier programs. For example, an initial policy of confinement was implemented in 1959–1960 as part of Diem's *agroville* program. Although billed as a counterinsurgency practice, Diem sought to impose a centralized control over the countryside. On paper, the plan called for the establishment of 80 large agrovilles and 400 smaller settlements; in actuality, only 22 were ever completed and occupied (McCollum, 1983: 107). Ironically, these encampments were reminiscent of the collectivized farms born under socialist governments. The agroville program was terminated in 1960, only to be reborn 1 year later under the advisement of the British counterinsurgency expert Robert Thompson. Prior to his work in Vietnam, Thompson had served in a variety of capacities, working to suppress communist insurgencies both in Malaya (present-day Malaysia) and the Philippines. In 1961 Thompson came to South Vietnam at the request of the U.S. government. Until his departure in 1965, Thompson advised American military and political officials on how to deal with the Vietcong.

CHAPTER THREE

1. The following account is taken from Youkimny Chan's autobiography, published in DePaul (1997).
2. As this manuscript was completed the trial for justice in Cambodia was finally underway. The Extraordinary Chambers in the Courts of Cambodia (ECCC) was established in 2006 to hold the senior leaders of the Khmer Rouge accountable for their crimes. Nuon Chea, Khieu Samphan, and Ieng Sary were arrested in late 2007 and await trial.
3. Removed from power, Sihanouk attempted to continue his fight from abroad. In declaring war against the new regime of Lon Nol, Sihanouk announced the formation of the National United Front of Kampuchea and agreed to an alliance with China, North Vietnam, the NLF, and the Khmer Rouge.
4. Chandler, *History of Cambodia*, 208.
5. Unidentified refugee quoted in Quinn (1989: 183).
6. You Huy, a chief of guards working at S-21, hand-wrote this statement at the bottom of a typewritten form listing biographical details on 18 prisoners executed on July 23, 1977 (quoted in Etcheson, 2005: 83).
7. Such an ontological understanding of humanity explains, in part, why the Khmer Rouge less frequently employed reeducation camps in the manner of the Vietnamese communists.
8. In this section I draw heavily on Foucault's understanding of sovereignty and the politics of life and death. Such a Eurocentric argument may appear discordant. However, I maintain that such a Eurocentric understanding is not entirely far-fetched when detailing the ideologies of the Khmer Rouge. Bear in mind that many of the leading ideologues and theorists of the Khmer Rouge were

French-educated. Many, including Khieu Samphan, Ieng Sary, and Pol Pot himself received educational training in Paris during the 1940s and 1950s; many received extensive training in both *French* and *European* politics and governance. These cadres were trained in the French language and studied French history. It is important to recognize, therefore, that the Khmer Rouge's understanding of revolution and state sovereignty is derived more from European examples than it is from indigenous Khmer understandings.

9. In a series of lectures delivered in 1976 (and appearing in the volume *Society Must Be Defended*), Foucault (2003: 77) provides a lengthy discussion of "race" and "race wars." The word "race" for Foucault, however, is "not pinned to a stable biological meaning." Nor, for that matter, is the term "completely free-floating." Rather, Foucault employs the term to designate a "certain historico-political divide." The term, as used in this section, therefore refers to a process of dividing, separating, and classifying people.

CHAPTER FOUR

1. Quoted in Nowrojee (1996).
2. Other news and opinion publications that spread the message of Hutu power included *Umurwanashyaka* (Le Militant); *Interahamwe* (Los Combattants solidaires); *Intera* (En avant); *Impanda* (Le Trompe d'appel); *Medaille Nyiramacibiri*; *Kamarampaka* (Le Dernier Mot); *Power-Pawa*; and *Umurava* (Honnêteté) (Chalk, 1999: 188).
3. It remains unclear as to who is responsible for the downing of the president's plane. Immediate blame was leveled at the RPF, reports of which were used to fuel the ensuing violence. More recent studies indicate that various factions within the Habyarimana regime were responsible (see Melvern, 2004: 260–266).
4. In a royal ritual known as the "Path of Inundation," Rwandan kings countered the problem of excessive celestial flow (rainfall) through the elimination of female "blocked beings," namely, women who failed to produce blood (menstruation) or maternal milk (Taylor, 1992: 37–40). Here, Taylor (p. 38) explains that "because the productivity of their bodies was blocked, they were thought to threaten the productive integrity of the entire Rwandan polity."
5. Quoted in Hinton (2002: 5).

REFERENCES

Adas, Michael. 2006. *Dominance by Design: Technological Imperatives and America's Civilizing Missions*. Cambridge, MA: Belknap Press of Harvard University Press.

Adelman, Howard. 2005. The Rwanda genocide. In Samuel Totten, ed., *Genocide at the Millennium*. London: Transaction, 31–54.

Agnew, John and Stuart Corbridge. 1995. *Mastering Space: Hegemony, Territory, and International Political Economy*. London: Routledge.

Alger, Chadwick. 1989. Peace studies at the crossroads: Where else? *Annals, AAPSS, 504*, 117–127.

Ali, Mohamed and Iqbal Shah. 2000. Sanctions and childhood mortality in Iraq. *The Lancet, 355*, 1851–1857.

Anglin, Mary K. 1998. Feminist perspectives on structural violence. *Identities, 5*(2), 145–151.

Appy, Christian G. 1993. *Working-Class War: American Combat Soldiers and Vietnam*. Chapel Hill: University of North Carolina Press.

Atack, Iain. 2001. From pacifism to war resistance. *Peace and Change, 26*(2), 177–186.

Aziz, Christine. 2003. Struggling to rebuild Iraq's health-care system. *The Lancet, 362*, 1288–1289.

Bailey, Adrian. 2005. *Making Population Geography*. London: Hodder Arnold.

Bailey, Adrian, Richard Wright, Alison Mountz, and Ines Miyares. 2002. (Re)producing Salvadoran transnational geographies. *Annals of the Association of American Geographers, 92*, 125–144.

Barker, Philip. 1998. *Michel Foucault: An Introduction*. Edinburgh, UK: Edinburgh University Press.

Barnaby, Frank. 1976, May. Environmental warfare. *Bulletin of the Atomic Scientists*, pp. 37–43.

Barnes, Trevor J. and Matthew Hannah. 2001. The place of numbers: Histories, geographies and theories of quantification. *Environment and Planning D: Society and Space, 19*, 404–408.

Barnett, Michael. 2002. *Eyewitness to a Genocide: The United Nations and Rwanda*. Ithaca, NY: Cornell University Press.

Barry, Brian. 2005. *Why Social Justice Matters*. Malden, MA: Policy Press.

Becker, Elizabeth. 1998. *When the War Was Over: Cambodia and the Khmer Rouge Revolution*. New York: Simon & Schuster.
Bell, David. 1995. [Screw]ing geography (censor's version). *Environment and Planning D: Society and Space*, 14, 139–153.
Bello, Walden. 2005. *Dilemmas of Domination: The Unmaking of the American Empire*. New York: Metropolitan Books.
Berkeley, Bill. 2002. Road to a genocide. In Nicolaus Mills and Kira Bunner, eds., *The New Killing Fields: Massacre and the Politics of Intervention*. New York: Basic Books, 103–116.
Binnie, Jon. 1997. Coming out of Geography: Towards a queer epistemology? *Environment and Planning D: Society and Space*, 15, 223–237.
Boffey, Philip M. 1970. Herbicides in Vietnam: AAAS study runs into a military roadblock. *Science*, 170, 42–45.
Boffey, Philip M. 1971. Herbicides in Vietnam: AAAS study finds widespread devastation. *Science*, 171, 43–47.
Booth, Karen M. 2006. Conceiving the nation: The "politics of the womb" in Kenya, the United States, Greece, and Ireland. *Journal of Women's History*, 18(2), 151–157.
Bordo, Susan. 1995. *Unbearable Weight: Feminism, Western Culture, and the Body*. Berkeley and Los Angeles: University of California Press.
Bourdelais, Patrice. 2004. The French population censuses: Purposes and uses during the 17th, 18th, and 19th centuries. *History of the Family*, 9, 97–113.
Bradshaw, Matt and Elaine Stratford. 2005. Qualitative research design and rigour. In Iain Hay, ed., *Qualitative Research Methods in Human Geography*. 2nd ed. New York: Oxford University Press, 67–76.
Brown, Ian. 2000. *Cambodia*. Oxford, UK: Oxfam.
Brunborg, Helge and Henrik Urdal. 2005. The demography of conflict and violence: An introduction. *Journal of Peace Research*, 42(4), 371–374.
Brunet, Ariane and Isabelle Solon Helal. 1998. Monitoring the prosecution of gender-related crimes in Rwanda: A brief field report. *Peace and Conflict: Journal of Peace Psychology*, 4, 393–397.
Buckingham, William A. 1982. *Operation Ranch Hand: The Air Force and Herbicides in Southeast Asia, 1961–1971*. Washington, DC: Office of the Air Force History.
Burnham, Gilbert, Riyadh Lafta, Shannon Doocy, and Les Roberts. 2006. Mortality after the 2003 invasion of Iraq: A cross-sectional cluster sample survey. *The Lancet*, 368, 1421–1428.
Cable, Larry. 1991. *Unholy Grail: The US and the Wars in Vietnam, 1965–8*. New York: Routledge.
Calderwood, Patricia E. 2003. Toward a professional community for social justice. *Journal of Transformative Education*, 1(4), 301–320.
Caldwell, John C. 2001. Demographers and the study of mortality: Scope, perspectives, and theory. *Annals of the New York Academy of Sciences*, 954, 19–34.
Carlton-Ford, Steve, Ann Hamill, and Paula Houston. 2000. War and children's mortality. *Childhood*, 7(4), 401–419.
Carmody, Moira. 2003. Sexual ethics and violence prevention. *Social and Legal Studies*, 12(2), 199–216.

Carney, Timothy. 1989. The unexpected victory. In Karl D. Jackson, ed., *Cambodia 1975–1978: Rendezvous with Death*. Princeton, NJ: Princeton University Press, 13–35.

Carter, George F. 1977. A geographical society should be a geographical society. *Professional Geographer*, 29(1), 101–102.

Castree, Noel. 2001. Socializing nature: Theory, practice, and politics. In Noel Castree and Bruce Braun, eds., *Social Nature: Theory, Practice, and Politics*. Oxford, UK: Blackwell, 1–21.

Cecil, Paul F. 1986. *Herbicidal Warfare: The RANCH HAND Project in Vietnam*. Westport, CT: Praeger.

Chalk, Frank. 1999. Radio broadcasting in the incitement and interdiction of gross violations of human rights, including genocide. In Roger W. Smith, ed., *Genocide: Essays toward Understanding, Early-Warning, and Prevention*. Williamsburg, VA: Association of Genocide Scholars, 185–203.

Chandler, David. 1991. *The Tragedy of Cambodian History: Politics, War and Revolution since 1945*. New Haven, CT: Yale University Press.

Chandler, David. 1999. *Voices from S-21: Terror and History in Pol Pot's Secret Prison*. Berkeley and Los Angeles: University of California Press.

Chandler, David. 2000a. *Brother Number One: A Political Biography of Pol Pot*. Rev. ed. Chiang Mai, Thailand: Silkworm Press.

Chandler, David. 2000b. *A History of Cambodia*. 3rd ed. Boulder, CO: Westview Press.

Chandler, David, Ben Kiernan, and Chanthou Boua. 1988. *Pol Pot Plans the Future: Confidential Leadership Documents from Democratic Kampuchea, 1976–1977*. Yale University Southeast Asia Studies, Monograph Series No. 33. New Haven, CT: Yale University Press.

Chappell, John E. Jr. 1977. On the nature of radicalism in geography. *Professional Geographer*, 29(4), 408–409.

Clark, Gordon L. and Michael Dear. 1978. The future of radical geography. *Professional Geographer*, 30(4), 356–359.

Clayton, Thomas. 1998. Building the new Cambodia: Educational destruction and construction under the Khmer Rouge, 1975–1979. *History of Education Quarterly*, 38(1), 1–16.

Clayton, Thomas. 2005. Re-orientations in moral education in Cambodia since 1975. *Journal of Moral Education*, 34(4), 505–517.

Clodfelter, Michael. 1988. *Mad Minutes and Vietnam Months: A Soldier's Story*. Jefferson, NC: McFarland.

Clodfelter, Michael, 1995. *Vietnam in Military Statistics: A History of the Indochina Wars, 1772–1991*. Jefferson, NC: McFarland.

Crane, Conrad C. 2002. "No practical capabilities": American biological and chemical warfare programs during the Korean War. *Perspectives in Biology and Medicine*, 45(2), 241–249.

Currey, Cecil B. 1988. *Edward Lansdale: The Unquiet American*. Boston: Houghton Mifflin.

Curtis, Bruce. 2002. Foucault on governmentality and population: The impossible discovery. *Canadian Journal of Sociology*, 27(4), 505–533.

Cutter, Susan L. 1995. The forgotten casualties: Women, children, and the environmental change. *Global Environmental Change*, 5(3), 81–194.
Dang, Thuy Tram. 2005. *Last Night I Dreamed of Peace: The Diary of Dang Thuy Tram*. Translated by Andrew X. Pham. New York: Harmony Books.
Davidson, Joyce. 2001. Pregnant pauses: Agoraphobic embodiment and the limits of (im)pregnability. *Gender, Place and Culture: A Journal of Feminist Geography*, 8(3), 283–297.
Davis, Peter, director. 1974. *Hearts and Minds* [Film]. Rainbow Pictures.
Dean, Mitchell M. 1999. *Governmentality: Power and Rule in Modern Society*. Thousand Oaks, CA: Sage.
Dear, Michael. 2001. The politics of geography: Hate mail, rebid referees, and culture wars. *Political Geography*, 20, 1–12.
Delaney, David. 1998. *Race, Place, and the Law, 1836–1948*. Austin: University of Texas Press.
Demeritt, David. 2001. Being constructive about nature. In Noel Castree and Bruce Braun, eds., *Social Nature: Theory, Practice, and Politics*. Oxford, UK: Blackwell, 22–40.
DePaul, Kim, ed. 1997. *Children of Cambodia's Killing Fields*. New Haven, CT: Yale University Press.
de Walque, Damien. 2005. Selective mortality during the Khmer Rouge period in Cambodia. *Populations and Development Review*, 31(2), 351–368.
de Walque, Damien. 2006. The socio-demographic legacy of the Khmer Rouge period in Cambodia. *Population Studies*, 60(2), 223–231.
Domosh, Mona and Joni Seager. 2001. *Putting Women in Place: Feminist Geographers Make Sense of the World*. New York: Guilford Press.
Dreyfus, Hubert L. and Paul Rabinow. 1983. *Michel Foucault: Beyond Structuralism and Hermeneutics*. 2nd ed. Chicago: University of Chicago Press.
Dunlop, Nic. 2005. *The Lost Executioner: A Journey to the Heart of the Killing Fields*. New York: Walker & Company.
Ebihara, May. 1990. Revolution and reformulation in Kampuchean village culture. In David A. Albin and Marlowe Hood, eds., *The Cambodian Agony*. 2nd ed. New York: M. E. Sharpe, 16–61.
Ebihara, May. 2002. Memories of the Pol Pot era in a Cambodian village. In Judy Lederwood, ed., *Cambodia Emerges from the Past: Eight Essays*. DeKalb: Center for Southeast Asian Studies, Northern Illinois University, 91–108.
Edelman, Murray. 1977. *Political Language: Words That Succeed and Policies That Fail*. New York: Academic Press.
Edkins, Jenny. 1999. *Poststructuralism and International Relations: Bringing the Political Back In*. London: Lynne Rienner.
Edwards, Paul N. 1996. *The Closed World: Computers and the Politics of Discourse in Cold War America*. Cambridge, MA: MIT Press.
Eisenstein, Zillah. 2007. *Sexual Decoys: Gender, Race and War*. New York: Zed Books.
Elden, Stuart. 2001. *Mapping the Present: Heidegger, Foucault, and the Project of a Spatial History*. London: Continuum.
Enslin, Penny. 2006. Democracy, social justice and education: Feminist strategies in a globalizing world. *Educational Philosophy and Theory*, 38(1), 57–67.

Enthoven, Alain and K. Wayne Smith. 1971. *How Much Is Enough?: Shaping the Defense Program, 1961–1969*. New York: Harper & Row.
Etcheson, Craig. 2005. *After the Killing Fields: Lessons from the Cambodian Genocide*. Lubbock: Texas Tech University Press.
Farwell, Nancy. 2004. War rape: New conceptualizations and responses. *Affilia: Journal of Women and Social Work*, 19(4), 389–403.
Fincher, Ruth. 1993. Commentary: Gender relations and the geography of migration. *Environment and Planning A*, 25, 1703–1705.
Findlay, Allan. 2003. Population geographies for the 21st century. *Scottish Journal of Geography*, 119(3), 177–190.
Findlay, Allan M. and Elspeth Graham. 1991. The challenge facing population geography. *Progress in Human Geography*, 15(2), 149–162.
Fisher, Berenice Malka. 2001. *No Angel in the Classroom: Teaching Through Feminist Discourse*. Lanham, MD: Rowman & Littlefield.
Flint, Colin. 2005. Introduction: Geography of war and peace. In Colin Flint, ed., *The Geography of War and Peace: From Death Camps to Diplomats*. New York: Oxford University Press, 1–15.
Folke, Steen. 1972. Why a radical geography must be Marxist. *Antipode*, 4(2), 13–18.
Foucault, Michel. 1972. *The Archaeology of Knowledge and The Discourse on Language*. New York: Pantheon Books.
Foucault, Michel. 1979. *Discipline and Punish: The Birth of Prison*. Translated by Alan Sheridan. New York: Vintage Books.
Foucault, Michel. 1980. *Power/Knowledge: Selected Interviews and Other Writings, 1972–1977*. Edited by Colin Gordon. New York: Pantheon Books.
Foucault, Michel. 1990. *The History of Sexuality: Vol. 1. An Introduction*. Translated by Robert Hurley. New York: Vintage Books.
Foucault, Michel. 2003. *'Society Must be Defended': Lectures at the Collège de France, 1975–1976*. Translated by David Macey. New York: Picador.
Gaile, Gary L. and Cort J. Willmott, eds. 1989. *Geography in America*. Columbus, OH: Merrill.
Gartner, Scott Sigmund and Marissa Edson Myers. 1995. Body counts and "success" in the Vietnam and Korean Wars. *Journal of Interdisciplinary History*, 25(3), 377–395.
George, Terry, director. 2005. *Hotel Rwanda* [Film]. MGM.
Gibson, James. 1986. *The Perfect War: Technowar in Vietnam*. Boston: Atlantic Monthly Press.
Glover, Jonathan. 1999. *Humanity: A Moral History of the Twentieth Century*. New Haven, CT: Yale University Press.
Gober, Patricia and James A. Tyner. 2004. Population geography. In Gary Gaile and Cort Willmott, eds., *Geography in America at the Dawn of the 21st Century*. Oxford, UK: Oxford University Press, 185–199.
Gottesman, Evan. 2003. *Cambodia after the Khmer Rouge: Inside the Politics of Nation Building*. New Haven, CT: Yale University Press.
Graham, Elspeth. 1999. Breaking out: The opportunities and challenges of multi-method research in geography. *Professional Geographer*, 51, 76–89.

Graham, Elspeth. 2000. What kind of theory for what kind of population geography? *International Journal of Population Geography*, 6, 257–272.
Graham, Elspeth. 2004. The past, present and future of population geography: Reflections on Glenn Trewartha's address fifty years on. *Population, Space and Place*, 10, 289–294.
Graham, Elspeth and Paul Boyle. 2001. Editorial introduction: (Re)theorizing population geography: Mapping the unfamiliar. *International Journal of Population Geography*, 7, 389–394.
Gregory, Derek. 1994. *Geographical Imaginations*. Cambridge, MA: Blackwell.
Gregory, Derek. 2004. *The Colonial Present: Afghanistan, Palestine, Iraq*. Cambridge, MA: Blackwell.
Griffiths, Ieuan L. L. 1995. *The African Inheritance*. New York: Routledge.
Harris, Ian M. and Mary Lee Morrison. 2003. *Peace Education*. 2nd ed. London: McFarland.
Harvey, David. 1973. *Social Justice and the City*. Baltimore: Johns Hopkins University Press.
Harvey, David. 1977. Communication on recent comments by Professor Carter. *Professional Geographer*, 29(4), 405–407.
Hawkins, John M. 2006. The cost of artillery: Elimination harassment and interdiction fire during the Vietnam War. *Journal of Military History*, 70, 91–122.
Hayslip, Le Ly (with Jay Wurts). 1993. *When Heaven and Earth Changed Places*. New York: Plume.
Hayslip, Le Ly and Dien Pham. 2006. Caught in the crossfire: The civilian experience. In Andrew Wiest, ed., *Rolling Thunder in a Gentle Land: The Vietnam War Revisited*. New York: Osprey, 136–155.
Hearden, Patrick J. 2005. *The Tragedy of Vietnam: Causes and Consequences*. 2nd ed. New York: Pearson Longman.
Herring, George C., ed. 1993. *The Pentagon Papers*. Abridged ed. New York: McGraw-Hill.
Herring, George C. 1996. *America's Longest War: The United States and Vietnam, 1950–1975*. 3rd ed. New York: McGraw-Hill.
Heuveline, Patrick. 1998. "Between one and three million": Towards the demographic reconstruction of a decade of Cambodian history (1970–1979). *Population Studies*, 52, 49–65.
Heuveline, Patrick and Bunnak Pock. 2006. Do marriages forget their past?: Martial stability in post–Khmer Rouge Cambodia. *Demography*, 43(1), 99–125.
Hick, Steven. 2001. The political economy of war-affected children. *Annals, AAPSS*, 575, 106–121.
Hintjens, Helen M. 1999. Explaining the 1994 genocide in Rwanda. *Journal of Modern African Studies*, 37(2), 241–286.
Hinton, Alexander L. 2002. The dark side of modernity: Toward an anthropology of genocide. In Alexander Laban Hinton, ed., *Annihilating Difference: The Anthropology of Genocide*. Berkeley and Los Angeles: University of California Press, 1–40.

Hinton, Alexander L. 2005. *Why Did They Kill?: Cambodia in the Shadow of Genocide*. Berkeley and Los Angeles: University of California Press.

Hirschman, Charles, Samuel Preston, and Vu Manh Loi. 1995. Vietnamese casualties during the American War: A new estimate. *Population and Development Review*, 21(4), 783–812.

Horne, John. 2002. Civilian populations and wartime violence: Towards an historical analysis. *International Social Science Journal*, 54(174), 483–490.

Horowitz, David. 2006. *The Professors: The 101 Most Dangerous Academics in America*. New York: Regnery Publishing.

Horowitz, David. 2007a. *Indoctrination U: The Left's War Against Academic Freedom*. New York: Encounter Books.

Horowitz, David. 2007b, March 18. Indoctrination U: Secular creationism. *Washington Times*. Retrieved June 1, 2007, at www.washingtontimes.com.

Hossein-Zadeh, Ismael. 2006. *The Political Economy of U.S. Militarism*. New York: Palgrave Macmillan.

Hubbard, Phil, Rob Kitchin, Brendan Bartley, and Duncan Fuller. 2002. *Thinking Geographically: Space, Theory and Contemporary Human Geography*. London: Continuum.

Hughes, Rachel. 2004. Memory and sovereignty in post-1979 Cambodia: Choeung Ek and local genocide memorials. In Susan E. Cook, ed., *Genocide in Cambodia and Rwanda: New Perspectives*. Yale Center for International and Area Studies: Genocide Studies Program Monograph Series, No. 1. New Haven, CT: Yale University Press.

Hynes, H. Patricia. 2004. On the battlefield of women's bodies: An overview of the harm of war to women. *Women's Studies International Forum*, 27, 431–445.

Jackson, Ben. 2005. The conceptual history of social justice. *Political Studies Review*, 3, 356–373.

Jackson, Karl D. 1989. The ideology of total revolution. In Karl D. Jackson, ed., *Cambodia 1975–1978: Rendezvous with Death*. Princeton, NJ: Princeton University Press, 37–78.

Jackson, Peter and Jan Penrose, eds. 1993. *Constructions of Race, Place and Nation*. Minneapolis: University of Minnesota Press.

James, Preston E. 1954. The geographic study of population. In Preston E. James and Clarence F. Jones, eds., *American Geography: Inventory and Prospect*. Syracuse, NY: Syracuse University Press, 106–122.

James, Preston E. and Geoffrey J. Martin. 1981. *All Possible Worlds: A History of Geographical Ideas*. 2nd ed. New York: Wiley.

Jenkins, Alan. 1985. Peace education and the geography curriculum. In David Pepper and Alan Jenkins, eds., *The Geography of Peace and War*. New York: Basil Blackwell, 202–213.

Joffé, Roland, director. 1984. *The Killing Fields* [Film]. Warner Bros.

Johansen, Hans Christian. 2004. Early Danish census taking. *History of the Family*, 9, 23–31.

Johnson, R. J. 1986. *Philosophy and Human Geography: An Introduction to Contemporary Approaches*. 2nd ed. London: Edward Arnold.

Jones, Huw R. 1990. *Population Geography*. 2nd. London: Paul Chapman.

Kamm, Henry. 1998. *Cambodia: Report from a Stricken Land*. New York: Arcade.

Kapp, Clare. 2003. Anarchy pushes Iraqi health system to brink of collapse. *The Lancet*, 361, 1351.

Karagiannakis, Magdalini. 1999. The definition of rape and its characterization as an act of genocide—A review of the jurisprudence of the International Criminal Tribunals for Rwanda and the Former Yugoslavia. *Leiden Journal of International Law*, 12, 479–490.

Karnow, Stanley. 1983. *Vietnam: A History*. New York: Penguin Books.

Keen, David. 2006. *Endless War?: Hidden Functions of the "War on Terror."* London: Pluto Press.

Kellow, Christine and H. Leslie Steeves. 1998. The role of radio in the Rwandan genocide. *Journal of Communication*, 48, 107–128.

Kende, Istvan. 1989. The history of peace: Concept and organizations from the late Middle Ages to the 1870's. *Journal of Peace Research*, 26(3), 233–247.

Kerkvliet, Benedict J. 2002. *The Huk Rebellion: A Study of Peasant Revolt in the Philippines*. Landham, MD: Rowman & Littlefield.

Kiernan, Ben. 1985. *How Pol Pot Came to Power: A History of Communism in Kampuchea, 1930–1975*. London: Verso.

Kiernan, Ben. 1996. *The Pol Pot Regime: Race, Power, and Genocide in Cambodia under the Khmer Rouge, 1975–1979*. New Haven, CT: Yale University Press.

Knox, Paul, John Agnew, and Linda McCarthy. 2003. *The Geography of World Economy*. 4th ed. London: Edward Arnold.

Kofman, Eleonore and Kim England. 1997. Editorial introduction: Citizenship and international migration: Taking account of gender, sexuality, and race. *Environment and Planning A*, 29, 191–194.

Kolko, Gabriel. 1994. *Anatomy of a War: Vietnam, the United States and the Modern Historical Experience*. New York: New Press.

Koo, Katrina Lee. 2002. Confronting a disciplinary blindness: Women, war and rape in the international polities of security. *Australian Journal of Political Science*, 37(3), 525–536.

Koskela, Hille and Rachel Pain. 2000. Revisiting fear and place: Women's fear of attack and the built environment. *Geoforum*, 31(2), 269–280.

Kraly, Ellen Percy and John McQuilton. 2005. The "protection" of Aborigines in colonial and early federation Australia: The role of population data systems. *Population, Space and Place*, 11, 225–250.

Krepon, Michael. 1974. Weapons potentially inhumane: The case of the cluster bombs. *Foreign Affairs*, 52(3), 595–611.

Kuhlke, Olaf. 2004. *Representing German Identity in the New Berlin Republic: Body, Nation, and Place*. Lewiston, NY: Edwin Mellen Press.

Lacoste, Yves. 1973. An illustration of geographical warfare: Bombing of dikes on the Red River, North Vietnam. *Antipode*, 5(3), 1–13.

Langguth, A. J. 2000. *Our Vietnam: The War, 1954–1975*. New York: Touchstone Books.

Laws, Glenda. 1997. Women's life courses, spatial mobility, and state policies. In John Paul Jones III, Heidi J. Nast, and Susan M. Roberts, eds., *Thresh-*

olds in *Feminist Geography: Difference, Methodology, Representation*. Lanham, MD: Rowman & Littlefield, 47–64.
le Billon, Philippe. 2001. Angola's political economy of war: The role of oil and diamonds, 1975–2000. *African Affairs*, 100, 55–80.
Lefebvre, Henri. 1991. *The Production of Space*. Oxford, UK: Blackwell.
Legg, Stephen. 2005. Foucault's population geographies: Classifications, biopolitics and governmental spaces. *Population, Space and Place*, 11, 137–156.
Lemarchand, René. 1999. Rwanda: The rationality of genocide. In Roger W. Smith, ed., *Genocide: Essays toward Understanding, Early-Warning, and Prevention*. Williamsburg, VA: Association of Genocide Scholars, 17–25.
Lerner, Melvin J. 1980. *The Belief in a Just World: A Fundamental Decision*. New York: Plenum Press.
Levene, Mark. 1999. Connecting threads: Rwanda, the Holocaust, and the pattern of contemporary genocide. In Roger W. Smith, ed., *Genocide: Essays toward Understanding, Early-Warning, and Prevention*. Williamsburg, VA: Association of Genocide Scholars, 27–64.
Li, Darryl. 2002. Echoes of violence. In Nicolaus Mills and Kira Bunner, eds., *The New Killing Fields: Massacre and the Politics of Intervention*. New York: Basic Books, 117–128.
Longhurst, Robyn. 1995. Geography and the body. *Gender, Place, and Culture: A Journal of Feminist Geography*, 2, 97–105.
Longhurst, Robyn. 1997. (Dis)embodied geographies. *Progress in Human Geography*, 21(4), 486–501.
Longhurst, Robyn. 2000. Geography and gender: Masculinities, male identity and men. *Progress in Human Geography*, 24(3), 439–444.
Longhurst, Robyn. 2001. *Bodies: Exploring Fluid Boundaries*. London: Routledge.
Maclear, Michael. 1981. *The Ten Thousand Day War: Vietnam, 1945–1975*. New York: Avon Books.
Magnarella, Paul J. 2002. Recent developments in the international law of genocide: An anthropological perspective on the International Criminal Tribunal for Rwanda. In Alexander Laban Hinton, ed., *Annihilating Difference: The Anthropology of Genocide*. Berkeley and Los Angeles: University of California Press, 310–322.
Maguire, Peter. 2005. *Facing Death in Cambodia*. New York: Columbia University Press.
Malkasian, Carter. 2004. Toward a better understanding of attrition: The Korean and Vietnam Wars. *Journal of Military History*, 68, 911–942.
Mam, Kalyanee. 2004. The endurance of the Cambodian family under the Khmer Rouge regime: An oral history. In Susan E. Cook, ed., *Genocide in Cambodia and Rwanda: New Perspectives*. Yale Center for International and Area Studies: Genocide Studies Program Monograph Series, No. 1. New Haven, CT: Yale University Press, 127–171.
Marston, John. 2002. Democratic Kampuchea and the idea of modernity. In Judy Ledgerwood, ed., *Cambodia Emerges from the Past: Eight Essays*. DeKalb: Center for Southeast Asian Studies, Northern Illinois University, 38–59.

Massey, Doreen. 1994. *Space, Place, and Gender*. Minneapolis: University of Minnesota Press.
Massey, Doreen. 2004. Geographies of responsibility. *Geografiska Annaler, 86B*(1), 5–18.
Mbembe, Achille. 2003. Necropolitics. *Pubic Culture, 15*(1), 11–40.
McCollum, James K. 1983. The CORDS pacification organization in Vietnam: A civilian military effort. *Armed Forces and Society, 10*(1), 105–122.
McDowell, Linda. 1999. *Gender, Identity and Place: Understanding Feminist Geographies*. Minneapolis: University of Minnesota Press.
McIntyre, Kevin. 1996. Geography as density: Cities, villages and Khmer Rouge orientalism. *Comparative Studies in Society and History, 38*(4), 730–758.
McKendrick, John H. 2001. Coming of age: Rethinking the role of children in population studies. *International Journal of Population Geography, 7*, 461–472.
McNee, Bob. 1984. If you are squeamish.... *East Lakes Geographer, 19*, 16–27.
Melvern, Linda. 2004. *Conspiracy to Murder: The Rwandan Genocide*. London: Verso.
Milgram, Stanley. 1963. Behavioral study of obedience. *Journal of Abnormal and Social Psychology, 67*(4), 371–378.
Milillo, Diana. 2006. Rape as a tactic of war: Social and psychological perspectives. *Affilia: Journal of Women and Social Work, 21*(2), 196–205.
Mills, Sara. 2003. *Michel Foucault*. London: Routledge.
Milne, David. 2007. "Our equivalent of guerrilla warfare": Walt Rostow and the bombing of North Vietnam, 1961–1968. *Journal of Military History, 71*, 169–203.
Milne, David. 2008. *America's Rasputin: Walt Rostow and the Vietnam War*. New York: Hill & Wang.
Mitchell, Don. 1995. The end of public space?: People's Park, definitions of the public, and democracy. *Annals of the Association of American Geographers, 85*, 108–133.
Mitchell, Don. 2000. *Cultural Geography: A Critical Introduction*. Oxford, UK: Blackwell.
Mitchell, Don. 2003. *The Right to the City: Social Justice and the Fight for Public Space*. New York: Guilford Press.
Monk, Janice and Susan Hanson. 1982. On not excluding half of the human geography. *Professional Geographer, 34*(1), 11–23.
Moss, George D. 1990. *Vietnam: An American Ordeal*. Englewood Cliffs, NJ: Prentice-Hall.
Mueller, John E. 1980. The search for the "breaking point" in Vietnam: The statistics of a deadly quarrel. *International Studies Quarterly, 24*(4), 497–519.
Nagar, Richa. 1998. Communal discourses, marriage and the politics of gendered social boundaries among South Asian immigrants in Tanzania. *Gender, Place and Culture: A Journal of Feminist Geography, 5*, 117–139.
Nagel, Caroline R. 1999. Social justice, self-interest and Salman Rushdie: Reassessing identity politics in multicultural Britain. In James D. Proctor and David M. Smith, eds., *Geography and Ethics: Journeys in a Moral Terrain*. New York: Routledge, 132–146.
Nagel, Caroline R. 2001. Hidden minorities and the politics of "race": The case

of British Arab activists in London. *Journal of Ethnic and Migration Studies*, 27, 381–400.

Nast, Heidi, J. and Steve Pile. 1998. Introduction: MakingPlacesBodies. In Heidi J. Nast and Steve Pile, eds., *Places Through the Body*. London: Routledge, 1–19.

Natter, Wolfgang and John Paul Jones. 1997. Identity, space and other uncertainties. In Georges Benko and Ulf Strohmayer, eds., *Space and Social Theory: Interpreting Modernity and Postmodernity*. Oxford, UK: Blackwell, 141–161.

Neale, Jonathan. 2003. *A People's History of the Vietnam War*. New York: New Press.

Neilands, J. B. 1970. Vietnam: Progress of the chemical war. *Asian Survey*, 10(3), 209–229.

Nevins, Joseph. 2003. Restitution over coffee: Truth, reconciliation, and environment violence in East Timor. *Political Geography*, 22, 677, 701.

Nevins, Joseph. 2005. *A Not-So-Distant Horror: Mass Violence in East Timor*. Ithaca, NY: Cornell University Press.

Newbury, David. 2002. Precolonial Brundi and Rwanda: Local loyalties, regional royalties. *International Journal of African Historical Studies*, 34(2), 255–314.

Newman, James L. and Gordon E. Matzke. 1984. *Population: Patterns, Dynamics, and Prospects*. Englewood Cliffs, NJ: Prentice-Hall.

Ngor, Haing with Roger Warner. 2003. *Survival in the Killing Fields*. New York: Carroll & Graf.

Nowrojee, Binaifer. 1996. *Shattered Lives: Sexual Violence during the Rwandan Genocide and Its Aftermath*. New York: Human Rights Watch.

Ogden, Philip. 1998. Population geography. *Progress in Human Geography*, 22(1), 105–114.

Olson, James, ed. 1987. *Dictionary of the Vietnam War*. New York: Peter Bedrick Books.

Opotow, Susan. 1990. Moral exclusion and injustice: An introduction. *Journal of Social Issues*, 46(1), 1–20.

Opotow, Susan. 2001. Reconciliation in time of impunity: Challenges for social justice. *Social Justice Research*, 14(2), 149–170.

Opotow, Susan, Janet Gerson, and Sarah Woodside. 2005. From moral exclusion to moral inclusion: Theory for teaching peace. *Theory into Practice*, 44(4), 303–318.

Osborne, Milton E. 1965. *Strategic Hamlets in South Viet-Nam: A Survey and a Comparison*. Southeast Asia Program, Data Paper No. 55. Ithaca, NY: Cornell University Press.

Pain, Rachel. 1997. Social geographies of women's fear of crime. *Transactions of the Institute of British Geographers*, 22(2), 231–244.

Pearce, Kimber Charles. 2001. *Rostow, Kennedy, and the Rhetoric of Foreign Aid*. East Lansing: Michigan State University Press.

Peet, Richard. 1977. The development of radical geography in the United States. *Progress in Human Geography*, 1, 240–263.

Peet, Richard. 1978. The dialects of radical geography: A reply to Gordon Clark and Michael Dear. *Professional Geographer*, 30(4), 360–364.

Peters, Gary L. and Robert P. Larkin. 1999. *Population Geography: Problems, Concepts, and Prospects*. 6th ed. Dubuque, IA: Kendall/Hunt.

Philo, Chris. 2001. Accumulating population: Bodies, institutions and space. *International Journal of Population Geography, 7*, 473–490.
Philo, Chris. 2005. Sex, life, death, geography: Fragmentary remarks inspired by "Foucault's population geographies." *Population, Space and Place, 11*, 325–333.
Pitts, Victoria. 2003. *In the Flesh: The Cultural Politics of Body Modification*. New York: Palgrave Macmillan.
Ponchaud, Francois. 1989. Social change in the vortex of revolution. In Karl D. Jackson, ed., *Cambodia, 1975–1978: Rendezvous with Death*. Princeton, NJ: Princeton University Press, 151–177.
Power, Samantha. 2002. *"A Problem from Hell": America and the Age of Genocide*. New York: Harper Perennial.
Prados, John. 1996. *Presidents' Secret Wars: CIA and Pentagon Covert Operations From World War II Through the Persian Gulf*. Chicago: Ivan R. Dee.
Pran, Dith, comp. 1997. *Children of Cambodia's Killing Fields: Memoirs by Survivors*. New Haven, CT: Yale University Press.
Prokosch, Eric. 1976. Technology and its control: Antipersonnel weapons. *International Social Science Journal, 28*(2), 341–358.
Prunier, Gerard. 1995. *The Rwandan Crisis: History of a Genocide*. New York: Columbia University Press.
Quinn, Kenneth M. 1989. The pattern and scope of violence. In Karl D. Jackson, ed., *Cambodia 1975–1978: Rendezvous with Death*. Princeton, NJ: Princeton University Press, 179–208.
Rehn, Elisabeth and Ellen Johnson Sirleaf. 2002. *Women, War, Peace: The Independent Expert's Assessment on the Impact of Armed Conflict on Women and Women's Role in Peace Building*. Washington, DC: United Nations Development Fund for Women.
Reza, A., James A. Mercey, and E. Krug. 2001. Epidemiology of violent deaths in the world. *Injury Prevention, 7*(2), 104–111.
Roder, Wolf. 1977. An alternative interpretation of men and women in geography. *Professional Geographer, 29*(4), 397–399.
Rodrigue, Christine M. 1977. Commentary on George F. Carter's "A geographical society should be a geographical society." *Professional Geographer, 29*(4), 407–408.
Ronayne, Peter. 2001. *Never Again?: The United States and the Prevention and Punishment of Genocide since the Holocaust*. Boulder, CO: Rowman & Littlefield.
Rostow, W. W. 1960. *The Stages of Economic Growth: A Non-Communist Manifesto*. Cambridge, UK: Cambridge University Press.
Rozee, Patricia D. and Mary P. Koss. 2001. Rape: A century of resistance. *Psychology of Women Quarterly, 25*, 295–311.
Sam, Roeun. 1997. Living in the darkness. In Kim DePaul, ed., *Children of Cambodia's Killing Fields*. New Haven, CT: Yale University Press, 73–81.
Sanders, Rickie. 2006. Social justice and women of color in geography: Philosophical musings, trying again. *Gender, Place and Culture: A Journal of Feminist Geography, 13*(1), 49–55.
SarDesai, D. R. 2005. *Vietnam: Past and Present*. 4th ed. New York: Westview Press.

Schulzinger, Robert D. 1997. *A Time for War: The United States and Vietnam, 1941–1975*. New York: Oxford University Press.
Secor, Anna. 2002. The veil and urban space in Istanbul: Women's dress, mobility and Islamic knowledge. *Gender, Place and Culture: A Journal of Feminist Geography*, 9, 5–22.
Seekins, Donald M. 1990. Historical setting. In R. R. Ross, ed., *Cambodia: A Country Study*. Washington, DC: US Government Printing Office, 1–72.
Seifert, Ruth. 1996. The second front: The logic of sexual violence in wars. *Women's Studies International Forum*, 19(1–2), 35–43.
Shawcross, William. 2002. *Sideshow: Kissinger, Nixon, and the Destruction of Cambodia*. Rev. ed. New York: Cooper Square Press.
Short, Philip. 2004. *Pol Pot: Anatomy of a Nightmare*. New York: Henry Holt.
Sibley, David. 1995. *Geographies of Exclusion: Society and Difference in the West*. London: Routledge.
Silvey, Rachel. 2004. On the boundaries of a subfield: Social theory's incorporation into population geography. *Population, Space and Place*, 10, 303–308.
Skjelsbaek, Inger. 2001. Sexual violence and war: Mapping out a complex relationship. *European Journal of International Relations*, 7(2), 211–237.
Smith, David M. 2000. *Moral Geographies: Ethics in a World of Difference*. Edinburgh, UK: Edinburgh University Press.
Smith, Roger W. 1999. Introduction. In Roger W. Smith, ed., *Genocide: Essays Toward Understanding, Early-Warning, and Prevention*. Williamsburg, VA: Association of Genocide Scholars, 3–14.
Stewart, Lynn. 1995. Bodies, visions, and spatial politics: A review essay on Henri Lefebvre's *The Production of Space*. *Environment and Planning D: Society and Space*, 13, 609–618.
Stone, Oliver, director. 1994. *Heaven and Earth* [Film]. Alcor Films.
Taylor, Christopher C. 1992. *Milk, Honey and Money: Changing Concepts in Rwandan Healing*. Washington, DC: Smithsonian Institution Press.
Taylor, Christopher C. 2002. The cultural face of terror in the Rwandan genocide of 1994. In Alexander Laban Hinton, ed., *Annihilating Difference: The Anthropology of Genocide*. Berkeley and Los Angeles: University of California Press, 137–178.
Thayer, Thomas C. 1985. *War without Fronts: The American Experience in Vietnam*. Boulder, CO: Westview Press.
Thion, Serge. 1983. The Cambodian idea of revolution. In David P. Chandler and Ben Kiernan, eds., *Revolution and Its Aftermath in Kampuchea: Eight Essays*. Yale University Southeast Asia Studies, Monograph Series No. 25. New Haven, CT: Yale University Press, 10–33.
Trewartha, Glenn. 1953. A case for population geography. *Annals of the Association of American Geographers*, 42, 71–97.
Tucker, Spencer C. 1999. *Vietnam*. Lexington: University of Kentucky Press.
Tully, John. 2005. *A Short History of Cambodia: From Empire to Survival*. New York: Allen & Unwin.

Tyner, James A. 1994. The social construction of gendered migration from the Philippines. *Asian and Pacific Migration Journal*, 3(4), 589–617.
Tyner, James A. 2002a. Narrating interracial relations and the negotiation of public spaces. *Environment and Planning D: Society and Space*, 20, 441–458.
Tyner, James A. 2002b. Scaled sexuality and the migration of Filipina overseas contract workers. *Philippine Population Review*, 1(1), 103–123.
Tyner, James A. 2004. *Made in the Philippines: Gendered Discourses and the Making of Migrants*. London: Routledge.
Tyner, James A. 2006a. *The Geography of Malcolm X: Black Radicalism and the Remaking of American Space*. New York: Routledge.
Tyner, James A. 2006b. *Oriental Bodies: Discourse and Discipline in the U.S. Immigration Policy, 1875–1942*. Lanham, MD: Lexington Press.
Tyner, James A. 2007. *America's Strategy in Southeast Asia: From the Cold War to the Terror War*. Boulder, CO: Rowman & Littlefield.
Tyner, James A. 2008. *The Killing of Cambodia: Geography, Genocide and the Unmaking of Space*. Aldershot, UK: Ashgate.
Tyner, James A. and Donna Houston. 2000. Controlling bodies: The punishment of multiracialized sexual relations. *Antipode*, 32(4), 387–409.
Underhill-Sem, Yvonne. 1999. Of social construction, politics and biology: Population geographies in the Pacific. *Asia Pacific Viewpoint*, 40, 19–32.
Underhill-Sem, Yvonne. 2001. Maternities in "out-of-the-way" places: Epistemological possibilities for retheorising population geographies. *International Journal of Population Geography*, 7, 447–460.
Valentine, Douglas. 1990. *The Phoenix Program*. New York: William Morrow.
Valentine, Gill. 1989. The geography of women's fear. *Area*, 21(4), 385–390.
Valentine, Gill. 1998. "Sticks and stones may break my bones": A personal geography of harassment. *Antipode*, 30, 305–332.
Van den Dungen, Peter and Lawrence S. Wittner. 2003. Peace history: An introduction. *Journal of Peace Research*, 40(4), 363–375.
Verwimp, Philip. 2004. Peasant ideology and genocide in Rwanda under Habyarimana. In Susan E. Cook, ed., *Genocide in Cambodia and Rwanda: New Perspectives*. Yale Center for International and Area Studies: Genocide Studies Program Monograph Series, No. 1. New Haven, CT: Yale University Press, 1–41.
Vickery, Michael. 1988. How many died in Pol Pot's Kampuchea? *Bulletin of Concerned Asian Scholars*, 20, 377–385.
Vriens, Lennart. 1997. Peace education: Cooperative building of a humane future. *Pastoral Care in Education*, 15(4), 25–30.
Waller, James. 2002. *Becoming Evil: How Ordinary People Commit Genocide and Mass Killing*. New York: Oxford University Press.
Walzer, Michael. 1977. *Just and Unjust Wars: A Moral Argument with Historical Illustrations*. New York: Basic Books.
Watts, Charlotte and Cathy Zimmerman. 2002. Violence against women: Global scope and magnitude. *The Lancet*, 359, 1232–1237.
Weeks, John R. 2005. *Population: An Introduction to Concepts and Issues*. 9th ed. Belmont, CA: Wadsworth/Thomson Learning.

Westing, Arthur H. 1971. Ecological effects of military defoliation on the forests of South Vietnam. *BioScience*, 21(17), 893–898.
Westing, Arthur H. 1975. Environmental consequences of the Second Indochina War: A case study. *AMBRO*, 4(5–6), 216–222.
Westing, Arthur H. 1980. *Warfare in a Fragile World: Military Impact on the Human Environment*. London: Taylor & Francis.
Westing, Arthur H. 1982. War as a human endeavor: The high-fatality wars of the twentieth century. *Journal of Peace Research*, 19, 261–270.
White, Paul and Peter Jackson. 1995. (Re)theorizing population geography. *International Journal of Population Geography*, 1, 111–123.
White, Stephen E., Lawrence A. Brown, William A. V. Clark, Patricia Gober, Richard Jones, Kevin E. McHugh, and Richard L. Morrill. 1989. Population geography. In Gary L. Gaile and Cort J. Willmotts, eds., *Geography in America*. Columbus, OH: Merrill, 258–289.
Willis, Kathie and Brenda S. A. Yeoh. 1999. Heart and wing, nation and diaspora: Gendered discourses in Singapore's regionalization process. *Gender, Place and Culture: A Journal of Feminist Geography*, 6(4), 353–372.
Winter, Deborah Du Nann. 1998. War is not healthy for children and other living things. *Peace and Conflict: Journal of Peace Psychology*, 4(4), 415–428.
Wisner, Ben. 1986. Geography: War or peace studies? *Antipode*, 18(2), 212–217.
Wright, Richard, Adrian Bailey, Ines Miyares, and Alison Mountz. 2000. Legal status, gender and employment among Salvadorans in the US. *International Journal of Population Geography*, 6, 273–286.
Yanagisawa, Satoko. 2004. Crossing the river: Health of mothers and children in rural Cambodia. *International Congress Series*, 1267, 113–126.
Yeoh, Brenda S. A. and Shirlena Huang. 2000. "Home" and "away": Foreign domestic workers and negotiations of diasporic identity in Singapore. *Women's Studies International Forum*, 23, 413.
Young, Iris M. 1990. *Justice and the Politics of Difference*. Princeton, NJ: Princeton University Press.
Young, Iris M. 1998. Harvey's complaint with race and gender studies: A critical response. *Antipode*, 30(1), 36–42.
Young, Iris M. 2001. Equality of whom?: Social groups and judgments of injustice. *Journal of Political Philosophy*, 9(1), 1–18.
Young, Marilyn B. 1991. *The Vietnam Wars, 1945–1990*. New York: HarperCollins.
Young, Robert J. C. 2003. *Post-Colonialism: A Very Short Introduction*. Oxford, UK: Oxford University Press.
Yuval-Davis, Nira. 1993. Gender and nation. *Ethnic and Racial Studies*, 16(4), 621–632.
Yuval-Davis, Nira. 1996. Women and the biological reproduction of "the nation." *Women's Studies International Forum*, 19(1–2), 17–24.
Zelinsky, Wilbur. 1966. *A Prologue to Population Geography*. Englewood Cliffs, NJ: Prentice-Hall.
Zinn, Howard. 2005. *Just War*. Milan: Edizioni Charta.

AUTHOR INDEX

Adas, Michael, 47, 60, 61, 62, 65, 69
Agnew, John, 28, 55, 65
Ali, Mohamed, 187
Appy, Christian G., 77, 79, 97, 102, 103, 202n4
Aziz, Christine, 187

Bailey, Adrian, 5, 6, 8, 9, 10, 11, 13, 15, 25, 189
Barker, Philip, 39
Barnaby, Frank, 93
Barnes, Trevor, 201n1
Barry, Brian, 44
Becker, Elizabeth, 117, 118, 121, 124, 125, 126, 133
Berkeley, Bill, 152
Binnie, Jon, 18
Boffey, Philip M., 89, 90, 91
Booth, Karen M., 181
Bordo, Susan, 172
Bourdelais, Patrice, 28, 29
Boyle, Paul, 6, 14, 18, 186
Bradshaw, Matt, 17
Brown, Ian, 127
Brunet, Ariane, 179
Buckingham, William A., 85, 86, 87, 88, 89
Burnham, Gilbert, 187

Cable, Larry, 77, 79, 98
Calderwood, Patricia, 189, 196
Caldwell, John C., 15, 27, 30
Carlton-Ford, Steve, 48

Carney, Timothy, 111
Carter, George F., 20
Castree, Noel, 96
Cecil, Paul F., 50, 84, 85, 86, 88
Chalk, Frank, 165, 166, 167, 205n2
Chandler, David, 1, 2, 3, 116, 119, 120, 122, 123, 127, 150, 204n4
Chappell, Jr., John E., 20
Clark, Gordon, 19, 20
Clayton, Thomas, 138
Clodfelter, Michael, 46, 47, 49, 50, 60, 83, 108
Corbridge, Stuart, 55, 65
Crane, Conrad C., 93, 202n7
Currey, Cecil B., 56, 57
Curtis, Bruce, 25, 26, 31, 201n1

Dang, Thuy Tram, 58, 66, 74, 81, 92, 97, 202n1
Dean, Mitchell M., 26, 27, 29, 30, 31
Dear, Michael, 18, 19, 20
Delaney, David, 33
Demeritt, David, 96
Demko, George, 11
DePaul, Kim, 203n1
Domosh, Mona, 23, 181
Dreyfus, Hubert L., 27, 28, 29, 31
Dunlop, Nic, 110, 143

Ebihara, May, 134, 135, 136, 137, 141, 145
Edkins, Jenny, 192
Edwards, Paul N., 59, 61

220

Author Index

Eisenstein, Zillah, 181
Elden, Stuart, 33
England, Kim, 6, 14
Enthoven, Alain, 60, 78, 79, 102
Etcheson, Craig, 111, 112, 204n6

Fincher, Ruth, 13
Findlay, Allan, 6, 12, 13, 14, 15, 43, 186, 187, 198
Fisher, Berenice M., 187, 195
Flint, Colin, 47, 107
Folke, Steen, 19
Foucault, Michel, 22, 23, 24, 25, 26, 31, 32, 33, 98, 99, 104, 105, 108, 146, 147, 148, 150, 172, 180, 184, 185, 201n1, 204n9

Gaile, Gary, 11
Gartner, Scott S., 77, 78
Gibson, James, 78
Glover, Jonathan, 42
Gober, Patricia, 5, 11
Gottesman, Evan, 120, 124
Graham, Elspeth, 6, 8, 12, 13, 14, 18, 22, 39, 186, 198
Gregory, Derek, 39
Griffiths, Ieuan L.L., 153
Grosz, Elizabeth, 24, 172

Hanson, Susan, 19
Haraway, Dona, 24
Harris, Ian M., 190, 194, 195, 197, 198, 199, 200
Harvey, David, 19, 20, 192
Hayslip, Le Ly, 97, 98, 107
Hearden, Patrick J., 52, 59
Herring, George C., 55, 67, 69, 70, 75, 77, 79, 100, 104
Heuveline, Patrick, 48, 140
Hintjens, Helen M., 161, 164, 166, 167
Hinton, Alexander L., 122, 123, 124, 126, 132, 133, 136, 138, 141, 142, 144, 145, 146, 205n5
Hirschman, Charles, 48
Horne, John, 48
Horowitz, David, 198
Hossein-Zadeh, Ismael, 47
Hynes, Patricia H., 180, 182

Jackson, Karl D., 111, 128, 129, 130, 131
Jackson, Peter, 7, 12
James, Preston E., 9, 26, 27

Jenkins, Alan, 200
Joffé, Roland, 45
Johansen, Hans Christian, 30
Jones, Huw R., 9
Jones, John Paul, 34

Kamm, Henry, 120, 121, 122, 124, 126
Kapp, Clare, 187
Karagiannakis, Magdalini, 179, 180
Karnow, Stanley, 52
Keen, David, 188
Kerkvliet, Benedict J., 56
Kiernan, Ben, 1, 115, 116, 120, 127, 131, 150
Knopp, Larry, 172
Knox, Paul, 28
Kofman, Eleonore, 14
Kolko, Gabriel, 69, 100, 101, 103, 104, 106, 107
Koskela, Hille, 4
Kraly, Ellen Percy, 157
Krepon, Michael, 70, 71, 72
Kuhlke, Olaf, 22

Lacoste, Yves, 92, 94, 95, 203n9
Langguth, A.J., 106, 107
Laws, Glenda, 23
Lawson, Victoria, 6, 14
Le Billon, Philippe, 96
Lefebvre, Henri, 34, 35, 128
Legg, Stephen, 22, 26, 28, 201n1
Lemarchand, René, 163, 165, 167, 170
Lerner, Melvin J., 41
Li, Darryl, 171
Longhurst, Robyn, 6, 18, 21, 23, 172, 184

Maclear, Michael, 56, 57
Magnarella, Paul J., 179
Mam, Kalyanee, 134, 135, 137, 138, 139, 140, 141, 142
Massey, Doreen, 196, 197
Mbembe, Achille, 146
McCollum, James K., 102, 203n12
McDowell, Linda, 21, 24, 172
McIntyre, Kevin, 128, 130, 131, 132
McKendrick, John H., 17, 43
Melvern, Linda, 154, 155, 157, 159, 160, 161, 163, 165, 167, 168, 169, 170, 171, 176, 205n3
Milillo, Diana, 182
Mills, Sara, 22, 25
Milne, David, 61, 64, 65, 66, 67, 68, 70

Mitchell, Don, 6, 35, 191
Monk, Janice, 19
Mueller, John E., 76, 80, 81

Nagar, Richa, 14
Nagel, Caroline R., 14, 190, 191
Nast, Heidi J., 21, 172
Natter, Wolfgang, 34
Neale, Jonathan, 49, 52, 59, 72, 75, 78
Neilands, J.B., 82, 83, 84, 85, 86, 89, 90, 91, 202n6
Nevins, Joseph, 40, 96
Newbury, David, 153, 154, 155, 156
Newman, James L., 18
Ngor, Haing, 3, 131, 144, 145
Nowrojee, Binaifer, 166, 180, 182, 183, 204n1

Opotow, Susan, 36, 39, 40, 41, 196

Pain, Rachel, 4
Pearce, Charles, 62
Peet, Richard, 19, 20
Peters, Gary L., 18, 74
Philo, Chris, 18, 22, 105, 201n1
Pile, Steve, 21, 172
Pitts, Victoria, 23
Ponchaud, Francois, 130, 131, 133, 137, 138, 140, 141, 143, 148
Power, Samantha, 151, 164, 166
Prados, John, 98, 203n11
Pran, Dith, 3, 45
Pratt, Geraldine, 6, 14
Prokosch, Eric, 71, 72, 73
Prunier, Gerard, 152, 156, 157, 158, 159, 160, 161, 166, 169, 170, 171, 176

Quinn, Kenneth M., 131, 133, 134, 135, 136, 141, 143, 145, 204n5

Rehn, Elisabeth, 181, 182
Reza, A., 4, 48
Roder, Wolf, 20
Rodrigue, Christine M., 20
Ronayne, Peter, 152, 155, 156, 157, 158, 169, 170, 171

Sam, Roeun, 38
Sanders, Rickie, 190, 191

SarDesai, D.R., 51
Schulzinger, Robert D., 53, 59, 69, 70, 74, 78, 79
Secor, Anna, 14
Seekins, Donald M., 115, 119
Shawcross, William, 112
Short, Philip, 116
Sibley, David, 17, 34, 35, 44, 122
Silvey, Rachel, 6, 14
Skop, Emily, 6
Smith, David M., 190, 194
Smith, Roger W., 40
Stewart, Lynn, 35
Stone, Oliver, 97

Taylor, Christopher C., 153, 173, 174, 175, 176, 177, 178, 179, 183, 184, 205n4
Trewartha, Glenn, 8, 9
Tucker, Spencer C., 53, 69

Underhill-Sem, Yvonne, 14, 22, 24

Valentine, Douglas, 103
Valentine, Gill, 4, 18, 20
Verwimp, Philip, 162, 163
Vriens, Lennart, 190, 194, 195, 197, 199, 200

Waller, James, 36, 37, 38, 39, 41
Walzer, Michael, 48
Weeks, John R., 28
Westing, Arthur H., 47, 48, 90, 94, 95
White, Paul, 7, 12, 186
White, Stephen E., 5, 9, 11, 12
Winter, Deborah Du Nann 48

Yanagisawa, Satoko, 3
Yeoh, Brenda, S.A., 14
Young, Iris M., 4, 35, 43, 191, 192, 193
Young, Marilyn B., 57, 58, 65, 69, 76, 77, 83, 101, 202n4
Young, Robert J.C., 16, 44
Yuval-Davis, Nira, 181

Zelinsky, Wilbur, 6, 9, 10, 11, 12, 19
Zinn, Howard, 48, 188, 189, 195, 199

Subject Index

Akayesu, Jean-Paul, 179
Akazu, 164
Anatomopolitics, 24, 32, 44
Angkar, 131, 133, 134, 135, 142
Arusha Accords, 169
Autonomy, 191

Basic demographic equation, 74
Biological warfare, 83–86, 93
Biopolitics, 31, 31, 44, 111, 147, 171, 182
Biopower, 32, 43, 44, 50, 108
Body/bodies, 21–33, 146, 148–149, 172, 177–178
   and bombs, 73
   discipline of, 24, 31, 42, 45, 99, 103, 104–105, 111, 134, 145, 188
   fluids, 23–24, 173–179, 184
   inscription of, 24, 172–175
   and napalm, 82–83
   and space, 24, 39, 98–99
Body counts, 46, 75–81, 103

Cambodia/Cambodian Genocide, 109–150, 176
   age–sex divisions, 137–138
   anti-urban practices, 128, 129–133
   daily life, 137–142
   ethnic tensions, 123–124
   families, 133–142
   historical context, 111–120
   killing of Vietnamese, 120–121
   political subjects, 142–149
   state-building, 127–129
Chemical warfare, 83–86, 202n6
Children, 3, 4, 138, 181, 187
Choeung Ek, 1–3
Cluster bombs, 49, 70–73, 104
   and effects on bodies, 73
Communist Party of Kampuchea, 118, 127, 133

Crisis of relevancy, 8
Critical race theory, 6
Culture of impunity, 40–41, 43, 47, 112, 126, 144, 177, 197

Darfur, 40, 187
Dehumanization, 37–38, 41, 49, 80, 149, 152, 175
Democratic Kampuchea, 1, 34, 109, 117, 120, 127, 134, 135, 137, 139, 143, 145, 148, 149. *See also* Cambodia
Depopulation, 75, 78, 129–133
Demography, 8, 15, 27, 29
Discipline, 25, 31, 45, 98, 104, 111, 134, 191
Disproportionate revenge, 141–142

Ecological warfare, 92, 95
Educating for peace, 194–199
Environmental destruction, 50, 81–92, 92–97
Environmental warfare, 86
Ethnic cleansing, 122, 146, 171

Feminism, 19–20, 24, 172

Gender, 13, 19, 181
Geneva Accords, 54, 55
Geneva Protocol, 84–85
Genital mutilation, 169, 178, 180, 181, 183–184
Genocidal rape, 182, 184
Geographic knowledge, 123
Geographical imaginations, 39–40, 49, 55, 77, 111, 122, 126, 129, 139, 142, 158, 172, 182, 188
Geographies of exclusion, 34
Geographies of experience, 33
Great Leap Forward, 127, 130

Habyarimana, Juvenal, 160–164, 167, 168, 170, 184
Hamlet Evaluation System, 102–103

Subject Index

Ho Chi Minh, 51, 53, 69, 81, 114
Holocaust, 2, 37–38
Human rights, 192–193
Hutu, 34, 37, 40, 151–185, 188

Ieng Sary, 111, 112, 117, 130
Imaginative geographies, 39–40, 49, 55, 77, 111, 122, 126, 129, 139, 142, 158, 172, 182, 188
Indiscriminate killing, 3, 48–49, 76, 104
  acceptable loss, 80–81, 88, 91
  and Boi Loi Woods, 87–88
Individualism, 143, 145
Interahamwe, 167, 171

Jim Crow Laws, 36
Johnson, Lyndon, 68, 73, 75
Justice, 108, 148, 191, 194
  scope of, 36
  theories of, 35, 190–191
Just war, 48
Just-world phenomena, 41–42

Kangura, 165–166
Kayibanda, Grégoire, 158, 159, 160
Kennedy, John F., 58–59, 66–67, 86, 108
Khieu Ponnary, 116, 117
Khieu Samphan, 111, 117, 119, 128, 130, 131, 132
Khieu Thirith, 117
Khmer People's Revolutionary Party, 114, 115, 116, 118
Khmer Rouge, 1–3, 4, 34, 37, 38, 109, 110, 117, 120, 127–150, 162, 171, 188
Killing
  acceptable loss, 91, 145
  civilians, 44, 48, 85, 121–121, 126, 171
  justification of, 40–41, 42, 66, 69, 107, 108, 126, 141, 145, 146, 147, 160, 174, 184–185, 193
  symbolic performance, 121, 126, 169, 172, 173–175, 177–178
  See also indiscriminate killing
Killing Fields, 1–3, 6
Knowledge, production of, 5, 26, 31, 60–62, 123, 188
Korean War, 77, 78, 93

Landsdale, Edward, 56–57, 66–67, 87
LeMay, Curtis, 68
Lon Nol, 117, 119–126, 129

Mao Zedong, 127
McNamara, Robert, 59–61, 73, 78, 99, 102, 108
Methodological conservatism, 18
Moral exclusion, 7, 36–42, 181, 188
  engagement, 36, 40–42
  extent, 36–39
  severity, 36, 39–40
Mortality, violence-related, 4

Napalm, 49, 82–83, 104
Nixon, Richard M., 74, 97, 108, 109, 193
Norodom Sihanouk, 113, 115, 117, 118, 119, 120
Nuon Chea, 112, 118
Nuremberg Laws, 166

Operation Menu, 109
Operation Pipestone Canyon, 97–98
Operation Ranch Hand, 87–92
Operation Sunrise, 101
Oppression, 4, 37, 67, 191, 195

Peace, 189, 190, 192, 200
Peace-building, 21, 32, 48, 187, 194–199
Phuc, Kim, 82
Place-death, 129–133
Political, 192, 193, 195
Politics, 192
Pol Pot, 42, 111, 116, 117, 118, 127, 130, 132, 143
Population(s)
  concept of, 27, 29
  construction of, 25–30, 37, 147, 185, 188
  control of 3, 97–104, 111
  governance, 30
  knowledge of, 31, 61
  registrations of, 46, 102–103, 105–107, 157–158, 160, 171
  regulation of, 31–32, 42, 45, 92, 107–108, 140, 182
  space and, 39, 134
Population geography, 5, 6, 186
  and bodies, 17–33
  crisis of relevancy, 8
  and genocide, 44, 111
  history of, 8–13
  methodological conservatism, 18
  philosophical reorientation, 15–17, 32, 42, 108, 187, 189, 195–199, 200
  production of, 37, 146, 150
  and social justice, 5, 187
  social theory and, 16
  and theory, 7–14, 32, 42–45
  and war, 44, 47–48, 50, 65, 107
Populous, 201n1
Postcolonialism, 6–7, 15–16, 21, 45
Poststructuralism, 6–7, 15–16, 21, 45, 172
Power, 25
Psychological warfare, 56–57

Rape, 179–184
Rostow, Walt W., 61–66, 67–70, 80, 86, 97, 99, 100, 104, 108, 193
Rostow Doctrine, 58–66, 68, 69, 73, 80, 98, 100
Rwanda/Rwandan Genocide, 151–185
  historical context, 153–162
  media representation, 152
  numbers killed, 152
  planned violence, 164–170, 185

sexual violence, 179–184
social groupings, 154–157

Saloth Sar. *See* Pol Pot.
"Search and destroy," 75–77
Sexuality, 18, 137, 140, 172, 174, 178
  and violence, 140, 166, 169, 179–184
Sieu Heng, 116, 117
Social categorization, 36–37, 100, 102, 105–107, 143, 144
Social engineering, 3, 34, 111, 127
Social groups, 34–35, 37, 143, 148, 158, 164, 170, 172, 188, 193
Social justice, 4, 5, 21, 43–44, 146, 187, 190, 192, 193, 194
Social reproduction, 137, 140
Social theory, 16
Societal injustices, 6, 32, 42, 43, 45, 96, 187, 191
Son Ngoc Minh, 114, 115, 116, 118
Son Ngoc Thanh, 113, 114
Sovereignty, and killing, 66, 146, 147, 174, 179–184, 204n8
Space(s), 33, 45, 105, 128, 196–197
  erasure of, 128, 134, 136, 146, 149
  representational, 34–35
  representations of, 34–35, 145, 164
  self and, 33, 145
  sovereignty, 55, 65, 66, 147
Spatial engineering, 127
Spatial practices, 172
  confinement, 38, 97–104, 108, 121, 136, 141
  exclusion, 42, 121, 122
  mobility, 161–162
  relocation, 56, 104, 131–133, 134, 136
Spatial purification, 122, 125, 142, 145, 148, 149, 171, 172
Stages of Growth, 63–66
Subjects, 22–24, 104, 105, 142–149
  femininity, 22
  masculinity, 22

Territorial trap, 55, 64–65, 80
Terror, 57, 97
Torture, 38, 145–147, 172–173, 177–178, 182
Tou Samouth, 116, 118
Toul Sleng, 2–3, 38
Tutsi, 34, 37, 40, 151–185, 188

Umuganda policy, 161–162

Vietnam/Vietnam War, 46–108
  aerial bombing, 66–67, 68, 94
  attrition, 75–81
  deaths, 49–50, 69
  environmental destruction, 50, 81–92, 92–97
  historical context, 51–54
  industrial war, 49–50
  pacification, 67, 98–104, 157
  Phoenix Program, 105–107, 171
  state-building, 54–58
  strategic hamlets, 38, 97–104, 203n12
Violence, 6, 32, 33–42, 44, 45, 96, 187, 189, 194–199
  bodily inscription of, 126, 143, 172–175, 178
  direct, 39, 141–142, 149, 158, 177–178, 180
  as performance, 126, 169, 172–173
  and sexuality, 140, 151, 166, 169, 179–184
  structural, 39, 149, 158, 180, 187

War
  deaths, 4, 47–48, 49–50, 69, 76, 84, 187
  embodied instruments of, 105
  nature and, 50, 81–92, 92–96
  strategic bombing, 48, 66–67, 108, 202n7
War rape, 44, 179–184
Westmoreland, William, 75, 76, 77, 78, 80, 97, 193
World War I, 84
World War II, 78, 80, 82, 92, 113, 158

About the Author

James A. Tyner is Professor of Geography at Kent State University. His research interests include mass violence, war, and social justice. The author of numerous books, articles, and book chapters, he is a recipient of the Glenda Laws Award from the Association of American Geographers, among other honors.